D. W. Griffith: Interviews

Conversations with Filmmakers Series

Gerald Peary, General Editor

D. W. Griffith

INTERVIEWS

Edited by Anthony Slide

University Press of Mississippi / Jackson

A prominent film scholar once asked me what it was about
D. W. Griffith that attracted such crazy zealots. I don't know
the answer, but I dedicate this book to four of them:

Barnet G. Bravermann
Ira Gallen
Arthur Lennig
Seymour Stern

www.upress.state.ms.us

The University Press of Mississippi is a member
of the Association of American University Presses.

Copyright © 2012 by University Press of Mississippi
All rights reserved
Manufactured in the United States of America

First printing 2012
∞

Library of Congress Cataloging-in-Publication Data

D. W. Griffith : interviews / edited by Anthony Slide.
     p. cm. — (Conversations with filmmakers series)
  Includes filmography and index.
  ISBN 978-1-61703-298-1 (cloth : alk. paper) — ISBN 978-1-61703-299-8 (ebook)
  ISBN 978-1-4968-5801-6 (paperback)
  1. Griffith, D. W. (David Wark), 1875–1948—Interviews. 2. Motion picture producers
and directors—United States—Interviews. I. Slide, Anthony.
  PN1998.3.G76D44 2012
  791.4302'33092—dc23   2012002777

British Library Cataloging-in-Publication Data available

Contents

Introduction

When I began writing books on film history some forty years ago, my greatest admiration was for D. W. Griffith, his films, and his leading players. My second book, published in 1973, was *The Griffith Actresses*, devoted to the major stars in the director's stock company, and while Griffith had long since died, I was able to know well some of his "discoveries," including Blanche Sweet, Margery Wilson, Miriam Cooper, and, of course, Lillian Gish. *The Griffith Actresses* was followed two years later by *The Films of D. W. Griffith*, coauthored with my mentor, Edward Wagenknecht. Since that time, many years—even decades—have gone by since I gave careful consideration to Griffith, and so I am happy, as I enter old age, to return to the "master" with this anthology of interviews. D. W. Griffith may have gone out of style, been assaulted, denigrated, and, quite frankly, "trashed" by many, and had his work and his career diminished, but I make no apologies for remaining his faithful and devoted admirer and defender.

I am still a few years younger than was Griffith when he gave his last interview in the spring of 1948, but like him, I respond, "I can say anything I want about Hollywood." And like Griffith, I am very aware how much those who have come along later have borrowed from my pioneering works—be they on the printed page rather than the illuminated screen. But enough of me; this book, as it should be, is about D. W. Griffith and his commentary in more than forty interviews published between 1914 and 1948.

I would like to believe that the interviews that follow constitute almost everything in which Griffith participated and which may be defined as interviews. Certainly, I have tried to be broad in my approach to the anthology, while at the same time discarding pieces which it would be impossible to classify under the heading of interviews. Sometimes the comments from Griffith in these interviews are few, sometimes repetitive. As Roberta Courtlandt wrote in the August 1915 issue of *Motion*

Picture Magazine, "One doesn't interview David Wark Griffith. He's too busy." Aside from the interview, or more honestly conversation, between Griffith and Walter Huston, which served as a prologue to the sound re-issue of *The Birth of a Nation,* the interviews here do not use the modern questions and answers format. They were conducted and published in an earlier time—prior to the invention of the audio tape—and are best described under the heading of "narratives." Indeed, one might argue that the motion picture–related "interview," as such, did not exist during Griffith's working lifetime.

One interview that will not be found here is that titled "An Interview with D. W. Griffith of Biograph" by Leonard Hall. While it is probably the most illuminating of early interviews, and one that, incredibly, is often cited as legitimate, it is, in reality, a fake. In August 1936, *The Stage* magazine decided to publish an anniversary issue in which various pieces would appear that might have been published twenty-five years ago, in 1911, if *The Stage* had existed back then. One such piece was that by Leonard Hall (on page 112), which, on closer inspection, could not have appeared in 1911 as one of the films cited was not produced until 1912.

It was not possible to reprint Frank Nugent's "Up the Years with D. W. Griffith," which appeared in the November 17, 1935, issue of the *New York Times.* In it, Griffith refers to the past as "ancient history," recalls Noel Coward's brief appearance in *Hearts of the World,* and identifies *The Thin Man* as the best film he has seen (some four times) in recent years, and pays tribute to its director, W. S. Van Dyke.

The earliest of the published interviews date from 1914 and the last from 1948, the year in which Griffith died. It is fascinating to read the piece in the June 1914 issue of *The Theatre*; technical descriptions today which are known to all, such as the close-up or the fade-out, did not exist back then, and the interviewer/writer struggles hard to come up with his own descriptive terms. While some of the interviews concentrate on specific films, including *The Birth of a Nation, Intolerance, Way Down East* (but not the ice floe sequence), and, most prominently, *Hearts of the World,* the subjects covered can be quite broad and surprising. Without bitterness, the director laments his failure to patent some of his innovations, most notably the close-up and the fade-out (although whether these could actually be patented is somewhat questionable). Modern readers and scholars will be surprised at the amount of attention that Griffith devotes to exhibition. As early as "The Making of a Masterpiece" by Edward Weitzel in the September 30, 1916, issue of the *Moving Picture World,* he is discussing the presentation, rather than the production, of

Intolerance. In several interviews he argues for what is today an established aspect of moviegoing, that of having separate performances. Not only does Griffith ask that the audience not be allowed in to a screening once it has commenced, but that latecomers be entertained in a separate theatre, showing comedies and newsreels, until his film and similar important works are ready to begin anew.

The interviewer most represented and one who seems very much at ease with his subject is Harry C. Carr, born in Tipton, Iowa, on March 27, 1877, who had joined the *Los Angeles Times* in 1897 and was a prominent figure in the entertainment world, not only as a writer and interviewer, but also as an occasional screenwriter. (One of his most important contributions to the screen is the 1926 production of *Old Ironsides*.) Beginning on November 18, 1924, Carr wrote a column headed "Lancer" for the *Los Angeles Times,* and in his last, he wrote, "death cuts down the famous by threes in Hollywood—Thelma Todd, John Gilbert, and Quien Sabe?" Shortly thereafter, he suffered a heart attack and died on January 10, 1936, at the age of fifty-eight. Happily, Carr has left us with an account of what it was like to interview D. W. Griffith:

> I don't believe that D. W. Griffith really likes being interviewed, but once caught, he always takes the utmost pains to see that the interviewer gets a thrill. You might not expect it of him but he gives the same attention to the kid reporter from the Farmers Almanac that he would to W. R. Hearst. Having been a newspaper man himself, he is keen enough to know that the newspaper business is a rapidly changing profession and that a green awkward reporter today may tomorrow be a big critic with your professional life in the hollow of his hand. So Griffith will always stop everything to be interviewed at any time—by anybody. He always stages a good show and makes a point of saying something that will work up into a spectacular story.
>
> He is so charming to them personally that every writer always goes away from the studio D. W.'s devoted friend for life. The more so, because they always approach the throne seared down to the bottom of their souls."[1]

Also represented here is another pioneering entertainment reporter from the *Los Angeles Times,* Grace Kingsley. She joined the newspaper in 1911, was its first motion picture editor, and for decades contributed a gossip column (titled "Hobnobbing in Hollywood" in the 1930s). She died, appropriately, in Hollywood on October 8, 1962, at the age of eighty-nine.

Other major entertainment writers of the period to be found here include Roberta Courtlandt, Hazel Simpson Naylor, and Frederick James Smith, all prominent in the fan magazine field. Writers from the trade papers who interviewed D. W. Griffith are George Blaisdell and Edward Weitzel. A legendary gossip columnist, Louella Parsons, published a 1922 interview with Griffith in the *Morning Telegraph*, one of a series of interviews with directors and leading players of the directors that are deserving of more attention from researchers and scholars.[2] It was actually Parsons's later competitor, Hedda Hopper, of whom the director was most fond. Hedda always had a soft spot for Griffith in that in the fall of 1915, he had hired her then-husband DeWolf Hopper, when he was down on his luck. Griffith was always assured of a friendly mention in Hedda's column. As Herb Sterne recalled for me, when he escorted Hedda to the 1946 Academy Awards, at which Griffith was one of the presenters, the director thanked the lady by pinching her bottom—much to the obvious delight of them both.

Herb Sterne was a close friend of both Griffith and Lillian Gish, and it is a pleasure to reprint his 1939 interview with the director, originally published in the *New York Times*. While Herb Sterne was a good friend to Griffith, it was Seymour Stern who was his officially anointed biographer, and while it is unfortunate that Seymour never sat down and formally interviewed the director, I am able to publish his notes on questions that he had prepared for Griffith a year before his death.

I have annotated the interviews both within the text and with the use of endnotes. I have tried to be sensible with such annotations, providing them only when appropriate, sometimes even explaining an antiquated term, and not purposely identifying every individual mentioned in the course of the interview. Hopefully, the reader is sufficiently versed in film and general history to be able to identify obvious individuals. Blatant typographical errors have been corrected, but I have made no effort to "modernize" a text by changing the manner in which a certain word was printed then rather than now (for example, "thru" rather than "through" is consistently used in the 1910s and 1920s).

The most drastic of my editing is reserved for Henry Stephen Gordon's series, "The Story of David Wark Griffith," that began publication in the June 1916 issue of *Photoplay*. I have retained all portions of the "Story" containing commentary by the director, but deleted sections which are, in all truth, not particularly important and which use overblown language that makes for heavy reading today.

Those readers with a keen knowledge and interest in Griffith's work will find many of his comments perceptive, and, under careful scrutiny, invaluable in terms of understanding how he functioned and what he was trying to achieve.

If there is an over-riding theme in the interviews, it is the director's search for truth and also for beauty. Often, he will identify *Broken Blossoms* as being far more important than, say, *The Birth of a Nation* or *Intolerance*. In a 1920 interview, in which the emphasis is on *Way Down East*, Griffith speaks of one beautiful, single effect such as "the movement of the wind upon the water, the swaying branches of a tree." It is a thought that stays with him through the end, as in his final interview, he talks of "the moving of wind on beautiful trees," and his arrogant belief that "We have lost beauty."

What can one say of the last interview? It is both tragic and infinitely moving. Griffith is sad and yet triumphant, saying exactly what he wants to say, aided by a double gin at his side. This editor has total empathy with the man. How much we owe Ezra Goodman for seeking out Griffith and getting that interview into print. As one reads it, we are reminded that Goodman wrote one of the best personal chronicles of Hollywood history, *The Fifty-Year Decline and Fall of Hollywood*, first published in 1961 and a book that still should be in print.

D. W. Griffith has quite a sense of humor, most notable in his 1928 comments to members of the Academy of Motion Picture Arts and Sciences; you can almost visualize the twinkle in his eye as he sets out to deflate the pomposity of the new organization. He is not a vain man, despite regretting that he failed to patent some of his cinematic "inventions," and while the interviews are at times intellectual in their references to Keats or to Browning, there is an innate simplicity to this great individual. This comes across most in the June 1916 piece by Henry Stephen Gordon, in which Griffith responds to a question, "About myself? . . . The public can not care about that topic; you cannot improve on what was written about a real man of note once: 'He was born, he grew a little, he slept a little, he ate a little, he worked a little, he loved a little—and then he died.'"

Ultimately, it must be acknowledged, the interviews fail to provide us with a complete picture of D. W. Griffith's life and work. What is here are, of necessity, fragments—some truthful commentary and some highly questionable. But then, as D. W. Griffith was fond of saying, quoting Pontius Pilate, "Truth? What is the truth?"

AS

Notes

1. Harry Carr, "The Confessions of an Interviewer," *Motion Picture Magazine*, March 1924, p. 82.

2. I am grateful to Bruce Long for bringing this series to my attention.

Chronology

1875	January 22, David Wark Griffith born on a farm near Crestwood, Oldham County, Kentucky, the youngest of four children, to Jacob and Mary (Oglesby) Griffith.
1885	Jacob Griffith dies suddenly.
1889	The Griffith family moves to Louisville, Kentucky.
1889	July 21, his sister Mattie Griffith dies.
1890	Begins full-time employment at J. C. Lewis Dry Goods Store in Louisville.
1893	Becomes a clerk at the C. T. Dearing Book Store, and, after being fired, at Flexner and Staadeker's Book Store in Louisville.
1896	Joins a theatrical touring company.
1897	Joins Meffert Stock Company in Louisville.
1897	Begins summer tour in Indiana and Kentucky with the Twilight Revellers; adopts stage name of Lawrence Griffith.
1899	Moves to New York.
1901	Tours in vaudeville playlet *In Washington's Time*.
1903	September–October, tours in *Miss Petticoats*.
1904	Meets Linda Arvidson while appearing with the Melbourne McDowell company at the San Francisco Opera House.
1904	Unable to find work as an actor, becomes a migrant worker in San Francisco area.
1905	Plays Alesandro in Los Angeles and touring version of *Ramona*.
1905	December 10, begins tour as member of Nance O'Neil's company.
1906	May 14, marries actress Linda Arvidson at Old North Church, Boston.

1906	Completes his play, *A Fool and a Girl*.
1906	Appears with his wife in *The One Woman*, touring the South, and meets its author, Thomas Dixon, Jr.
1906	August 24, his sister Annie Wheeler Griffith dies.
1907	January 10, his poem, "The Wild Duck," appears in *Leslie's Weekly*.
1907	Spring, appears in historical pageant *Pocahontas* in Norfolk, Virginia.
1907	September 12, James K. Hackett produces Griffith's play *A Fool and a Girl* in Washington, D.C., starring Fannie Ward, her husband-to-be Jack Dean, and Alison Skipworth.
1908	Tries unsuccessfully to sell a scenario to the Edison Company.
1908	January, hired by director J. Searle Dawley to appear in the Edison film *Rescued from an Eagle's Nest*; also appears at Edison in *Cupid's Pranks*.
1908	Hired as an actor by the American Biograph Company.
1908	July 14, his first film as a director, *The Adventures of Dollie*, released.
1909	June 10, *The Lonely Villa* released.
1909	October 4, *Pippa Passes or, The Song of Conscience*, released.
1909	October 28, *Lines of White on a Sullen Sea* released.
1909	December 13, *A Corner in Wheat* released.
1910	January, begins annual winter visit with company to Southern California.
1910	His elder brother, Jacob Wark Griffith dies.
1911	March 23, *The Lonedale Operator* released.
1911	June 12 and June 15, *Enoch Arden* released.
1912	March 28, *The Girl and Her Trust* released.
1912	September 9, *An Unseen Enemy* released.
1912	October 31, *The Musketeers of Pig Alley* released.
1913	June 21, *The Mothering Heart* released.
1913	David W. Griffith Corporation formed.
1913	September 29, full-page advertisement appears in the *New York Dramatic Mirror* promoting him as "Producer of All Great Biograph Successes."
1913	October 1, officially leaves the American Biograph Company.
1913	December, begins production on his first Reliance-Majes-

	tic feature, *The Escape*, final scenes for which were shot at 4500 Sunset Boulevard, Los Angeles.
1914	March 28, *The Battle at Elderbush Gulch* released (filmed in the spring of 1913).
1915	January 1,. as *The Clansman*, *The Birth of a Nation* previews at the Loring Opera House, Riverside, California.
1915	February 8, as *The Clansman*, *The Birth of a Nation* opens at Clune's Auditorium, Los Angeles.
1915	February 18, screens *The Birth of a Nation* at the White House at request of President Woodrow Wilson. Legend has it that at the end of the screening the President said, "It is like writing history with lightning. And my only regret is that it is all so terribly true."
1915	March 3, *The Birth of a Nation* premieres at the Liberty Theatre, New York.
1915	May, announces plans to make a film on *The Quest of the Holy Grail*.
1915	July 28, with Thomas H. Ince and Mack Sennett forms distribution company, Triangle Film Corporation, headed by Harry E. Aitken.
1915	September 4, formal announcement that films supervised by Griffith for Triangle to be identified as Fine Arts productions, with studios at 4500 Sunset Boulevard.
1915	November 7, release of first Fine Arts production, marking the screen debut of Douglas Fairbanks, *The Lamb*, written by D. W. Griffith.
1915	December 11, his mother, Mary Oglesby, dies.
1916	D.W.G. Corporation formed.
1916	August 6, *Intolerance* previews at the Loring Opera House, Riverside, California.
1916	September 5, *Intolerance* opens at the Liberty Theatre, New York.
1916	November, produces one-reel film, *A Day with Governor Whitman*, in appreciation of the New York governor's vetoing of a motion picture censorship bill.
1917	Spring, invited by British Government to visit Europe and make propaganda film about World War I.
1917	March 18, sails for Europe on SS *Baltic*.
1917	March 31, announcement of Griffith's disposal of his

	stock in Triangle and his signing a long-term contract with Artcraft Pictures Corporation (dated March 16, 1917).
1918	January 29, signs new contract with Famous Players-Lasky Corporation, amending previous contract following the merger of Artcraft Pictures and Famous Players.
1918	March 12, *Hearts of the World* premieres at Clune's Auditorium, Los Angeles.
1918	April 4, *Hearts of the World* premieres at 44th Street Theatre, New York.
1919	February 5, signs articles of incorporation of United Artists, along with Charlie Chaplin, Douglas Fairbanks, and Mary Pickford.
1919	May 13, *Broken Blossoms* premieres at the George M. Cohan Theatre, New York.
1919	May, D. W. Griffith Repertory Season at the George M. Cohan Theatre, New York, which includes *The Fall of Babylon* and *The Mother and the Law*, adapted from *Intolerance*.
1919	June, agrees to produce a short film record of the Centenary Celebration of the Methodist Minute Men at Columbus, Ohio, titled *The World at Columbus*.
1919	August 11, revised "peace edition" of *Hearts of the World* premieres at the George M. Cohan Theatre, New York.
1919	December 10, while shooting exteriors for *The Idol Dancer* and *The Love Flower*, sets sail from Fort Lauderdale to Nassau, and because of a tropical storm, the trip takes three days and rumors circulate that the director has been lost at sea.
1919/1920	Acquires the Henry Flagler estate at Mamaroneck, Long Island, and this becomes his new studio.
1920	D. W. Griffith Corporation formed.
1920	Secures option to film Joseph Hergesheimer's novel, *Java Head*, subsequently filmed in 1923 by Paramount.
1920	September 3, *Way Down East* premieres at the 44th Street Theatre, New York.
1921	December 28, *Orphans of the Storm* premieres at the Tremont Theatre, Boston.
1922	January 2, 1922, *Orphans of the Storm* premieres at the Apollo Theatre, New York.
1923	Summer, plans blackface comedy, *His Darker Self*, to star

	Al Jolson, but the latter quits and film subsequently released in March 1924 with Lloyd Hamilton.
1924	December 4, *Isn't Life Wonderful* premieres at the Town Hall, New York.
1927	Shoots additional scenes and handles some re-editing of the Duncan Sisters vehicle, *Topsy and Eva*.
1929	February 3, talks about "success in the movies" on television station WZAXD-Schenectady and radio station WGY-New York.
1931	December 10, his last film, *The Struggle*, premieres at the Rivoli Theatre, New York.
1933	April 19, ends relationship with United Artists Corporation.
1933	Broadcasts radio series, *D. W. Griffith's Hollywood*; series cancelled after thirteen weeks.
1934	March 22, his sister Virginia Ruth Griffith dies.
1935	March 5, Biltmore Hotel, Los Angeles, receives a Special Academy Award "for his distinguished creative achievements as director and producer and his invaluable initiative and lasting contributions to the progress of the motion picture arts"; also presents Best Actor and Best Actress Awards to Victor McLaglen and Bette Davis.
1935	Summer, in United Kingdom with plans to direct remake of *Broken Blossoms*; it is eventually directed by Hans Brahm, released in U.K. in 1936, and opens in New York at the Belmont Theatre, January 13, 1937.
1936	February 28, divorces Linda Arvidson.
1936	March 2, marries Evelyn Baldwin, at the Brown Hotel, Louisville.
1936	Summer, invited by director W. S. Van Dyke to shoot a scene for *San Francisco* (probably nothing more than a publicity stunt).
1939	June, joins Hal Roach organization with announced plan to direct *One Million B.C.*, but leaves the project.
1939	August, receives first honorary life membership from the Screen Directors Guild (later the Directors Guild of America).
1940	November 12, beginning of a retrospective at New York's Museum of Modern Art, together with an exhibition of original documents and photographs in second floor gal-

	lery; curator Iris Barry publishes first book-length study of the director, *D. W. Griffith: American Film Master*.
1942	December, producer Harry Sherman abandons plans to remake *The Birth of a Nation*, "knowing that it would be objectionable to Negroes."
1945	Writes a treatment based on his time with the Twilight Revellers and a small portion is used by George Cukor in his 1960 film, *Heller in Pink Tights*.
1945	Receives Honorary Doctorate from University of Louisville.
1946	March 7, Grauman's Chinese Theatre, Hollywood, presents Academy Awards for Best Cinematography to Harry Stradling and Leon Shamroy.
1946	September 13, separates from Evelyn Baldwin Griffith.
1947	October 10, divorces Evelyn Baldwin and moves into Hollywood Knickerbocker Hotel.
1948	January 22, to celebrate his seventy-third birthday donates some volumes used for research on *The Birth of a Nation* and *Hearts of the World* to the Hollywood Public Library; they are subsequently destroyed in a fire.
1948	July 23, suffers a cerebral hemorrhage in the lobby of the Hollywood Knickerbocker Hotel.
1948	July 24, 8:42 A.M., dies at Temple Hospital, Los Angeles; that same day, attorney Lloyd Wright files will, revealing estate of between $20,000 and $50,000.
1948	July 25, body lies in state at A. W. Brown & Sons, morticians.
1948	July 27, Memorial Service at Hollywood Masonic Temple, after which body is flown for burial at Mount Tabor cemetery, Centerfield, Kentucky.
1950	May 15, remains transferred to new plot in order to accommodate memorial from Directors Guild of America.
1959	Homer Croy publishes first Griffith book-length biography, *Starmaker: The Story of D. W. Griffith* (Duell, Sloan & Pearce).
1959	March 20, thirty-six films and sixteen scenarios owned by Griffith are offered for sale at auction in Los Angeles; they are sold to Killiam Shows, Inc., the only bidder, for $21,000.

1961	August, announcement that the D. W. Griffith/Fine Arts studio is to be razed for the building of a supermarket.
1975	Edward Wagenknecht and Anthony Slide publish first complete filmography and survey of Griffith's work, *The Films of D. W. Griffith* (Crown).
1975	February 20, Blanche Sweet, escorted by Anthony Slide, opens the D. W. Griffith Theatre in New York.
1975	May 27, U.S. Postal Service issues commemorative stamp in his honor; film clips for the event are prepared by Anthony Slide.
1984	Richard Schickel publishes the definitive biography, *D. W. Griffith: An American Life* (Simon & Schuster).
1994	May, British Board of Film Classification rules that video versions of *The Birth of a Nation* can only be released with a lengthy disclaimer calling the film "inflammatory" and referencing Griffith's "unthinkable racial prejudice" and "distortion of history."
1999	December, the national board of the Directors Guild of America votes unanimously and without input from its members to end the use of the name "D. W. Griffith Award" for its highest honor, and it is renamed the DGA Lifetime Achievement Award.
2000	January, National Society of Film Critics protests action of DGA in a public letter, labeling it "an erasure and rewriting of American film history."

Filmography

This list includes feature films only. Complete credits and synopses for all the feature films, as well as a complete list of all the Biograph shorts directed by Griffith, with release dates, can be found in *The Films of D. W. Griffith* by Edward Wagenknecht and Anthony Slide, Crown Publishers, 1975. The best known of the Biograph shorts are also listed in the chronology, with release dates, as are the most prominent of the feature films with full information as to premiere locations and dates.

1914
JUDITH OF BETHULIA
Producer/Distributor: American Biograph
Director/Screenplay: **D. W. Griffith**, based on the narrative poem "Judith and Holofernes," and the subsequent play *Judith of Bethulia*, by Thomas Bailey Aldrich, both of which were based on the Book of Judith in the Old Testament Apocrypha.
Titles: Frank Wood
Cinematographer: Billy Bitzer
Editor: James Smith
Cast: Blanche Sweet (Judith), Henry B. Walthall (Holofernes), Mae Marsh (Naomi), Robert Harron (Nathan), Lillian Gish (young mother), Dorothy Gish (crippled beggar), Kate Bruce (Judith's maid), G. Jiquel Lanoe (the eunuch)
Four reels

THE BATTLE OF THE SEXES
Producer: Reliance-Majestic
Distributor: Mutual/The Continental Feature Film Company
Director: **D. W. Griffith**
Based on *The Single Standard* by Daniel Carson Goodman
Cinematographer: Billy Bitzer

Editors: James Smith and Rose Richtel
Cast: Lillian Gish (Jane Andrews), Owen Moore (Frank Andrews), Mary Alden (Mrs. Frank Andrews), Fay Tincher (Cleo, the siren), Robert Harron (the son)
Five reels

THE ESCAPE
Producer: Reliance-Majestic
Distributor: Mutual
Director: **D. W. Griffith**
Screenplay: Paul Armstrong, based on his play
Cinematographer: Billy Bitzer
Editors: James Smith and Rose Richtel
Cast: Blanche Sweet (May Joyce), Mae Marsh (Jennie Joyce), Robert Harron (Larry Joyce), Donald Crisp ("Bull" McGee), Owen Moore (Dr. von Eiden), F. A. Turner (Jim Joyce), Ralph Lewis (senator), "Tammany" Young (McGee's henchman)
Seven reels

HOME, SWEET HOME
Producer: Reliance-Majestic
Distributor: Mutual
Director: **D. W. Griffith**
Screenplay: H. E. Aitken and **D. W. Griffith**
Cinematographer: Billy Bitzer
Editors: James Smith and Rose Richtel
Cast (Prologue and Epilogue): Henry B. Walthall (John Howard Payne), Josephine Crowell (his mother), Lillian Gish (his sweetheart), Dorothy Gish (his sister), Fay Tincher (the worldly woman)
Cast (The First Story): Mae Marsh (Apple Pie Mary), Spottiswoode Aitken (her father), Robert Harron (the easterner), Miriam Cooper (his fiancée)
Cast (The Second Story): Mary Alden (the mother), Donald Crisp, James Kirkwood and Jack Pickford (her sons), Fred Burns (the sheriff)
Cast (The Third Story): Courtenay Foote (the husband), Blanche Sweet (the wife), Owen Moore (the tempter), Edward Dillon (the musician), Betty Marsh (the baby)
Six reels

THE AVENGING CONSCIENCE
Producer: Reliance-Majestic

Distributor: Mutual
Director/Screenplay: **D. W. Griffith**, suggested by "The Tell-Tale Heart"
and other works by Edgar Allan Poe
Cinematographer: Billy Bitzer
Editors: James Smith and Rose Richtel
Cast: Henry B. Walthall (the nephew), Blanche Sweet (the sweetheart),
Josephine Crowell (her mother), Spottiswoode Aitken (the uncle),
George Siegmann (the Italian), Ralph Lewis (the detective), Mae Marsh
(maid at the garden party), Robert Harron (the grocer's boy)
Six reels

1915
THE BIRTH OF A NATION
Producer/Distributor: Epoch Producing Corporation
Director: **D. W. Griffith**
Screenplay **D. W. Griffith** and Frank Woods, based on the novel and
play *The Clansman* by Thomas Dixon, Jr.
Cinematographer: Billy Bitzer
Assistant Cinematographer: Karl Brown
Editor: James Smith
Cast: Lillian Gish (Elsie Stoneman), Mae Marsh (Flora Cameron, the Lit-
tle Sister), Henry B. Walthall (Colonel Ben Cameron, the Little Colonel),
Miriam Cooper (Margaret Cameron), Mary Alden (Lydia Brown), Ralph
Lewis (the Hon. Austin Stoneman), Walter Long (Gus), Robert Harron
(Tod Stoneman), Elmer Clifton (Phil Stoneman)
Twelve reels

[In 1915 and 1916, Griffith "supervised" or "produced" all the films made
by Fine Arts. His contribution to these productions is uncertain in that
Griffith himself denied any involvement in later years. Listed below are
those films for which Griffith has a definite credit.]

PILLARS OF SOCIETY
Screenplay: **D. W. Griffith**

THE LAMB
Based on *The Man and the Test* by Granville Warwick (**D. W. Griffith**)

THE LILY AND THE ROSE
Screenplay: Granville Warwick (**D. W. Griffith**)

1916

LET KATIE DO IT
Based on a novel by Granville Warwick (**D. W. Griffith**)

THE MISSING LINKS
Based on a story by Granville Warwick (**D. W. Griffith**)

THE WOOD NYMPH
Screenplay: Granville Warwick (**D. W. Griffith**)

DAPHNE AND THE PIRATE
Screenplay: Granville Warwick (**D. W. Griffith**)

HOODOO ANN
Screenplay: Granville Warwick (**D. W. Griffith**)

AN INNOCENT MAGDALENE
Based on a story by Granville Warwick (**D. W. Griffith**)

THE MARRIAGE OF MOLLY O'
Screenplay: Granville Warwick (**D. W. Griffith**)

INTOLERANCE
Producer/Distributor: Wark Producing Corporation
Director/Screenplay: **D. W. Griffith**
Cinematographer: Billy Bitzer
Assistant Cinematographer: Karl Brown
Editors: James and Rose Smith
Cast (Of All Ages): Lillian Gish (the Woman Who Rocks the Cradle)
Cast (The Modern Story): Mae Marsh (the Dear One), Fred Turner (her father), Robert Harron (the Boy), Sam De Grasse (Arthur Jenkins), Vera Lewis (Mary T. Jenkins), Miriam Cooper (the Friendless One), Walter Long (the Musketeer of the Slums)
Cast (The Judaean Story): Howard Gaye (the Christ), Lillian Langdon (Mary, the Mother), Olga Grey (Mary Magdalene), Bessie Love (the bride of Cana), George Walsh (the bridegroom)
Cast (The French Story): Margery Wilson (Brown Eyes), Eugene Pallette (Prosper Latour), Spottiswoode Aitken (Brown Eye's father), Ruth Handforth (Brown Eye's mother), Josephine Crowell (Catherine de Médici)
Cast (The Babylonian Story): Constance Talmadge (the Mountain Girl),

Elmer Clifton (the Rhapsode), Alfred Paget (Belshazzar), Seena Owen (Attarea, the Princess Beloved), Carl Stockdale (King Nabonidus), Tully Marshall (High Priest of Bel), George Siegmann (Cyrus the Persian), Elmo Lincoln (the mighty man of valor)
Fourteen reels

DIANE OF THE FOLLIES
Screenplay: Granville Warwick (**D. W. Griffith**), based on the play *Trelawny of the Wells* by Arthur Wing Pinero

1918
HEARTS OF THE WORLD
Producer: Paramount-Artcraft/D. W. Griffith, Inc.
Distributor: Paramount
Director: **D. W. Griffith**
Screenplay: M. Gaston de Tolignac, translated into English by Captain Victor Marier (both pseudonyms for **D. W. Griffith**)
Cinematographer: Billy Bitzer
Editors: James and Rose Smith
Cast: Adolphe Lestina (the grandfather), Josephine Crowell (the mother), Lillian Gish (the Girl), Robert Harron (the Boy), Jack Cosgrave (the Boy's father), Kate Bruce (the Boy's mother), Ben Alexander (the Littlest Brother)
Twelve reels

THE GREAT LOVE
Producer/Distributor: Paramount-Artcraft
Director: **D. W. Griffith**
Screenplay: Captain Victor Marier (**D. W. Griffith**)
Cinematographer: Billy Bitzer
Cast: Robert Harron (Jim Young of Youngstown), Henry B. Walthall (Sir Roger Brighton), Gloria Hope (Jessie Lovewell), Lillian Gish (Susie Broadplains), Maxfield Stanley (John Broadplains)
Seven reels

THE GREATEST THING IN LIFE
Producer/Distributor: Paramount-Artcraft
Director: **D. W. Griffith**
Screenplay: Captain Victor Marier (**D. W. Griffith**) and S. E. V. Taylor
Cinematographer: Billy Bitzer

Editor: James Smith
Cast: Lillian Gish (Jeanette Peret), Robert Harron (Edward Livingston), Adolpe Lestina (Leo Peret), David Butler (Monsier Le Bébé), Elmo Lincoln (the American soldier)
Six reels

1919
A ROMANCE OF HAPPY VALLEY
Producer/Distributor: Paramount-Artcraft
Director: **D. W. Griffith**
Screenplay: Captain Victor Marier (**D. W. Griffith**), based on a story by Mary Castelman
Cinematographer: Billy Bitzer
Editor: James Smith
Cast: Lydia Yeamans Titus (Auntie Smiles), Robert Harron (John L. Logan, Jr.), Kate Bruce (Mrs. Logan), George Fawcett (John L. Logan, Sr.), Lillian Gish (Jennie Timberlake), George Nichols (her father)
Six reels

THE GIRL WHO STAYED AT HOME
Producer/Distributor: Paramount-Artcraft
Director: **D. W. Griffith**
Screenplay: S. E. V. Taylor and **D. W. Griffith**
Cinematographer: Billy Bitzer
Editor: James Smith
Cast: Adolphe Lestina (Monsieur France), Carol Dempster (Atoline France), Frances Parkes (the chum), Richard Barthelmess (Ralph Grey), Robert Harron (James Grey), George Fawcett (Edward Grey), Kate Bruce (Mrs. Edward Grey)
Six reels

TRUE HEART SUSIE
Producer/Distributor: Paramount-Artcraft
Director: **D. W. Griffith**
Screenplay: Marian Fremont
Cinematographer: Billy Bitzer
Editor: James Smith
Cast: Lillian Gish (Susie May Trueheart), Robert Harron (William Jenkins), Walter Higby (William's father), Loyola O'Connor (Susie's aunt), George Fawcett (the stranger), Clarine Seymour (Bettina Hopkins), Kate

Bruce (Bettina's aunt)
Six reels

SCARLET DAYS
Producer/Distributor: Paramount-Artcraft
Director: **D. W. Griffith**
Screenplay: S. E. V. Taylor
Cinematographer: Billy Bitzer
Editor: James Smith
Cast: Richard Barthelmess (Alvarez, a bandit), Eugene Besserer (Rosie Nell), Carol Dempster (Lady Fair, her daughter), Clarine Seymour (Chiquita), Ralph Graves (Randolph, a Virginia gentleman), George Fawcett (the sheriff), Walter Long (King Bagley)
Five reels

BROKEN BLOSSOMS
Producer: D. W. Griffith, Inc.
Distributor: United Artists
Director and Screenplay: **D. W. Griffith**, based on "The Chink and the Child" in *Limehouse Nights* by Thomas Burke
Cinematographer: Billy Bitzer
Special Effects: Hendrik Sartov
Additional Cinematography: Karl Brown
Editor: James Smith
Cast: Lillian Gish (Lucy Burrows), Richard Barthelmess (the Yellow Man), Donald Crisp (Battling Burrows), Arthur Howard (his manager), Edward Peil (Evil Eye), George Beranger (the Spying One)
Six reels

THE GREATEST QUESTION
Producer/Distributor: First National
Director: **D. W. Griffith**
Screenplay: S. E. V. Taylor, based on a story by William Hale
Cinematographer: Billy Bitzer
Editor: James Smith
Cast: Lillian Gish (Nellie Jarvis, known as "Little Miss Yes'm"), Robert Harron (Jimmie Hilton), Ralph Grave (John Hilton, Jr.), Eugenie Besserer (Mrs. Hilton), George Fawcett (John Hilton, Sr.), Tom Wilson (Uncle Zeke), George Nicholls (Martin Cain), Josephine Crowell (Mrs. Cain)
Six reels

1920

THE IDOL DANCER

Producer/Distributor: First National

Director: **D. W. Griffith**

Screenplay: S. E. V. Taylor, based on the story "Blood of the Covenanters" by Gordon Ray Young

Cinematographer: Billy Bitzer

Editor: James Smith

Cast: Richard Barthelmess (Dan McGuire), Clarine Seymour (Mary, otherwise known as White Almond Flower), Creighton Hale (Walter Kincaid), George MacQuarrie (Rev. Franklin Blythe), Kate Bruce (Mrs. Blythe), Porter Strong (Peter, a native minister), Anders Randolf (the Blackbirder)

Seven reels

THE LOVE FLOWER

Producer: D. W. Griffith, Inc.

Distributor: United Artists

Director and Screenplay: **D. W. Griffith**, based on the story "The Black Beach" by Ralph Stock

Cinematographer: Billy Bitzer

Editor: James Smith

Cast: Carol Dempster (Stella Bevan), Richard Barthelmess (Jerry Trevethon), George MacQuarrie (Thomas Bevan), Anders Randolf (Matthew Crane), Florence Short (Mrs. Bevan), Crauford Kent (Mrs. Bevan's lover), Adolphe Lestina (Bevan's old servant)

Seven reels

WAY DOWN EAST

Producer: D. W. Griffith, Inc.

Distributor: United Artists

Director: **D. W. Griffith**

Screenplay: Anthony Paul Kelly, elaborated by **D. W. Griffith**, from the stage play by Lottie Blair Parker and Joseph R. Grismer

Cinematographers: Billy Bitzer and Hendrik Sartov

Editors: James and Rose Smith

Cast: Lillian Gish (Anna Moore), Mrs. David Landau (her mother), Florence Short (the eccentric aunt), Lowell Sherman (Lennox Sanderson), Burr McIntosh (Squire Bartlett), Kate Bruce (Mrs. Bartlett), Richard Barthelmess (David Bartlett), Vivia Ogden (Martha Perkins), Porter Strong

(Seth Holcomb), George Neville (Reuben Whipple), Edgar Nelson (Hi Holler), Mary Hay (Kate Brewster), Creighton Hale (Professor Sterling), Emily Fitzroy (Maria Poole)
Thirteen reels

1921

DREAM STREET
Producer: D. W. Griffith, Inc.
Distributor: United Artists
Director: **D. W. Griffith**
Screenplay: Roy Sinclair (**D. W. Griffith**), based on two stories, "Gina of the Chinatown" and "The Sign of the Lamp," in *Limehouse Nights* by Thomas Burke
Cinematographer: Hendrik Sartov
Editors: James and Rose Smith
Set Designer: Charles M. Kirk
Cast: Carol Dempster (Gypsy Fair), Ralph Graves (James "Spike" McFadden), Charles Emmett Mack (Bill McFadden), Edward Peil (Sway Wan), W. J. Ferguson (Gypsy's father), Porter Strong (Samuel Jones), George Neville (Tom Chudder), Charles Slattery (the police inspector), Tyrone Power, Sr. (a preacher of the streets), Morgan Wallace (the masked violinist)
Eleven reels

1922

ORPHANS OF THE STORM
Producer: D. W. Griffith, Inc.
Distributor: United Artists
Director: **D. W. Griffith**
Screenplay: Gaston de Tolignac (**D. W. Griffith**), based on *The Two Orphans* by Adolphe Dennery and Eugene Cormon
Cinematographers: Hendrik Sartov, Paul Allen, and Billy Bitzer
Editors: James and Rose Smith
Art Director: Charles M. Kirk
Set Designer: Edward Scholl
Cast: Lillian Gish (Henriette Girard), Dorothy Gish (Louise), Joseph Schildkraut (Chevalier De Vaudrey), Frank Losee (Count de Linieres), Catherine Emmett (Countess de Linieres), Morgan Wallace (Marquis de Praille), Lucille La Verne (Mother Frochard), Sheldon Lewis (Jacques Frochard), Frank Puglia (Pierre Frochard), Creighton Hale (Picard), Leslie

King (Jacques-Forget-Not), Monte Blue (Danton), Sidney Herbert (Robespierre)
Thirteen reels (later cut to twelve)

ONE EXCITING NIGHT
Producer: D. W. Griffith, Inc.
Distributor: United Artists
Director and Screenplay: **D. W. Griffith**, based on the original story
"The Haunted Grange" by Irene Sinclair (**D. W. Griffith**)
Cinematographer: Hendrik Sartov
Cast: Carol Dempster (Agnes Harrington), Henry Hull (John Fairfax),
Porter Strong (Romeo Washington), Morgan Wallace (J. Wilson Rock-
maine), C. H. Crocker-King (the neighbor), Margaret Dale (Mrs. Har-
rington), Frank Sheridan (the detective)
Eleven reels

1923
THE WHITE ROSE
Producer: D. W. Griffith, Inc.
Distributor: United Artists
Director: **D. W. Griffith**
Screenplay: Irene Sinclair (**D. W. Griffith**)
Cinematographers: Billy Bitzer, Hendrik Sartov, and Hal Sintzenich
Set Designer: Charles M. Kirk
Cast: Mae Marsh (Bessie "Teazie" Williams), Carol Dempster (Marie Car-
rington), Ivor Novello (Joseph Beaugarde), Neil Hamilton (John White),
Lucille La Verne ("Auntie" Easter), Porter Strong (Apollo)
Twelve reels (later cut to ten)

1924
AMERICA
Producer: D. W. Griffith, Inc.
Distributor: United Artists
Director: **D. W. Griffith**
Screenplay: John Pell, based on an original story by Robert W. Chambers
Cinematographers: Hendrik Sartov, Billy Bitzer, Marcel Le Picard, and
Hal Sintzenich
Editors: James and Rose Smith
Art Director: Charles M. Kirk
Cast: Neil Hamilton (Nathan Holden), Erville Anderson (Justice Mon-

tague), Carol Dempster (Nancy Montague), Charles Emmett Mack (Charles Philip Edward Montague), Lee Beggs (Samuel Adams), John Dunton (John Hancock), Arthur Donaldson (King George III), Frank Walsh (Thomas Jefferson), Lionel Barrymore (Captain Walter Butler) Fourteen reels (later cut to eleven)

ISN'T LIFE WONDERFUL
Producer: D. W. Griffith, Inc.
Distributor: United Artists
Director and Screenplay: **D. W. Griffith**, based on the short story by Major Geoffrey Moss in his book *Defeat*
Cinematographers: Hendrik Sartov and Hal Sintzenich
Cast: Carol Dempster (Inga), Neil Hamilton (Paul), Helen Lowell (the grandmother), Erville Alderson (the professor), Frank Puglia (Theodor), Marcia Harris (the aunt), Lupino Lane (Rudolph)
Nine reels

1925
SALLY OF THE SAWDUST
Producer: D. W. Griffith, Inc.
Distributor: United Artists
Director: **D. W. Griffith**
Screenplay: Forrest Halsey, based on the play *Poppy* by Dorothy Donnelly
Cinematographers: Harry Fischbeck and Hal Sintzenich
Editor: James Smith
Art Director: Charles M. Kirk
Cast: Carol Dempster (Poppy), W. C. Fields (Professor Eugene McGargle), Alfred Lunt (Peyton Lennox), Erville Alderson (Judge Foster), Effie Shannon (Mrs. Foster), Charles Hammond (Mr. Lennox, Sr.)
Ten reels

"THAT ROYLE GIRL"
Producer: Famous Players-Lasky
Distributor: Paramount
Director: **D. W. Griffith**
Screenplay: Paul Schofield, based on the novel by Edwin Balmer
Cinematographers: Harry Fischbeck and Hal Sintzenich
Editor: James Smith
Art Director: Charles M. Kirk
Cast: Carol Dempster (Joan Daisy Royle), W. C. Fields (her father), James

Kirkwood (Deputy District Attorney Calvin Clarke), Harrison Ford (Fred
Ketlar, the King of Jazz), Marie Chambers (Adele Ketlar)
Ten reels

1927
THE SORROWS OF SATAN
Producer: Famous Players-Lasky
Distributor: Paramount
Director: **D. W. Griffith**
Screenplay: Forrest Halsey, based on the novel by Marie Corelli
Adaptation: John Russell and George Hull
Titles: Julian Johnson
Cinematographer: Harry Fischbeck
Art Director: Charles M. Kirk
Cast: Adolphe Menjou (Prince Lucio de Rimanez), Ricardo Cortez (Geof-
frey Tempest), Lya De Putti (Princess Olga), Carol Dempster (Mavis
Claire), Ivan Lebedeff (Amiel), Marcia Harris (the landlady), Lawrence
D'Orsay (Lord Elton)
Nine reels

1928
DRUMS OF LOVE
Producer: Art Cinema Corporation
Distributor: United Artists
Director: **D. W. Griffith**
Screenplay: Gerrit J. Lloyd
Cinematographer: Karl Struss
Assistant Cinematographers: Harry Jackson and Billy Bitzer
Editor: James Smith
Set Designer: William Cameron Menzies
Cast: Mary Philbin (Princess Emanuella), Lionel Barrymore (Duke
Cathos de Alvia), Don Alvarado (Count Leonardo de Alvia), Tully Mar-
shall (Bopi, the court jester), Eugenie Besserer (Duchess de Alvia), Charles
Hill Mailes (Duke of Granada), William Austin (Raymond of Boston)
Eight reels

THE BATTLE OF THE SEXES
Producer: Art Cinema Corporation
Distributor: United Artists
Director: **D. W. Griffith**

Screenplay: Gerrit J. Lloyd, based on *The Single Standard* by Daniel Carson Goodman
Cinematographers: Karl Struss and Billy Bitzer
Editor: James Smith
Cast: Jean Hersholt (Judson), Phyllis Haver (Marie Skinner), Belle Bennett (Mrs. Judson), Don Alvarado ("Babe" Winsor), Sally O'Neil (Ruth Judson), William Bakewell (Billy Judson), John Batten (a friend of the Judsons)
Ten reels

1929
LADY OF THE PAVEMENTS
Producer: Art Cinema Corporation
Distributor: United Artists
Director: **D. W. Griffith**
Screenplay: Sam Taylor, based on the story "La Paiva" by Karl Volmoeller
Titles: Gerrit J. Lloyd
Dialogue: George Scarborough
Cinematographer: Karl Struss
Assistant Cinematographer: Billy Bitzer
Editor: James Smith
Set Designer: William Cameron Menzies
Cast: Lupe Velez (Nanon del Rayon), William Boyd (Count Karl von Armin), Jetta Goudal (Countess Diane des Granges), Albert Conti (Baron Finot), George Fawcett (Baron Hausemann), Henry Armetta (Papa Pierre), Franklin Pangborn (M'sieu Dubrey, the dancing master), William Bakewell (a pianist)
Seven reels (silent)/Eight reels (sound)

1930
ABRAHAM LINCOLN
Producer: Feature Productions
Distributor: United Artists
Director: **D. W. Griffith**
Screenplay and Production Adviser: John W. Considine, Jr.
Continuity and Dialogue: Stephen Vincent Benét and Gerrit J. Lloyd
Cinematography: Karl Struss
Editors: James Smith and Hal C. Kern
Art Director: William Cameron Menzies
Cast: Walter Huston (Abraham Lincoln), Una Merkel (Ann Rutledge),

Kay Hammond (Mary Todd Lincoln), E. Alyn Warren (Stephen A. Douglas), Hobart Bosworth (General Lee), Fred Warren (General Grant), Henry B. Walthall (Colonel Marshall), Frank Campeau (General Sheridan), Frances Ford (Sheridan's aide), Lucille La Verne (midwife), Ian Keith (John Wilkes Booth), Oscar Apfel (Secretary of War Stanton)
97 minutes

1931
THE STRUGGLE
Producer: D. W. Griffith, Inc.
Distributor: United Artists
Director: **D. W. Griffith**
Screenplay: Anita Loos, John Emerson, and **D. W. Griffith**, based on an original screenplay by Loos and Emerson
Cinematographer: Joseph Ruttenberg
Editor: Barney Rogan
Cast: Hal Skelly (Jimmie Wilson), Zita Johann (Florrie, his wife), Charlotte Wynters (Nina, a cabaret girl), Evelyn Baldwin (Nan Wilson), Jackson Halliday (Johnnie Marshall), Edna Hagan (Mary, Jimmie's daughter), Claude Cooper (Sam, Jimmie's friend), Arthur Lipson (Cohen, the insurance collector), Helen Mack (a catty girl)
87 minutes

D. W. Griffith: Interviews

At the Sign of the Flaming Arcs

George Blaisdell/1914

From the *Moving Picture World*, January 3, 1914, 52. "At the Sign of the Flaming Arcs" was the overall title of a weekly series.

It was a wise person who remarked that a really big man is never pomp-ous. Which saying is recalled to mind by a mighty pleasant half hour's chat on an early Saturday afternoon with David W. Griffith. It is a re-markable fact that the most striking figure in the motion picture in-dustry—the man who in whole truth may be said to have done more than any other to advance and bring us now to the day of the universal recognition of the greatness of the screen as a factor in the amusement world—it is, we repeat, a remarkable fact that for so many years the iden-tity of this man should practically have been unknown outside of trade circles. The reason is simple. It was the policy of his employers that the public had no legitimate right to any knowledge of the personality of the men and women who made and appeared in their pictures. There was no belief in, there was utter repudiation of, the theory that the in-terest of the public was heightened in the productions of a company by the knowledge of the human elements entering into the construction of them—even if that information be restricted to the names of producers and players. In line with this business practice of the Biograph Compa-ny—it is now nearly a year since its abandonment by the way—was the unusual disinclination of Mr. Griffith for publicity. He apparently cared little for it. This attribute was forcibly brought to the attention of the director's associates just after his recent alliance with the Mutual forces. They advised him to make public by means of an advertisement in the trade press a list of some of the successful pictures produced under his guidance. It was only after repeated urging that he consented.

The writer had gone to the Broadway studio of the Reliance Company to have a talk with Henry [B.] Walthall. He had met Philip Mindil, old-time newspaper man and all-around live wire, who is at the head of the Mutual's most efficient publicity bureau. Mr. Mindil is good to meet. When a man delays his departure for a half holiday on a sunny afternoon in the height of the Christmas shopping season just to entertain an intruding scribe and retains his affability you respect him.

Hopp Hadley, secretary of the Screeners and associated with Mr. Mindil, undertook to guide us about the studio. Near to the Broadway end of the building Jim [James] Kirkwood was seated in a comfortable chair, his long frame sunk into its depths as he meditatively watched and guided the rehearsal of the players under him. We wandered to the Sixteenth Street part of the studio. Under lights fiercer than any that ever beat on a throne stood Blanche Sweet and Mae Marsh rehearsing a scene of Paul Armstrong's *The Escape* [1914]. In the play the two are sisters. Miss Sweet uttered no word. Her lips did not move. She looked. You felt that she was thinking. Miss Marsh, a slip of a girl, looking even younger than she actually is—and she is in the teens—indulged in pantomime. Her lips moved, but she spoke not. A slight cough indicated the tuberculosis taint of the character she was portraying. It was all very interesting.

For a quarter of an hour we stood by the camera just behind a tall man seated comfortably, a big brown fedora hat pulled over his eyes serving as a shade from the lights. He was talking into a megaphone. It was a mild, conversational tone. At times there would be a lull. Then again there would be advice, but the voice was not raised. So this was the man who so thoroughly inspires his players that they in turn may penetrate and stir the hearts of their audiences; who by his magnetism binds to him with hoops of steel these same players. It is a rare trait, this secret of commanding unbounded loyalty, an unusual equipment, especially in one of pronounced artistic temperament. It is a cordial handshake Mr. Griffith has for a stranger. It was early in the conversation that he referred to the Biograph picture, *Man's Genesis*, released a year ago last July. The director said that within a few feet were two of the principals of the cast of that story. They were Miss Marsh and Robert Harron. It was the latter who had played Weakhands, but the writer had not recognized him. You are not long talking with Mr. Griffith before you realize that his chief aim is to reproduce life as it is—the avoidance of the stagey, the artificial, the affected. He said sometimes in a picture, when a screen player was over-acting, he would be inclined to shudder at the remark of some enthusiast nearby. "Isn't that splendid acting!" He said that successful stage actors were not necessarily good screen players. He instanced one well-known actor who had come to him for engagement, but who was only employed on an extra basis until the result of his work might be judged on the screen.

Asked as to the recent statement attributed to him about young players, Mr. Griffith smiled. "I was not quite accurately reported," he said. "What I meant was a youthful player for a youthful part. If the character calls for a girl of eighteen, I don't like to see it portrayed by a woman of thirty. When large figures are used the player is necessarily close to the camera. Then every line of the face is revealed." Mr. Griffith agreed that it is difficult if not practically impossible to fool the camera. He said that of course if a player has to indicate more than one age a resort to makeup is compulsory. Reference was made to some of the girls who have been so successful under Mr. Griffith's direction, including among others being Miss [Mary] Pickford.

"Yes," said Mr. Griffith, "the public notes the successes, but it has no knowledge of the hundreds who are tried and fail to show the possession of that indefinite quality, that something in here"—as he tapped his temple—"which gives them the power to impart to others a clear realization of a given situation." Mr. Griffith told how for two years he had tried to secure a player in a certain branch of dramatics commonly supposed to be oversupplied, but had failed.

During the conversation Mr. Griffith made a statement than which none could more clearly reveal the size of the producer—his unstinted praise of work done in a studio other than his own. We had been talking of the great respect shown by experienced stage players for the remorseless camera. The writer told how at the invitation of Producer [Edwin S.] Porter he was standing alongside the camera in the Famous Players studio when Mrs. [Minnie Maddern] Fiske was rehearsing a scene in *Tess of the D'Urbervilles* [released September 1913]. The great actress who in her long career had from the stage faced thousands was, when she was preparing for the record of her work on the screen, perturbed by the interested scrutiny of but one. She intimated to [director] Mr. [J. Searle] Dawley her desire that there should be no audience. "By the way," we asked Mr. Griffith, "did you see the work of Mrs. Fiske in *Tess*?"

"I did," he replied. "I think it was the most wonderful performance I ever saw on the screen—surely one of the most wonderful. It moved me and it held me, for its art and for its life."

David W. Griffith Speaks

Robert E. Welsh/1914

From the *New York Dramatic Mirror*, January 14, 1914, 49, 54.

There is a gray-haired, cigar-chewing city editor in my mind just now whose only guide in the writing of headlines is, "Say something that will tempt them to read the article through." What could better carry out this gospel than the line, "David W. Griffith Speaks?" He who knows not of David W. Griffith should be abashed at his temerity in wandering into the motion picture section [of this trade paper devoted to all aspects of entertainment], and he who knows David W. Griffith needs no other incentive to read. For as the statisticians say, "Were film progress to be measured in miles, the steps of advancement contributed by David W. Griffith placed end on end would gird the earth." That is the way the Statistics Editor would say it, to the motion picture student "David W. Griffith" would be enough. Explanation is superfluous, for to film men this name is what is called in algebra a "known quantity." But enough of lame comparisons, you say, away with the preliminaries; you want to hear David W. Griffith, not a mere manipulator of the typewriter keys.

Well and good, by special request, we omit the overture and raise the curtain. With the aid of Frank Woods, the Spectator,[1] I have hunted my elusive quarry down and now have him backed into a swivel chair. To call David W. Griffith a director is but half stating the truth, yet we seek the tangible as a topic for conversation and begin to talk about the direction of pictures. Remembering Mr. Griffith's early stage experience I ask him which he deems the harder work, directing for motion pictures or the spoken drama.

A wry smile lights his dark, sharply cut features, and you can already guess the answer. In fact, the very atmosphere of the Union Square studio is sufficient answer. "Directing for motion pictures, undoubtedly," he replies. "The stage director who knows absolutely nothing of pictures will throw up his hands in dismay when he begins to learn the many difficulties that surround picture work. For one thing, the director's work is, in a sense, never done. After long rehearsals, and diligent study of the scene, he cannot congratulate himself because it appears to be finely going when the camera's crank turns. There are a multitude of pitfalls before the film will be shown on the screen. Perhaps your film stock was poor, there is a danger in the developing of the negative, or making the positive prints. Then when the picture is seen on the screen you find that a stray ray of light has spoiled a much desired effect, or any one of a dozen little details that the stage directly is entirely free from."

A big man is David W. Griffith, on a big job, and with a big viewpoint. This is a discovery that you make after only a few minutes conversation with him. You note from the infrequency with which he mentions "my company, and my this and my that." It is a broader outlook that David Griffith has, and in his words you detect that broad-gauged respect and love for the new art—the motion picture. Mention of the stage director has brought to mind the ever-waking conflict, "the stage versus the motion picture," and we speak of the attitude that many adherents to the old testament hold towards the motion picture. Aha, that has struck the mark. Mr. Griffith had been leaning back in his leather-cushioned chair. Now his feet come down to the floor with a bang, and his hand taps the desk for emphasis.

"That is all wrong," he says, the words sharply cut as he is speaking fastly. "When the present day stage can show one-half to its credit that the motion picture can, then will be the time for criticism, assuredly today is not the time. The shoe is on the other foot. It is the stage that should be defended when in comparison with the motion picture.

"Suppose, for instance, that you were Milton, or Browning,[2] or any of the poets whose work has lived for generations after them. Say that you have written *Paradise Lost* and wished to have it produced on the stage. To whom would you go? In your natural enthusiasm after the completion of a great work, to whom would you go and even expect a production. Can you imagine your reception in the average manager's office with a manuscript of a classic under your arm? Or supposing the impossible, that you had secured a production, of what manager would you expect a performance that would contain any of the poetry, any of the soul of your work?"

Giving the due allowance for the difficulty with which I imagine that

I am Browning or Milton, I confess that the prospect of peddling *Paradise Lost* along Broadway is not alluring. Mr. Griffith smiles with me as we imagine the poet's plight.

"Ah," he continues, "but the motion picture has taken all of these works, has deemed none of them too 'highbrowed,' and has 'got them across.' Perhaps the production was not always perfect, or wonderfully artistic, but the big idea was still there, still intact, and it reached the hearts of the spectators. The motion picture today is doing daily more than the stage of today can think of doing. Before the stage attempts to criticize the photoplay let it do one part of what the motion picture is doing for the enjoyment, uplift, and education of the people.

"Stage directors and players often criticize the picture and its methods of work. And why? Because the picture is true to life, it is not 'theatrical.' The motion picture is an art, since it approaches more closely real life. It is this viewpoint that many people reared in the life of the spoken drama cannot get. They say that we picture directors do not know the 'rules,' the technique of the drama. We know enough of the rules and the technique to avoid them, for real life is not run by 'rules.' The motion picture technique is what technique really means, a faithful picture of life. Unless you do the thing as it was done before, as it has been done for years, you violate the 'rules'; to my mind you violate the real essence of technique when you do not do it as it is done in real life. The motion picture, properly presented, should be a picture of real life, entrances and exits should be regulated as they would be in real life, not according to set rules, and emotions should be depicted as they would be in real life.

"You say that some stage players look down on the motion picture. I say that I would not have the average stage player in a picture of mine. Mrs. [Minnie Maddern] Fiske's work in *Tess of the D'Urbervilles* [released September 1913] was wonderful; Sir Johnson Forbes-Robertson being a great artist, I imagine should be able to do some good work in pictures, but we are speaking now of the average player. It would take them years to grasp one-tenth of the knowledge of the picture art that young members of our company already know. Aside from the value of a few big names I would much rather have real picture people in my plays. Where is the player that by a mere flash of the eyes, a passing of the hand over the forehead could convey half the emotion to the spectator that Blanche Sweet or Mary Pickford could give? Where is the stage player who studies real life and who duplicates real life as these players of the screen do?"

"Blanche Sweet. Mary Pickford." These names bring to mind another thought, and I ask Mr. Griffith for the secret by which he chooses and develops screen stars. Here we make another discovery. This man of the mind-stunning salary, this director with the power of a dictator, possesses the modesty of a hermit.

"It is learning, step by step, that brought about the 'close-up.' We were striving for real acting. When you saw only the small full-length figures it was necessary to have exaggerated acting, what might be called 'physical' acting, the waving of the hands and so on. The close-up enabled us to reach real acting, restraint, acting that is a duplicate of real life. But the close-up was not accepted at once. It was called many names by men who now make use of it as a matter of course. 'Why,' said one man well known in the film world, 'that man Griffith is crazy, the characters come swimming in on the scene.'"

From talk of the close-up we come naturally to the switchback and the score of other innovations to the credit of this smiling, somewhat boyish, man in the chair before me. The evolution of the switchback as told by David Griffith proves the contention that the film is more akin to printed fiction than to the spoken drama.

"You remember," he continues, "in Dickens and other writers of his period the plan of saying, 'While all these dire happenings were occurring to our heroine, far away another scene fraught with interest was being enacted?' You remember how a chapter would end leaving you at the highest pitch of expectancy, while the author told of happenings somewhere else, but bearing on the main issue? This was the reason for the switchback, to draw the threads of the narrative together, to accelerate the action, to heighten the action. But the switchback can be abused, and is being abused. In many pictures I think the director used the switchback merely because he knows of nothing else to do at that particular moment, he used the switchback to hinder the action, to hold up the story, but all that is wrong. The switchback I use with fear. Each scene, even when only a snatch of a few feet of film, is carefully rehearsed time after time, and down to the finest details. The switchback must be as perfect as any portion of the story, and above all, it must give a very good, sound, reason for its existence before I will attempt to use it."

All this talk you say and we have not found out anything about David W. Griffith, the man, the individual. We have not discovered his age, how he came to enter pictures—oh! We've missed any one of a dozen stock interviewing details. But no, you have found the real David Griffith, the present-day Griffith. You've found, as I found, that David W. Griffith was as big in thought and word, as you expected. There is one thing you can't discover, and that is the David Griffith of the future. Still in his prime, there is a strong note in his words, an optimistic tone that make you hesitate to prophesy, to place any limitations on the future of this man.

"The future?" he replies to your question. "The future of the picture is a topic that usually makes me go into ecstasies. The big things it is possible for the picture to do makes one feel at a loss for words. Just think of what it would mean as an educational force. Think what could be done with the picture if it came into the hands of a great political party with a big issue like that of slavery before the voters. Think of the possibilities as a newspaper, with up-to-the-minute illustrated news of the world. Think of the big stories that are yet to be filmed, the history of the world yet to be told in pictures for future centuries. And all these things are not so far in the future as you may imagine. I'll wager that in a year from now, even you with some knowledge of the film business and rosy expectations of what is likely to happen, will come to me and admit that you are absolutely surprised, that you had not the faintest expectation of the things that will have happened during the coming year."

Will we? The words of David W. Griffith have unusual weight; I think we will. Let's watch 1914 and see.

Notes

1. Frank Woods was a film critic with the *New York Dramatic Mirror*, writing a column as "The Spectator," prior to becoming D. W. Griffith's story editor.

2. D. W. Griffith filmed Browning's "Pippa Passes" at Biograph in 1909.

A Poet Who Writes
on Motion Picture Films

Theatre Magazine/1914

From *Theatre Magazine*, June 1914, 311–12, 314, 316.

It has been quite the fashion to say that the motion picture profession (art if you prefer) is in its infancy. This is true, for no invention since the printing press has contained such possibilities for future development. But the implication that the business of making motion pictures is to-day of small moment is not true. If money talks, here are items which are convincing.

Several American directors are paid over twenty thousand dollars a year; a number over ten thousand. One has refused an offer which meant a salary in excess of that of the President of the United States. The owners, many of them starting with nothing, are millionaires several times over. Leading actors everywhere are paid from one hundred to three hundred dollars a week, and this—leading actors in the spoken drama please take notice—for fifty-two weeks a year. One girl, under twenty, has for some time been making a salary equal to that of a bank president.

It is not easy to comprehend the size of their audience. To say that ten million people a day go to picture shows in this country alone is to speak within the truth, but it is difficult to visualize such an audience. Just the effort is inspiring. It is not possible to estimate the world's attendance, but it must run up to many millions more.

All this both causes and is caused by rapid development in the profession. Aside from purely mechanical improvements, numerous as they have been, the past few years has seen a progress in the art of pictures plays which has meant practically a new form of dramatic expression. This has been so largely the work of one person that to-day he stands the acknowledged leader.

Yet for a long time even the name of the producer who is revolutionizing motion pictures by his work for a company organized by himself was unknown except to the elect. And in fact, even now, in spite of the pressure of the public's interest in the affairs of those who serve it, little is known of the man himself except his name. And yet to David Wark Griffith do motion pictures owe much of the wonderful artistic advance they have made in the past six years.

Mr. Griffith is peculiarly an inspiration to other directors, and the perfection of his technique is, of course, more keenly appreciated by them than by the larger audience, the public, which knows little of the means by which the effect it applauds is produced. By directors throughout the profession he is accorded first place, without question or quibbling; by the members of his company he is followed with a devotion that has knit them into an unsurpassed organization; and the public at large has responded to his work as it has to no other one man.

A boyhood bent for writing poetry, shared with youth the world over, was realized to the extent of one or two acceptances by leading magazines. He smiles at it now, and evidently sees no connection between that early ambition and his present work. But the writer, seeking to analyze his achievements, felt on hearing this that the keynote had been sounded.

In the last analysis, Mr. Griffith approaches the theme of a play essentially as a poet. The director who produced *Pippa Passes*, *A Blot on the 'Scutcheon*, *Enoch Arden* (the first two-reel photoplay), *A Pueblo Legend*, *Man's Genesis*, *The Wanderer*,[1] as he did, could be nothing less. Certainly his standard is far removed from the theatrical. Its jargon does not mark his speech nor do its confining traditions limit his method of plot development, vividly dramatic though that method is. Indeed, he denies that motion pictures can be served by looking to the current stage for inspiration.

"Moving pictures can get nothing from the legitimate stage," he says, "because American directors and playwrights have nothing to offer. The former are, for the most part, conventional and care nothing for natural acting. They don't know how to make use of even the material they have, limited as that is. Of course, there are a few, a very few exceptions. As for American playwrights, we can get our ideas from the same sources as they. We need to depend on the stage for our actors and actresses least of all. How many of them make you believe they are real human beings? No, they 'act,' that is, they use a lot of gestures and make a lot of sounds such as are never seen or heard anywhere else. For range and delicacy, the development of character, the quick transition from one mood to another, I don't known an actress now on the American stage, I don't care how great her reputation, who can begin to touch the work of some of the motion picture actresses. And I'll give you the names if you want them.

"As far as the public is concerned, there is no real competition between the stage and the motion picture. It doesn't exist. The latter makes an appeal which the former never has and never can hope to meet, not only because of its physical limitations, but because most of its managers, directors, and actors are bound by tradition. They don't know human emotion. They don't know human nature and they don't care to find out about it. James A. Herne,[2] who wrote plays with real people in them, is only just beginning to be rightly appreciated years after his death. Wonderful Mrs. Fiske is, of course, one of the exceptions, too."

With this faith in the possibilities of the medium in which he works, it is hardly necessary to say that each of the several steps in the development of motion pictures which he has originated has enhanced their poetic and their natural as opposed to their theatric value. Each has served to bring them closer to Nature, further from the playhouse. This is the Alpha and Omega of his ambition. The poetic element which accompanies this advance is inevitable, but he seems quiet unconscious of it, or at least not to have analyzed it.

He traces his descent from a long line of Welsh and Irish patriots—the romantic daring Celtic type, which had ideals, and fought and died for them. Griffith is a name with which Welsh history fairly bristles, and there has been a David Wark from the time when it was "ap-Griffith" in the sturdy clans among the Welsh mountains to the present holder of the name. His immediate family have been Southerners for four generations, and he himself is a Kentuckian—the son of Brigadier-General Jacob Wark Griffith of the Confederate Army. With such a gallant heritage, it was only natural that the stage should have appealed to the romanticism and poetry of the Celt in him, and that these, combined with the executive, courage, and single-hearted devotion which inspired his ancestors in their various courses, should have brought him to his present development.

Eight years on the stage, during which time he also wrote for magazines and began a playwright's career with a play produced by James K. Hackett, preceded his entrance into motion pictures, where he is now in his eighth year. He became a director of the Biograph Co. after a few months of acting, and Biograph photoplays soon began to show the effects of his eager originality.

He was the first director to set his scenes in the midst of great stretches of territory—with the characters standing out on the sky-line, barely to be seen in the distance, then sweeping down into the valleys below with a rush that stirs the imagination. There is an epic quality to work of this kind which is wonderfully effective, but Mr. Griffith employs it now but seldom, and then only in themes which would be hampered by any less dashing handling. His evolution has been steadily from crowds to individuals, and the next step carried it so far as to be revolutionary.

This was the introduction of the large figures. Not only was the illusion heightened by making the characters life-size or larger, but it permitted the use of quiet, slow, natural action and subtle expression—obviously a complete change in the technique of picture acting, without which picture plays could never have become what they are now. Stated concisely, it put a premium on brains and lessened the importance of muscular energy as a means of character interpretation.

Scarcely a month passes that a Griffith picture does not introduce some bit of action, novelty in the mechanics of photography or form of expression that makes his métier more flexible. Now it would be forest scenes which looked like one exquisite Corot after another. Or a device to raise suspense to the nth power, as when he introduced endless flash scenes. Again, and often, it was a device to heighten pathos or to bring out the lyrical quality of what would otherwise seem matter-of-fact, as in fading the scene to darkness, or opening black and lightening gradually. One can hardly credit the strength of the illusion created by this in some situations, such as the passing of a night of sorrow and the dawn of a new day. These are a few instances from many that might be listed.

Practically all of Mr. Griffith's devices have been adopted or adapted by directors both in this country and abroad, so that wherever he may see a photoplay, by whomsoever made, the picture "fan" is looking at technique largely developed by this American producer.

Next in importance to the large figures is the pioneer work he is doing in releasing a film in whatever length may be necessary to tell the story properly. Only writers who have seen their plays stretched to the breaking point or hacked into a distorted jumble to fit the iron-bound measure of a thousand feet can appreciate what this will mean to the photoplay as a thing of logical development and construction.

As with themes, settings and camera work, so with the members of his company. He knows how to get the best results from his material, whether it is a temperamental actor or a strip of celluloid film. His company has been a real school for both actors and directors, and the list of well-known members of the profession who owe much to his training and influence would be impressive.

To see him at work in a location, correcting the last detail in the sweep of a battle scene, for example; or in the studio, molding a plot through the development of one or two characters (work vastly more difficult and to his liking) is to understand something of the reason of his success. He is keen, quick to praise, compelling, enthusiastic, and poised. Apparently, when things go wrong; when, let us say, a hundred supers ride furiously away in the wrong direction, out of earshot, it may seem to the careless observer that the Chief is pretty thoroughly perturbed about it, and the supers will certainly get that impression on their return. In reality it has not so much touched the surface of a poise as strongly entrenched as it is rare. Then, there is a sense of humor, truly Celtic in both its abundance and the aptness of its expression; and a memory so highly trained that he directs without manuscript or notes. To do that with the spoken drama, four acts played consecutively by a cast of fifteen or twenty, within the four walls of a theatre, is not so difficult. Just kindly think what it means with a play of three hundred scenes, all those in one setting being taken at one time, regardless of the numerical sequence, with two hundred actors scattered over several acres of land. To accomplish all this with due regard to the thousands of details involved is nothing less than marvelous.

As implied, the productions for which Mr. Griffith is responsible are, in the last analysis, poetic, but it is not poetry which is transcendental or which is satisfied with vague generalities concerning beauty and art. Like the greatest of the poets whose written word he has visualized, it is humanity which interests him. And, like that poet, in all that touches the human heart he finds material to his hand and interprets even the sordid and weak in human nature in the light of an idealism founded on understanding.

Notes

1. *Pippa Passes or, The Song of Conscience*, released October 4, 1909; *A Blot on the 'Scutcheon*, released January 29, 1912; *Enoch Arden*, released June 12 and June 15, 1911; *A Pueblo Legend*, released August 29, 1912; *Man's Genesis*, released July 11, 1912; *The Wanderer*, released May 3, 1913.

2. James A. Herne (1839–1901) is best known for *Hearts of Oak* (1879) and *Shore Acres* (1892).

Editorials in Films

New York Dramatic Mirror/1914

From the *New York Dramatic Mirror*, July 1, 1914, 21.

[This unsigned piece is adapted from a longer article in which the main commentary is from Ned Finley, an actor/writer/director most closely associated with the Vitagraph Company.]

Just as there were "sermons in stones" a long time ago, so there were "editorials in films" back in the early days of pictures, but the helter-skelter march of progress in a new art drove along other avenues and the "film editorial" was allowed to languish. David W. Griffith was probably among the first to produce pictures of this type and it was Frank Woods, [critic for the *New York Dramatic Mirror* who wrote under the name of] "The Spectator," who christened them "film editorials." Director Griffith's productions were in thousand foot lengths and told *The Story of Wheat*,[1] *The Story of Coal*, and so on with many industries. The reels all followed the same general tone of treatment, and *The Story of Wheat* may be taken as an example. This tale opened on Western plains, with scenes of the harvest in the wheat fields of Kansas. Then to the mills, and on to the bake-shops of the cities and into the homes of rich and poor the camera followed from the yellow kernel to the loaf of bread. All this was interesting enough, but it was mainly intended as sugar-coating, the producer's moral was reserved for the last. With a swirl, the scenes swung to the wheat pit, and an attempt to corner the market. The lesson was driven home in the contrast between the idyllic beauty of the early views and the greed and strife of the financiers, followed by the universal suffering attendant upon a successful corner. It was a film editorial with a "punch."

"I liked to work on those pictures," said Mr. Griffith to the writer, "and some day I hope to get back to them and do some really big things, for I think that some of the greatest work of the motion picture is to be done along those lines. Think of the value of motion pictures of this kind to a political party with a big issue before the voters. The perfect motion picture editorial will take its place in the making of history along with the press and stage."

Note

1. Actually *A Corner in Wheat*, based on the Frank Norris novel *The Octopus* and story "A Deal in Wheat," released November 3, 1909.

D. W. Griffith Answers
Two Vital Questions

Robert Grau/1914

From *The Theatre of Science* (New York: Broadway Publishing, 1914), 85–87.[1]

"You ask me: 'Do you think the stage and its craft are the best means of productivity for the camera man?' No, I do not. The stage is a development of centuries, based on certain fixed conditions and within prescribed limits. It is needless to point out what these are. The motion picture, although a growth of only a few years, is boundless in its scope, and endless in its possibilities. The whole world is its stage, and time without end its limitations. In the use of speech alone is it at a disadvantage, but the other advantages of the motion picture over the stage are so numerous and powerful that we can well afford to grant the stage this one point of superiority. The conditions of the two arts being so different, it follows that the requirements are equally dissimilar. Stage craft and stage people are out of place in the intense realism of motion-picture expression, but it may well be that a little motion-picture realism would be of immense advantage to the stage.

"To your second question, 'After the plays of other days are exhausted, who will supply the needs of thirty thousand theatres?' I would refer you to the opinion expressed in the foregoing paragraph. The plays of other days are not essential to the motion picture, and I am not sure that they are not proving a positive harm. If motion-picture producers had no access to stage plays, they would be obliged to depend upon their own authors for their material, and, since the picture dramas that would thus result would be composed entirely for picture production, they could not fail to much more nearly reach a perfection of art than could ever be hoped for while writers and directors are trying in vain to twist stage dramas into condition for picture use. When the plays of others days, and of these days are exhausted, as they will be, motion pictures will come into their own. They are valued now only for advertising purposes, and, when a stage play is reproduced in pictures with any success, it is inevitably found that often the plot and always the manner of treatment have been entirely departed from."

Note

1. This pioneering work is dedicated to David Wark Griffith, "Whose genius in the perfection of that Motion Picture Art contributes significance to this Volume."

D. W. Griffith Producer
of the World's Biggest Picture

New York American/1915

From the *New York American*, February 28, 1915, City Life and Dramatic Section, 9.

If your mental picture of "Dave" Griffith is that of a man of the bludgeon type, you are mistaken. The biggest man in the moving picture business today is a curious mingling of the man of leisure, man of the world, and the dreaming poet.

Yet his quarrel with life is that "They," the indeterminate word with which he includes people and conditions of today, "keep him running around." He clutches two telegrams that looked, as he said, like the afternoon editions of newspapers, as he talked to the interviewer across the luncheon table at a Broadway hotel and confided that the only man on earth of whom he is afraid, his secretary, might enter the room any minute.

"It's amazing the way that man keeps me running around," he said. "I hope he's taking a nap, a nice long one, that will keep him away from me all afternoon." He has the poet's quality of wanting to be left alone while he is dreaming his poet's dreams and getting a little pleasure in a good joke or a story, and those pestiferous persons who keep you "running around" sadly interface with both.

Yet, in defiance of these leanings, and in large part because of them, he is conceded to be the greatest producer of motion pictures in the world. The most poetic, the most daring, the most artistic, and the most stupendous works have had their inception in his brain and been worked out under his direction. This week there will be shown at the Liberty Theatre [New York] the largest film drama yet conceived, a film 13,058 feet long, a three-hour entertainment, during which no less than 18,000 people come before the eyes.

"Why call it *The Birth of a Nation?*" the interviewer asked.

"Because it is," was the sufficient answer from the lean, smiling man across the table, who has been called the "David Belasco of the Motion Pictures." "The Civil War was fought fifty years ago. But the real nation has only existed the last fifteen or twenty years, for there can exist no union without sympathy and oneness of sentiment. While Thomas Dixon's novel *The Clansman* is the basis of the play, we don't get to that until the film is half done. The author himself was good enough to say that the novel was so small a part of it that he thought it should not be considered. He said that in his novel he had taken a small section of the subject, a racial war. But we have gone back to the Civil War itself. We have shown the burning of Atlanta and the assassination of Lincoln. The birth of a nation began, according to an authority [Woodrow Wilson?], with the Ku Klux Klans, and we have shown that. We are using many veterans who served in the war."

"What do you think is the biggest thing in the big picture?"

"The burning of Atlanta, perhaps. More probably the battle of Petersburg, with the armies in the trenches. Yes, that is the biggest."

"And the littlest?"

"The littlest thing, in one sense, is the sigh of General Lee as the papers of surrender were signed. And, too, the fact that they had to pass the pen around and dip it into several bottles before they could get enough ink to sign it.

"We took some of the pictures in the region around Los Angeles, some of them in Mexico, others in various southern states. I traveled 15,000 miles in making the picture."

"Is it your greatest work, and are you content with it?"

"It is the biggest thing I have undertaken, but I shall not be satisfied until I do something else. I can see the mistakes in this. I am, like all other human beings, aiming at perfection."

"And that is the reason we never achieve our ambitions. But *The Birth of a Nation* received very high praise from high quarters in Washington."

"Yes, I was gratified when a man we all revere, or ought to, [Woodrow Wilson] said it teaches history by lightning."

"They say a great many things about you. One is that you came into the world of moving pictures when they were despised, and that you raised them to dignity. I have heard that if it hadn't been for the transfusion of your blood into it the motion picture art would have died."

"If that were true I wouldn't be ashamed of it. I believe in the motion picture not only as a means of amusement, but as a moral and educational force. Do you know that there has been less drinking in the past five years, and that it is because of motion pictures? It is absolutely true. No man drinks for the sake of drinking. He drinks because he has no place to go. Man is a moving animal. The bigger the man the more he has need of activity. It isn't so with women. Their natures are different. The motion pictures give man a place to go beside the saloons. He drops in to see a picture. He has been somewhere. He has seen something. He comes out and goes home in a different state than if he had gone to a saloon. The domestic unities are preserved.

"As for improprieties in motion pictures, they do not exist. What motion pictures have you seen that revealed the anatomical wonders that a Broadway musical comedy or burlesque show frankly discloses? I recall no motion picture that deals in any way with the nude save one, and that should never have been produced. There was once the claim that the playhouses were kept too dark for propriety. That criticism was made long ago, and it was never true. The requirements for motion picture lighting are such that you must be able to see a face twenty feet from the picture.

"If I had a growing son I would be willing to let him see motion pictures as he liked, because I believe they would be an invaluable aid to his education. They would stimulate his imagination, without which no one will go far. They would also give him a fund of knowledge, history and otherwise, and all good. And they would shape his character along the most rigid plane of human conduct. In moving pictures the code of conduct is hard and fast. No one need fear that it will deviate from the Puritan plane."

"And the physical side of it? When will motion pictures be so made that they will not strain the eyes?"

"They have improved greatly in that respect within a year. They are constantly improving. Even now some of them do not tire the eyes any more than do the figures in a play."

"What is your vision of the motion pictures of the future?"

"I expect that in five years pictures will be made at a cost of a million dollars. *The Birth of a Nation* cost half a million. And I expect audiences will pay not merely what they are paying for a legitimate drama today, but as much as they pay for grand opera—five dollars a seat."

Five Dollar Movies Prophesied

Richard Barry/1915

From the *New York Times*, March 28, 1915, SM16. This interview was also published in the *Editor*, April 24, 1915, 407–10.

David Griffith is today the biggest figure in the moving picture world. As the creator who is stalking ahead of the procession and lifting it literally by its own boot straps, he is now a marked man throughout filmdom. He has done more subtle things, more delicate things on the screen than any other man.

However, it was not in his capacity as a showman that I approached Mr. Griffith. While he is a producer without a rival and a generalissimo of mimic forces whose work has never been equaled, it was as a thinker, pondering the new problems of filmland, a triumphant Columbus of the screen, that he talked with me for the *Sunday Times* recently.

"It is foolish to think that the moving picture has reached its climax of development," said he. "We have the moving picture theatre as well built and as well run as any other theatre; we have the moving-picture show that brings two dollars a seat; we have the foremost writers of the world working for us. So people are prone to think we have gone the limit and there is nothing more to be done. But I tell you that moving pictures are still only in their swaddling clothes."

"Would you mind predicting something about the maturity of this promising infant," I suggested.

He smiled that courteous, humorous, knowing smile of the Southerner (his father was a Kentucky Colonel, brevetted Brigadier General of Volunteers by the Confederate States of America). He said that he had been obliged to predict so much for motion picture while talking of their possibilities to capitalists that he would welcome the chance to go into the prophecy business where it costs nothing to make good.

"But," he added seriously, "I am not a dreamer in the sense that I see fantastic things unlikely of realization. I haven't dreamed an impossible thing in seven years—since I started in pictures. That is the beauty of this work. It makes dreams come true.

"My first prediction is that a moving picture will be made within three or four years for which the entrance money will be five dollars and six dollars a seat. It is easy to predict that."

"But will the public pay five dollars a seat merely to see a picture?"

"They are already doing it—to ticket speculators. When I first proposed asking two dollars a seat for my new film not a single man in the theatrical business could be found to say I was making a sound business move. Regular theatres on all sides were cutting prices, not advancing them, and fifty cents a seat had always heretofore been considered a record price for the best films.

"The public is quick to see values. If they are willing to pay five cents to see a picture that costs five hundred dollars to produce and fifty cents to see a picture that cost fifty thousand dollars to produce, they are willing to pay two dollars to see one that costs half a million to produce.

"And when we can put on a picture that will cost $2 million to produce the public will be willing to pay five dollars a seat for it."

"Two million dollars!" I exclaimed. "Where are you going to get the money and how are you going to spend it?"

"If you had asked me a year ago where we could get the money I would have believed it would be impossible," replied Mr. Griffith, "for up to that time an investment of fifty thousand dollars was considered utterly daring for a picture; but the days of little things in the pictures are gone by forever. When I started in the business only seven years ago a producer who spent five hundred dollars on a picture was considered very extravagant. Not today. We spend that much on a single scene that runs less than a minute, and then often throw it away because it doesn't fit or is not just right.

"The experimental work on a big picture costs thousands of dollars. The trying out of new effects to see if they will reproduce is a costly process, and when one has the inventive faculty and is anxious to produce new things he is likely to bankrupt his promoters."

The mellow smile came back to the Griffith countenance. "However," he added, "that is the only known way to get the big, big, new effects."

"What will happen to the regular theatre when its prices are being cut while yours are advancing?"

"The regular theatre," he continued, "will, of course, always exist, but not, I believe, as now. The pictures will utterly eliminate from the regular theatre all the spectacular features of production. Plays will never again appeal to the public for their scenery, or their numbers of actors and supernumeraries. Pictures have replaced all that.

"The only plays the public will care to see in the regular theatre will be the intimate, quiet plays that can be staged in one or two settings within four walls, and in which the setting is unimportant, while the drama will be largely subjective. Objective drama, the so-called melodrama, will be entirely absorbed in the pictures.

"The audience for these old-fashioned theatres will be drawn from old-fashioned people who remember the days of old and how plays were produced by [David] Belasco and [Charles] Frohman when 'I was a boy.' The new generation will be wedded to the movies. You won't be able to satisfy them with anything else."

"What of the written and spoken word that is so vital to true drama? Do you intend to kill that, too?"

"On the contrary, we intend to vitalize it. The bane of the drama is verbosity, but we can't produce any picture without some words. In one of my pictures [*The Birth of a Nation*] we throw on the screen seven thousand words, in which there are at least four pages from Woodrow Wilson's history of the United States. That is more words than are used in the average short story.

"We are coming to pay more and more attention to the words we use on the screen. The art of writing for the pictures is developing almost as rapidly as the art of acting for them. And the great rewards to be gained there by a writer will be a powerful incentive for him to learn to tell his story more crisply, more tellingly, more alluringly, than he ever could, even in the best spoken drama."

"But this will mean a great revolution in our methods of thought?"

"Of course," answered the multi-parous[1] Griffith, "the human race will think more rapidly, more intelligently, more comprehensively than it ever did. It will see everything—positively everything.

"That, I believe, is the chief reason that the American public is so hungry for motion pictures and so loyal to a good one when it comes along. They have the good old American faculty of wanting to be 'shown' things. We don't 'talk' about things happening, or describe how a thing looks; we actually show it—vividly, completely, convincingly. It is the ever-present, realistic, actual now that 'gets' the great American public, and nothing ever devised by the mind of man can show it like moving pictures."

At this point the director, who counts that day lost whose low descending sun finds no new idea hatched, produced an illumination for the future right out of his egg (we were at breakfast).

"The time will come, and in less than ten years," he went on, "when the children in the public schools will be taught practically everything by moving pictures. Certainly they will never be obliged to read history again.

"Imagine a public library of the near future, for instance. There will be long rows of boxes of pillars, properly classified and indexed, of course. At each box a push button and before each box a seat. Suppose you wish to 'read up' on a certain episode in Napoleon's life. Instead of consulting all the authorities, wading laboriously through a host of books, and ending bewildered, without a clear idea of exactly what did happen and confused at every point by conflicting opinions about what did happen, you will merely seat yourself at a properly adjusted window, in a scientifically prepared room, press the button, and actually see what happened.

"There will be no opinions expressed. You will merely be present at the making of history. All the work of writing, revising, collating, and reproducing will have been carefully attended to by a corps of recognized experts, and you will have received a vivid and complete expression.[2]

"Everything except the three R's, the arts, and possibly the mental sciences can be taught in this way—physiology, chemistry, biology, botany, physics, and history in all its branches."

Seven years ago this man who talks thus glibly of "revolutions" was an actor out of work, and a director without a prospect. He was walking along Broadway as are thousands of others today.

While now his annual salary is reputed to be one hundred thousand dollars, Griffith at that time was so hard up that he clutched desperately at the chance to earn fifteen a week as an extra man in "pictures." His play, *A Fool and a Girl*, had been produced out of town by James K. Hackett and had run one consecutive week. He had been an actor in California and once had received as much as twenty-seven dollars a week.

Yet he was just turned thirty, in perfect health, with an excellent education. He walked to the office of a little motion-picture concern, the Kalem Company, and asked its manager, Frank Marion, for a job as an extra man. Usually in those days actors changed their names before dropping so low; not Griffith.

He also kept his nerve. Griffith said to Marion: "I believe motion pictures might be dignified and put on a par with the spoken drama. It is my opinion you've got to change your whole style of acting. At present it's only horseplay and not true to life. Moreover, you don't use the right kind of stories and your photography is rotten."

"I'm afraid I can't use you," said Marion, "you seem to be a bit visionary."

The next place Griffith applied was the office of the Biograph Company, up in the Bronx.[3] He kept his opinions to himself and he got a job at fifteen dollars a week.

What happened after that is a vital part of the history of moving pictures.

To say that Griffith almost single-handedly revolutionized the moving-picture business is only to repeat what many of its students and historians have said before. He introduced naturalistic acting and he began, in a small way, the development of handling crowds that has led to the half-million-dollar picture with eighteen thousand people and fifteen hundred horses.

As soon as he had induced the Biograph people to let him direct in his own way his advancement was rapid. Within four years his annual salary with Biograph was said to be fifty thousand dollars. The Mutual bought him away only at a published price of a hundred thousand dollars a year and a percentage of the profits.

Many of the big stars of the pictures, from Mary Pickford to Blanche Sweet, were "discovered" by Griffith, and a large number of the best directors have learned their trade under him.

For seven years he has been leading the motion-picture procession. If he makes one-quarter the "discoveries," "improvements," and "revolutions" in the business in the next seven years that he has in the past seven, then the prophecies of today may be less absurd than was his comment to the manager who first refused him because he was "visionary.

Notes

1. An obsolete word meaning "give birth to" or "produce."

2. Griffith's notion is reminiscent of the 1953–57 CBS television series *You Are There*, hosted by Walter Cronkite, which recreated all manner of events from the past.

3. Actually at 11 East 14th Street. The company did not move to its new studio in the Bronx until 1913.

Interviews with Prominent Directors: "And the Greatest of These Is"—David W. Griffith

Roberta Courtlandt/1915

From *Motion Picture Magazine*, August 1915, 90–92.

One doesn't interview David Wark Griffith. He's too busy. One simply stands about the studio, wherever he may be working in the open, and gathers up the verbal pearls of wisdom which fall from his clean-cut, aggressive-looking mouth.

Unquestionably the greatest director of Motion Pictures in the United States (which, of course, means the world), he is an intensely "human" man, one in whom great trust may be reposed. Always courteous, first of all a gentleman, he has risen rapidly to a position in the picture world where he may know that his wishes are carried out as promptly and as respectfully as if commands.

He is Southern all thru, having been born in Louisville, Ky., and it was in this town that he first saw a theatrical performance, at the ripe age of sixteen. And then it was decidedly against the wishes of his parents who were bitterly opposed to the stage and its connections. After seeing a performance of Henry Irving and Ellen Terry, in Louisville, he made up his mind that he, too, would be an actor.

And his ambition was shortly realized. He soon began writing plays, drifted to New York, and there, while temporarily short of funds, gladly accepted work as an extra with the Biograph Company. And there he stayed until a short time ago, when he left them to make the Mutual pictures even more famous. The pictures which he produces personally, at present, are really his own, and are released under his own name. Thus the "Griffith Brand" has quickly sprung to fame and popularity. *The*

Battle of the Sexes caused a sensation in the picture world when released some time ago. It has been followed by *The Avenging Conscience* and *The Birth of a Nation*, which was lately released. Wherever it has been shown, it has met with applause equally as great as, if not greater than, *The Battle of the Sexes*.

Mr. Griffith has had wonderful success at training young people with no stage experience to become the most successful and popular players of the day. And his company is made up of young people. In fact, there is no company in the business today whose cast numbers so many young people as Mr. Griffith's. Scarcely one of the girls has passed twenty years of age. There's charming little Lillian Gish, not quite nineteen, whose face is known and admired the world over, and her clever little sister, two years younger, Dorothy, the inimitable comedienne; Mae Marsh, whose work in some recent pictures, as well as past successes has endeared her to all; and Blanche Sweet, who, as the Biograph Blonde, had won fame and honors galore at an age when most girls are thinking of putting up their hair and wondering if mother will permit that nice young man on the next corner to take them to the theater. And there's ever so many more. Space forbids my mentioning them all, but they are too well known to need it.

Mr. Griffith has a strong disapproval of the words "silent drama" as applied to motion pictures, for he says of all mediums of expressing thought the Motion Picture is the loudest, and its message is received by multitudes.

"Suppose," he says, this eyes glowing with fire and the earnestness of his speech, "suppose one reads a book, perhaps an old classic. Nine out of ten people will forget it a few hours later. Show the same book in Motion Pictures and see how long the memory lasts. Where hundreds read the book, perhaps thousands will see the picture. And where ten people will remember the book, a thousand will remember the picture."

He has very decided ideas as to "types," and when he has a scenario calling for a certain type, he is untiring until he has found it. He also watches carefully the costumes and make-up of the players and criticizes freely, but his company are thankful for his interest and repay it by a loyalty that is as rare as it is beautiful.

"I had rather spend a week coaching and training a young, inexperienced girl who has no knowledge of picture acting, but who looks the part which she is to play, than to spend ten minutes reading 'business' to a capable stage actress. Why? Because the girl, inexperienced tho she is, *looks* the part; while the actress from the stage would be a matured woman, who would act splendidly, but who would look foolish as the innocent young ingénue. It takes years to acquire stage experience, where it takes months in Motion Pictures, if the aspirant has dramatic ability."

When assigning parts or rehearsing his company in the bringing out of some intricate bit of acting, Mr. Griffith will often assume the troublesome role in question, go into the scene and work out every gesture, showing the player exactly how it should be done. Often the very bit of acting that arouses a picture audience to enthusiasm and causes them to applaud eagerly the genius of the player was worked out in some bare-looking, unattractive "set" by the "Greatest Director in Motion Pictures."

He writes a large number of his scripts, having had experience of play-writing to back him up in this second effort, and often works in the studio or field without a script either in hand or pocket. It is all in his brain, and he needs no copy.

Under the hand of any save an artist, *The Avenging Conscience* would have developed into a "blood-and-thunder" feature. But as it is, we have a six-reel dramatic gem. Who save a Griffith could have thought of, or have had the courage to add, the intensely interesting touch preceded by the subtitle, "Nature is one long system of murder," and which shows the survival of the fittest among ants, flies, and spiders?

I repeat there is only one David Wark Griffith! Would that there were more, and then, perhaps, the Utopia of perfect pictures would not be so far away, after all!

The Story of David Wark Griffith: Part One

Henry Stephen Gordon/1916

From *Photoplay*, June 1916, 35–37, 162–65. This interview is adapted from part one of Gordon's six-part series, "The Story of David Wark Griffith." Part six of the series appeared under the title "The Real Story of *Intolerance*." The page numbers given above relate to this adaptation; the full citation reads pp. 28–37, 162–65.

His personal story consists of fragmentary bits; a few facts noted during a few moments' talk; a few more another time; his horror of egotism is extreme; he cannot believe that the world is interested in himself or his past, nor what may be intimate information about his personality, and he has learned to be cautious; he hasn't written poetry since he was eighteen.

He has but one trait of the prima donna nature; he does not tell his age; some publications of a Who's Who order put his birth [incorrectly] in 1880; this may or may not be correct.

"About myself?" he replied when asked for details. "The public can not care about that topic; you cannot improve on what was written about a real man of note once: 'He was born, he grew a little, he slept a little, he ate a little, he worked a little, he loved a little—and then he died.'

"My family? I do come of good stock; my mother was a Shirley-Carter, my father was Colonel Jacob Wark Griffith of the Confederacy; old comrades of his in the war have told me he was known in the army as 'Thunder Jake,' because he never went into a charge but what his voice could be heard above the din of guns and combat, urging on his men.

"About the first thing I remember was my father's sword; he would put it on to amuse me. The first time I saw that sword was when my father played a joke on an old negro, once his slave but who with the heads of four other negro families refused to leave the plantation; those four families were four important factors in keeping the Griffith family poor.

"Down South the men usually wore their hair rather long; this negro, who in our better days had been the plantation barber, had been taken to Louisville, ten or twelve miles from our home at Bairdstown, and had seen the Northern men with their close-cropped hair; when he came back he got hold of my brother and cut his hair close, Northern style.

"When father saw this he pretended to be enraged; he went into the house, donned his old uniform, buckled on his sword and pistols, and had the negro summoned.

"Then, drawing the sword, he went through the technical cuts and thrusts and slashes, threatening the darkey all the time with being cut into mince meat.

"The old Uncle was scared pale, and I took it seriously myself until a wink and a smile from father enlightened me.

"So that sword remains the first memory I have of existence.

"We were all somewhat studious; father was a highly educated man, and an elder sister, Mattie, was a brilliantly cultured woman; she it was who gave the children their basic education; my parents always directed our studies and our thoughts towards the noble; the great in literature.

"Mattie found in her father an intellect that met her requirements and a character that she adored; she never married, and would say, either jokingly or seriously, I was never certain which, but suspect the latter, that she never had found a man equal to her father, and that none of less quality would every satisfy her as a husband.

"Personally, I have not bothered about an ancestry; it is likely though that I was impressed in my childhood with certain family traditions which had come down through the mist of former generations; one was that *ap* Griffith, a Welsh Prince of Wales, was the founder of one side of the house, and that a Lord Brayington who revolted with Monmouth and later emigrated under duress to Virginia, was a founder of the other side of the American Griffiths.

"I used to be told of a great-grandfather in Virginia, a stormy, fierce old man who refused to allow the word England to be spoken in his presence and who, as far as he could, barred the door to anything English.

"My grandfather was a Captain David Griffith, who fought in 1812.

"It happens I do know a lot about my father, from what I have been told by Southern soldiers. Colonel Polk Johnson told me of his regiment never having surrendered, and of his having been brevetted Brigadier General.

"After I left home I walked through Kentucky and Tennessee once when I had a job as traveling correspondent and canvasser for the *Baptist Weekly,* and I met a man named, I think, Holly, who had served with father; I sat up all night with him listening to his stories about Colonel Griffith, whom he pronounced to be the bravest man he had ever seen in action.

"'There was a Yankee supply train,' said Holly, 'that Colonel Jo Wheeler had tried to capture with the regiment of another Colonel, who had been driven off by the escort of the train; but the wagons were still within striking distance and Jo Wheeler very much wanted the bacon and ammunition they contained.

"'An orderly called your father, and Jo said to him, "Colonel, can you capture that Yankee wagon train?"

"'Your father saluted and turned to go.

"'"Why don't you answer me, Colonel Griffith?" said General Jo.

"'"I'll answer you in five minutes," said your father, and in that time he had the train on its way into our camp.'

"This incident I have found verified in Jefferson Davis's *Rise and Fall of the Confederacy.*

"My first and last ambition, until Fate turned me into a picture man, was to be a writer. I determined on that when I was six years old. My father's sword and its early effect on my mind, his noble career, his wounds, for he was shot all to pieces, did impart a martial trend to my character, but there was no war, and the scholarly atmosphere of my home, I suppose, was responsible for my inclination to become a great literary man.

"As soon as I was big enough I began my own personally conducted tour of Life; I went to Louisville and got a job as a reporter on the *Courier-Journal.* I did not meet Marse Henry [pen name of editor and politician Henry Watterson] then. I wish I could have done something to make him notice me, but I did not; in some way I was put to work writing notes about theatrical matters. With my night police assignment and a general hunt for items, I determined to become a dramatist.

"I received emphasis for that inspiration on seeing my first theatrical performance; in it was Peter Baker, who sang "America's National Game." Then I saw Julia Marlowe and Robert Taber in *Romola.*

"That settled everything; I was to be a great dramatist. First it was necessary to secure some advice, so I called on the stage manager of the company at the Louisville theater and told him of my scheme of life.

"He approved it thoroughly and solemnly; but he explained to me that no man could ever write a good play who was not an actor; he cited

Shakespeare and Moliere, and Dion Boucicault and Gus Thomas and as he was an authority I accepted his advice, thereby breaking a universal, time-honored rule, and becoming an actor. I played in stock in Louisville, and after many ups and downs, I had some good engagements.

"My first part was the Clergyman in *Trilby*. I wasn't twenty then and I was paid eight dollars a week; then, later, I joined Walker Whiteside on tour through Iowa. I never have since then been in sympathy with Iowa ideas. After that I had a wide experience in characters, heavies and leads.

"It wasn't all so long ago, yet I played one season with Helen Ware before she was discovered, and then with J. E. Dodson as de Maupret to his Richelieu, and was given a good notice by Alan Dale, which confirmed my suspicion that I was quite a good actor. It secured me as well an increase in salary. Then came a season with Nance O'Neil in Shakespeare and Ibsen in Boston; the reviewers gave me corking good notices there—but of course Shakespeare and Ibsen couldn't be roasted in Boston.

"And reviewers are not always over perceptive; there was a time when I was with Nance O'Neil and McKee Rankin right here in Los Angeles at the Mason Theatre, when Rankin was ill one night; I had been playing Magda's preacher lover, but when Rankin did not appear I was thrown into his part of the father. I stuffed out my clothes and went through the part with no change of name on the programme. The next morning's papers had most eulogistic notices of Mr. Rankin's thoroughly artistic acting, and the world looked very brilliant to me that day.

"All the time my determination to be a dramatist was unshaken. I had, before getting deep in the theater, written two poems and a story; one of the poems I had sent to John Sleicher, editor of *Leslie's* weekly, and he bought it; he paid me thirty-five dollars!

"Ah! When *Leslie's* came out with my poem in it—that was the one day of all life. It was called 'To a Wild Duck.' It was a serious poem and not written on that subject because I was hungry. I bought a copy of the magazine and entered a subway train; I read the verses carelessly, registering indifference, and rolled the paper up and put it in my coat pocket; but—I couldn't stand it; it seemed as if everyone in the car would know I had written that poem, but I had to read it again; I pulled the paper out of my pocket, scanned the advertisements, and then as if by accident turned over to the poem and savored Victory again.

"Can I remember it? Huh! Let me see. The first line ran, 'See how beautifully—' 'See how beautifully—' No, it's all gone; I'm not even sure of the first line! And that was the happiest moment of my life—with what caused it forgotten. There might be something of a theme for a poem in that situation.

"Naturally I wrote another poem, and sent it to *McClure's*. It came back; but you must pardon me, for a poet has to be proud, while a picture man may be very modest; it came back, but with a personal letter from Colonel McClure saying the committee of five editors who passed on contributions had voted three to two against accepting the verses, but would I be good enough to send in some more.

"I did not; but I sold a story that same month, and I began to write Sunday 'Sup' [Supplement] stuff; I couldn't sell these specials myself, but I became acquainted with a very popular newspaper woman who was paid a high space rate; I would give her my stories and specials, and she would put her 'byline' on them, sell them, and give me half the money.

"And then I wrote my first play, *the* play.

"It was called *A Fool and a Girl*.

"I decided when it was finished that it was a good play, and I took it to James K. Hackett, who read it. 'My boy,' he said in his vigorous way, 'this is one of the best plays I have ever read; I'll produce it.'

"That day of the first poem appearing was as nothing; I must have been unbearably happy—until I met Mr. Hackett's stage director.

"He read the play; he turned to me when he had finished reading and said, 'Your play's rotten. It will never go; the governor's blowing himself in by giving you a production. Why, man alive! You make your characters talk and behave like real people. Rotten!'

"Then he censored the play; he improved it; he deprived it of the sin of picturing real men and women on the stage and changed them into people of the theatrical mind.

"But even at that it flivvered.

"I was sure it was because the stage director had changed it, but—I knew Wilfred Lucas then, who is with me now, and I asked him to read the play; he did so, but he has always refrained from telling me what he thought of it.

"Come to think it over, there was something of a coincidence about that play and *The Clansman*; the play had an important character who was a white man with a strain of negro blood.

"It was good training while that play was put on; I lost twenty pounds of flesh a week, and my temper.

"I learned how to suffer, a knowledge that often has come in useful to me in the picture business.

"If you've ever had any disagreeable portion of your life, you understand the times of stress, the episodes where you licked or were licked, we look back upon—having passed them—with keen joy.

"That is why Béranger's song about being happy at twenty in a garret always has been, and always will be, beloved by all men."

"Yes, but your ordeals as an actor cannot equal what the stories of your life as a book agent, as an iron puddler, your brakebeam tours, your comradeship study of tramps, taught you; tell me of those times; to be a rich success is considerable; to have been a brave vagabond of Fortune is to have been much more. Tell me of those episodes," I asked.

He smiled whimsically. "This is a curious world we are in," he replied; "while we are in it, we must be careful what we say lest others say about us what is not careful, after we are gone.

"I will think it over for your next visit."

The Story of David Wark Griffith: Part Two

Henry Stephen Gordon/1916

From *Photoplay*, July 1916, 124–32. This interview is adapted from part two of Gordon's six-part series, "The Story of David Wark Griffith." Part six of the series appeared under the title "The Real Story of *Intolerance*." The page numbers given above relate to this adaptation; the full citation reads pp. 122–32.

He [Griffith] grinned. "I will not unfold all the secrets of my young life," was his response, "and as to being a book agent, I refuse to incriminate myself. I stand mute. But I admit selling the *Encyclopedia Britannica*; that isn't a book, it is a freight commodity.

"I did not sell very many—but even an occasional sale carried a very fat commission and enabled me to pack a meal ticket with my sample bindings, and to travel in railway cars in place of underneath them on a brakebeam.

"I early learned to use means to discover the men who would likely want to listen to a seller of books; and had my friends and acquaintances trained to report to me information that might lead to a dicker.

"There was a day when some one told some one else to tell me that Cousin Janie had said to Uncle Sawyer that Jim Dodson had heard Sam Roller from down river say that there was a man living at Burgoyne côte house who owned a Bible and a dictionary, and who wanted an encyclopedia."

Griffith told the rest of the story just as an amusing effort of a man hard put to it. But it thoroughly illustrates the resiliency of his mind, and—it may be valuable to book agents.

"My man lived in a country of pork and 'sides' diet," he said. "It was a hard grinding school I had been through; one that had taught me to think before acting. Knowing the value put on fresh meat in that region,

I gambled quite a bit of my resources and bought a lot of good steaks. I could have used those steaks myself to advantage—but business is business and strategy is strategy.

"In a buggy with my bundle of steaks and my sample bindings and pages, we started one evening for my man.

"There were not any roads thereabout when it rained. And it rained. We upset, we were bogged, but we managed to make progress until, while driving through a thick woods, a panther agilely dropped to the seat beside me from an overhanging tree, and I dropped out of the buggy. The beast had sniffed the odor of those steaks.

"There was a pretty scrap while it lasted, but the panther was dislodged before the steaks were swallowed, and we drove on.

"The farmer gave me shelter for the night, and for breakfast I presented my steaks, and before lunch I had made my sale."

This incident put Griffith in a reminiscent mood, and he kept on—oblivious of the notes being taken.

"Success does not make a fellow feel a bit proud, even if he realizes, as any honest, successful man must realize, how little there really is to achievement," he observed.

"For a long time I was proudest over a journey I made from Minneapolis to my home on a capital of fifteen cents; and I still had the fifteen cents when I reached my destination.

"That was one of my early adventures on 'blind baggage' cars and brakebeams.

"I had been acting, when the ghost which had limped sadly for some weeks failed to walk, even with crutches.

"Luck had been favorable; I had made a living and had sent some money home, but back of the situation was a formidable oath I had taken when I struck out for myself that never would I ask for help from those I had left behind; as for meals and shelter, during a financial squall, that was different, and my thoughts and my feet turned toward the old plantation.

"There is considerable alertness required to swing onto a 'blind baggage' at the maximum of speed, to combine the minimum chance of discovery. When it happened that I was thrown off a train, I did odd jobs wherever I found myself, until the chance came rolling down the track again for another stage of the journey.

"Along with the experience was a knowledge gained of the great army of vagabonds who constantly migrate simply from the love of wandering, the enjoyment of the savor of change. During those years I met in more or less intimacy all kinds and conditions of men—all kinds; what Kipling wrote of the Colonel's Lady and Judy O'Grady being just alike under the skin is equally true about the intellect of the 'pike' and the university gentle; the yegg and the poet, the peripatetic and the stationary philosopher.

"No matter how contorted one way or another the soul may be, the man is still a man and with recognizable traits of relationship to all men.

"Somewhat illustrative of the domination of circumstances over mental attitudes is just another instance of—at the time—great pride to me.

"This was an occasion around the warm cinders which had been drawn from the fire boxes of the locomotives in a roundhouse; the company was an assembly of tramps—hobos they are called now—and I was given the center of the stage, the best place at the ashes, and called on for a monologic account of the longest uninterrupted blind baggage ride then on record, something over two hundred miles out of Chicago.

"Louisville had again attracted me. A company had gone broke in Chicago and I with it. The way to arrive at a place, I had learned, is to start for it; so I walked from Downtown in Chicago to Englewood, and there a train whizzed along so fast that the crew was not watching, feeling that no ticketless tourist would take the chance. This one did, and landed safely. It was a wild night stormy and freezing; the crew of the train stuck to their snug quarters, not knowing their flying bailiwick had been invaded, until one brakeman made a perfunctory inspection. I also had grown careless from long immunity and sleepiness.

"Consciousness returned violently when I was assailed by two bulging red fists, accompanied by much language. We made an even match; but a second brakeman hovered along and then it was all over. I reposed gracefully on a snow bank with many minor injuries to my person and a realization that Louisville was a great deal farther away than when I had been in Chicago.

"Something led me to walk a bit, and I came to the round-house, the pile of warm cinders and the gallant company of the Knights of Disindustry. When my story was heard there was acclaim, unenvious and generous comment, and the warmest place by the cinders.

"Which is generally more than a man is given when he succeeds with people who are—not hoboes."

There are many peppery stories about the studios of Griffith's courage and strength. Any man who has a Duke of Wellington nose can be relied on for courage; as for Griffith's physical strength, a glance at him shows litheness, not massive, but a very athletic example of bodily architecture, and the celebrity of movement which frequently arrives so rapidly as to defeat more potent but more sluggish muscles.

It is possible that he is a bit proud of his sturdy sinews. He climbs about all manner of places in his studio in order to study perspective, or whatever it is a director has to study, and it is axiomatic about the place that he never has asked any man or woman to do a "stunt" that included the precarious without first doing the same thing himself.

There was one occasion when this chronicler saw that trait bloom out.

There was a "set" arranged for an escaped lion to wander into a hotel office with panicky results among the guests, principal of whom was De Wolf Hopper. The lion was in his cage, ready to be prodded onto the scene; the "set" was surrounded by heavy wire barricades, the cameraman being encased in a tooth-proof wire redoubt; several extra people and the beast's trainer were on the scene ready for rehearsal, and Mr. Hopper was outside the barrier waiting his cue. He was quite willing to go on with the lion, but there is really no use in cluttering up things until your call comes, and, anyway, the lion animal is perfectly harmless. Then came the story from an old-time attaché of the studio in graphic detail of how that same lion a year before had with neatness and dispatch removed two ribs from an actor while feeling playful.

Just before the director was to begin, Griffith walked on the scene, fussed about with the lion, pulled his ears and frolicked with him.

Everyone else then made friends with the animal, and the play went on with Mr. Hopper. Well, of course he knew all the time the lion was a good sort, and there's never any danger with a lion if you make him understand you're not afraid of him—Come here, Nero old top!

There is a story told by his pals of the Biograph of how Griffith, requiring some exercise, had a middleweight prize fighter come to box with him, and how at the first lesson Griffith knocked the bruiser down and out.

One man told the story and then whispered that the fighter had been doing some acting himself; that he felt there would be more money in the lessons if the employer were to be thoroughly convinced of his own latent superiority. Such things have been known to occur. Royalty rarely finds a courtier skillful enough to be victor in a bridge set-to; it isn't done. If that boxer was not knocked down at once by his employer he is a very poor fighter—with his mind.

But the somewhat slender, very agile picture-creator is quite able to take care of himself under all conditions; he proved this in his early directing, when roughnecks formed the artists of the lens and when the methods and etiquette of a second mate were essential to the handling of the crew of a movie.

It was when Griffith himself told of another venture into the land of ferocious effort that it was made evident why his surprising elasticity of physical resource is what it is.

"Nothing had changed my decision to be the world's greatest literary man," he explained while still discussing his life before the studio gave shelter; "and I felt that as a preparatory study, before I could have the world of letters at my feet, it might be useful to know a little more about certain phases of life commonly unfamiliar.

"My other adventures had been made of necessity; this was one of choice, for the knowledge of the working man—the toiler—I thought would be valuable.

"There was no financial need spurring me to ride hard over the rough spots in the highway of existence; a comfortable sum of a few hundred dollars had been accumulated by some occasional good fortune in the theater, and my duties toward those at home had been met.

"To be a puddler [working with clay and water to compact it] in a foundry, to do the real 'muscle-stretching,' bone-bending work, and to live among the men who did such work, was my ambition, and naturally I went to Tonawanda. I didn't work at puddling first, but shoveling ore out of a ship's hold into the crane buckets.

"There were no union restrictions as to hours or anything; the pay was not by the day but by the piece; so much money for every ton of ore shoveled; it was good enough pay, so good that if a man would work until he dropped in his tracks he could pick up twenty dollars or so at a piece.

"It was work under tremendous competitive conditions; I mean the competition of emulation.

"Men would shovel down in that grimy, stuffy hold until they dropped in their tracks from utter exhaustion; then they would be chucked into one of the steel buckets, hoisted to the deck and flung to one side, to come to, or go to, as they listed.

"Under that stint system that work was probably the hardest in the world; for young men it was beautifully healthful; it was not long before I found myself capable of shoveling ore for twenty-four hours at a stretch. In some traits the men were as hard and exhausting as the life; they were naturally circumscribed, and if their daily existence was an orgy of labor, their life when released from toil was just as strenuous in their efforts to win relief.

"So, in one way or another, under this or that circumstance, my life flowed on, with no approachment to that laurel wreath of literature; I was acting most of the time, and essaying a few other lines of livelihood."

There is a singular lack of information as to Griffith's stage career; the few testimonies at hand all trend to the one definition of his exceptional ability, which appeared to be handicapped by disinclination to do roles in certain prescribed manners and methods.

Those few actors who have known him when he was a "talkie" agree that his work was exceptionally clever, and most of them qualify it by the term "original," which in theater patter usually means that an actor has a brain.

That as a rule is a drag to his progress. Stage directors have brains—always; and if an actor should have the habit of thinking, you can see it would be very embarrassing for the director; therefrom has grown the obvious fact that actors seldom think for themselves; they prefer to hold their jobs.

There is reason to believe Griffith learned to be one of the latter class of histrions—also that he did not like to be.

James Neill, who used to be a stock king in the West in those years when Chicago was still spoken of as a Western city, once employed Griffith; it was in one of the Neill stock companies, at that period known in Chicago as the Neill Alhambra Stock.

Mr. Neill had several stock companies then, and when he visited his Chicago theater he found them doing *The Ensign* [by William Haworth] with a particularly good Abraham Lincoln.

"In *The Ensign*," says Mr. Neill in telling about the incident, "we never gave Lincoln any lines, just as few words as we could get by with in the scene. It was thought that the public would resent any attempt to carry Lincoln as far as really acting on the stage, so the part was kept almost entirely pantomimic—what we call in the pictures 'registering'—and I noticed the admirable way the young fellow playing Lincoln did this very 'registering' stuff.

"I asked my stage director, who was Oscar Eagle, about the actor and he told me he was a 'rather bright young fellow named Griffith,' and somehow the matter dropped, and he never came into my mind again until a short time ago.

"I had been doing pictures, but the company I was working for cut down, and I wanted a position.

"The first place I called was the Griffith studio, and when I saw him I at once remembered our Lincoln in *The Ensign* years ago. Mr. Griffith recalled the circumstance to me, and I rather apologized—for we had only paid him eighteen dollars a week.

"'It was a poor salary we paid you, Mr. Griffith,' I said.

"'It was a very good salary,' he replied, 'for I needed it tremendously, and it was much more than I was worth then, for I was a beginner.'

"No, I did not go to work for Griffith, thought he made it evident that I probably could have done so; but before I could get farther with the application something else came to hand, and I have not had occasion to see him since.

"He has always been spoken of in the profession by those who knew him in his acting days as 'a gifted young man.'"

. . . Griffith likes those reminiscent glances at what were cruel but savory experiences.

As to the ore-shoveling he said: "It was corking good. I feel the benefit of it every day I live; it gave me physical resilience, fortitude, and some little muscle which has been of particular value to me many times.

"Every phase of life is good for you if you face it all rightly, with fine cheer.

"For tramps, artists, ironworkers, actors, writers—all of us—are alike in our souls; it was in knowing all manner of men that I derived my most useful education."

"And then came the movies?" he was asked.

"And then came the photoplay," was his reply.

You mustn't use the word "movies" to some of the picture people any more. They like to refer to the early films as "movies" but believe it is not sufficiently dignified or expressive of the artistic films of today.

"It happened very casually, as most events do occur, for it proved to be an event to me," he went on. "It was one day in Chicago when with a friend I was knocking about town with no purpose in immediate view; he suggested that we go to a picture show.

"Never having seen one, the suggestion was inviting. We went; it was some boreful affair, exactly what, I have forgotten; my friend liked it greatly, but I found it silly, tiresome, inexcusable. It was in no way worth while.

"But the great interest the audience evinced impressed me, and made me think; it seemed that if a thing which could attract the public as that picture did were to be done, it should be done better.

"'What do you think of it?' asked my friend.

"'That any man who enjoys such a thing should be shot at sunrise,' was my response.

"He looked at me in wonder and talked on, explaining why the picture was great; and when we went out he called my attention to the line of people waiting to enter the theater.

"Things did not go very well just then for me; I found myself out of work, and all the time pictures were being talked of, and unconsciously that interested audience and the line of people waiting outside stuck in my mind.

"Probably then, as now, there was no egotism in my thinking that I could write far better scenarios than were being shown, and that the acting of the pictures could be improved.

"As to whether I seriously at that time gave any studied effort to the new profession I cannot say; it is probable that unconsciously I gave it all considerably more attention than I then realized. For it was a prospect, and the feeling that you can do something perhaps a little better than it is being done makes interest acutely active.

"Finally I wrote a scenario and took it to the Edison studio. I left it and was told I would receive an answer.

"That scenario is still on file there, I presume; I never heard anything of it since."

There have been several notable philosophers who have ascribed the quality of success to the faculty of saying "No." Truly, "No" has saved many dollars and delirium tremens. But the ready negative in creative affairs has lost more fortunes for its users than "Yes" ever has gained.

. . . The biography of that Edisonian who filed the Griffith scenario and forgot about its existence because it was "bum," would make interesting reading; it was probably so very negative that he said, "It was no good nohow."

Griffith's knuckles were calloused by that time, so he did not suffer particular disappointment at no results from the Edison folk.

But with head up and straight-eyed, he wrote another scenario and took it to the Biograph. They bought it for fifteen dollars and said he might bring some more if he liked.

He liked very much.

And he wrote more; the money came at the generous—then—rate of fifteen dollars for a half-reel and twenty-five for a full-reel picture.

"I managed to make enough to live on—with the aid of Hope," he says of those days; and then he got the chance to stage *The Adventures of Dol-*

lie [released July 14, 1908], and that made him a Biograph fixture, and his life work was begun.

Dollie was quite an absurd young thing, flippantly of the Bertha M. Clay type, who found her habitat in nickelodeons; but Dollie dead, now buried in an unnamed grave of forgetfulness, played the part of Providence; Dollie brought the brain to its haven, where it could bigly work out its destiny.

She graciously opened the door of the Biograph studio to Griffith, a door that was not to be closed on him until he shut it himself and entered wider, more shining portals of consummate effort.

The Story of David Wark Griffith: Part Three

Henry Stephen Gordon/1916

From *Photoplay*, August 1916, 82–84, 86–88. This interview is adapted from part three of Gordon's six-part series, "The Story of David Wark Griffith." Part Six of the series appeared under the title "The Real Story of *Intolerance*." The page numbers given above relate to this adaptation; the full citation reads pp. 78–84, 86–88.

He [Griffith] was given Arthur Marvin as his first photographer.

Marvin was described by Griffith as an expert photographer who was seldom afflicted with exuberance of ambition.

He would sometimes refer to himself as "the captain of the good ship 'Take-It-Easy,' with nine decks and no bottom, which sails on forever, and forever sails on."

He probably did have some hankering for [Billy] Bitzer's job; not enviously, but in confidence in his own ability; but his master's certificate as skipper of "Take-It-Easy" forbade any such event.

"There was one occasion," says Griffith in talking over this companion of his early fighting days, "when Marvin took great satisfaction in what he considered 'putting it over Bitzer.'

"We were taking a canoeing scene; the hero and the heroine floating calmly down a river in the canoe, toward the eternal happiness that is popularly ascribed to be an inevitable consequence of true love.

"Marvin in order to take the scene at its best point had to stand in water up to his chin, while turning the crank of his camera.

"It did result in a very beautiful scene, and Marvin was highly pleased, remarking as he blandly looked at the record, 'There's a bit of work that Bitzer never could do.'

"I was strong for Bitzer then as now, and also was strong for Marvin, but I could not refrain from asking Marvin why he thought Bitzer could not have done the scene as well as he.

"'He couldn't do it; not in a thousand years,' was Marvin's reply.

"When I pressed him for an explanation of his fancied superiority to Bitzer, he grinned and said, 'Well, Governor, I took that picture with the water just swashing past my lower lip; now I'm three inches taller than Bitzer, so you see if he undertook it, what would happen to him.'"

Marvin in his easy, unquestioning fashion was docile; this was then a quality of inestimable value for Griffith, who was doing new things.

That Griffith is a big man as well as an artist is shown by his sticking to his first photographer; later on he had Bitzer; he was given anyone or anything he asked for.

But when he quit the Biograph, Martin quit with him; when he made his own pictures, Marvin worked with him at Hollywood; and until the day came when the good ship "Take-It-Easy" that was to "sail forever and forever sail," insisted on driving into the last port with Marvin's soul its only cargo, it was Griffith who, until those nearer to the dead in kinship could come to him, did all that could be done to make the voyage free from tempest, and who sent along a fervent prayer that the Great Consignee would make it easy for poor old "Take-It-Easy."[1]

It was now that the door of Happiness began to swing a bit open for this man combating Fortune. . . .

"Those early Biograph days," says Griffith, "were the most picturesque since the time of Molière and Villon; true, there was no 'sleeping under the end of a star' and there were no medieval vagrancy classifications for us; but there were the freedom, the change of scene, and the coursing about the country as Romans, pirates, royalty, great lovers, and great villains; some days we would be playing at Commodore Benedict's great country place up the [Long Island] Sound or at [Ernest] Seton-Thompson's home, and again would be chasing down a punch scene on the Bowery or in the midst of the human sewer seepage of Rivington street.

"There was the unusual interest in the new form of amusement, the Movies; we were generally treated with respect and given welcome and the consideration due to artists; but there were the sharp contrasts which give to life its personal dramatic fillip.

"It was in one of these expeditions that I discovered Cuddebackville, the most beautiful, altogether the loveliest spot in America."

"Where is it?" eagerly asked the interviewer.

"I forget exactly; somewhere about a hundred miles from New York;

I don't think you can find it in a Gazetteer for I don't even know how to spell the name[2]; I don't want it found, and spoiled, for I hope some time to see it again, still untroubled by trippers, unmoved by flying tissue paper picnic napkins, untainted by cigarette-smoking advanced minds.

"Cuddebackville is a place where Goldsmith could have written as he did of Auburn; which Tennyson would have peopled with the lovely majesty of romance; and where in our small way we found a perfect 'location' for scenes for a film of *The Last of the Mohicans*[3]; the film is now and happily forgotten, but no one of that company can ever forget Cuddebackville.

"That place illustrated what was the charm of that life; there we were in the dress and demeanor of the Leather Stocking days, acting on a stage that was set by the One stage director to a perfection that even Cooper could not have described.

"There is a quality about the light there, particularly a twilight that I have never found elsewhere; it is transcendentally illuminative for pictures.

"It was a natural place for romance, and here it was, I believe, that Mary Pickford's romance began.

"[Owen] Moore and Mary were in the company; there were moonlight canoeing parties, there was every quality that develops, nurtures, and fructifies romance.

"Mary was very young, and the most beautiful, charming girl known to the stage or pictures; the lake at Cuddebackville never had reflected so fair a visage in the gentle mirror of its bosom.

"She is more beautiful as a woman now; but she is remembered there as dressed in a colleen's raiment in another picture that is also like the *Mohican* happily forgotten—save for Mary's part in it.

"What a pity that picture cannot be made again as pictures are now made!

"There was an old gentleman named Godfrey [perhaps correctly Goddefroy], who had a place nearby, something of the order of an English country seat; and he said of Mary: 'If Thackeray could only have seen this girl, and had let his heart work while he was writing of her, he would be the only man in the world who could do justice to her beauty and charm.'

"The whole world loved her; everyone does now who sees her. Mary to us all is like a sunbeam, like a rose-white cloudlet in a clear sky, like—well like nothing other than Mary.

"Everyone loves her, and everyone is glad that she married the man she loved [Owen Moore at this time, not Douglas Fairbanks]."

Before we leave Cuddebackville, I'll tell you how it was discovered; it may be that you will want to do a picture there, so you will like to know the Griffith manner of finding what he wants—and getting it.

Someone had whispered the secret to him of Cuddebackville's beauty, and when he came to direct *The Last of the Mohicans* he knew that was a "location" he must have.

He asked the management of the Biograph to send him and his company there.

It was with scorn and wonder that the request was heard and rejected.

"A hundred miles of travel, railway fares, all manner of expenses, for a rural scene? Bosh! Go up above Harlem for it."

Griffith made no reply; he has always been of the Oh!-what's-the-use type, when breasted by imperviousness.

For some weeks he had been employed, and his pay had been raised as his value became imperative; never foolishly lavish he had saved quite a little "bank roll," and with this, dismantling his entire fortification against adversity, he paid all the cost of the excursion himself, and that with full knowledge that the items would never be passed on an expense account. But he got the scenes he had to have.

He was gambling?

No more than the insiders were gambling when a year or more ago they bought Bethlehem Steel.

Griffith knew, and was playing a cinch hand, with Fortune looking over his shoulder and chuckling sardonically at the manager who had refused the railway fares and grub expenses for the trip to Cuddebackville.

"Go to Harlem!"

He was on his way to his niche in the Hall of Fame; he paid his fare then, but the world has been paying it ever since.

For he had found his Aladdin's lamp by thinking.

He had learned that the path ahead was only to be found by discarding all sign posts left by past travelers; by ignoring all experience; in forgetting what everyone had been doing; and by giving the lie to all tradition as to the manner and method in which things should be done.

"I found that picture-makers were following as best as they could the theory of the stage," he says of this period of his work.

"A story was told in pictures, and it was told in regular progression; it is bad stage technique to repeat; it would be bad stage technique to have an actor show only his face; there are infinite numbers of things we do in pictures that would be absurdities on the stage, and I decided that to do with the camera only what was done of the stage was equally absurd.

"My first anarchistic effort was what we now call the 'close-up.' This made me laughed at again at first; but I had become used to jeers, and feeling I was right I kept at it; what caused the fizzle at first was that in my attempt to get the actors closer to the camera I misjudged distance and their heads did not show in the film."

He laughed grimly. Perhaps if you recall some actor's heads you have seen in a film you may grasp the full significance of that laugh.

W. [William] C. [Christy] Cabanne,[4] one of Griffith's most trusted and highly gifted directors [at the Fine Arts Company], tells of how the idea came to his Chief.

"When Griffith began to direct," says Mr. Cabanne, "we used to act as people do on the stage; preserving distances, and as the story seemed to demand standing quite a distance from the camera.

"'What's the good of this?' he said one day; 'your legs and your feet do not act; it's your faces that tell the story,' and he marked new limit lines and had us stand so close to the camera that it seemed the result would certainly look foolish."

Probably that first attempt with the headless actors did seem to prove that Griffith was as crazy as the anvil chorus players termed him; just as Columbus did not have to study long to make the egg stand on end, Griffith had no trouble in arranging the close-up so that the actors' heads and faces *would* show.

He tried it again, and focused the camera so that all the legs were cut off.

Then came the single close-up; the large, many-times-magnified face with full expression.

And then the "switchback"; this is probably the most effective innovation in picture-making; judged by its quick adoption and persistent use by all other producers, it is invaluable.

"'The switchback,'" says Griffith, "enabled me to follow the story with exactitude and at the same time preserve in the mind of the spectator an unimpaired continuity, with added emphasis.

"For example, a character says to another: 'I hate you;' you show the speaker's face, and then switch in the face of the man to whom the remark is made with its expression, and then perhaps a bit of a previous scene which laid the foundation for the hatred.

"That method is now used in a million different manners, and in a way has possibly transformed the entire procedure of picture-making."

It was not long before his brain, unshackled from what had been done by others, intent only on doing what ought to be done, devised the "fade-in" and "fade-out," a feature which combines with nice accuracy the utmost of realism and the ultimate of idealism; then the men who had been calling Griffith crazy and worse, "swiped" his novel ideas and are using them with the calm serenity which is a characteristic of theatrical piracy.

These startling developments did not come all at once, and with every step forward Griffith took, his competitors took one backward in terming him "ridiculous," varied in expression in all the eloquently vituperative patter which rivalry possesses in stage controversies.

One man, a Mr. [Jeremiah J.] Kennedy in the Biograph, stood by him at first; as the orders from exhibitors piled up others gave him support, and the glad hand began to swing toward him.

He took it serenely, and shook it genially, for he does not know what malevolence is.

No one then dreamed of what he still had in mind, no one contemplated a four- or five-reel picture much less a thirteen-reel like *The Birth of a Nation*; neither did Griffith dream it.

He knew.

Notes

1. Arthur Marvin died on January 28, 1912, at the age of fifty; Griffith was still with Biograph at that time.

2. The name is incorrectly spelt in the published piece.

3. Griffith is probably referring to *Leather Stocking*, released September 27, 1909. However, it was not the first film shot in Cuddebackville.

4. The correct pronunciation of the director's last name has always been something of a mystery. In this interview, it appears with an acute accent over the "e" which certainly suggests that the final "e" is pronounced.

The Story of David Wark Griffith: Part Four

Henry Stephen Gordon/1916

From *Photoplay*, September 1916, 85–86, 146, 148. This interview is adapted from
part four of Gordon's six-part series, "The Story of David Wark Griffith." Part Six
of the series appeared under the title "The Real Story of *Intolerance*." The page
numbers given above relate to this adaptation; the full citation reads pp. 79–86, 146,
148.

Just Gold was Griffith's second picture.[1] In making *Dollie* he had followed
the scenario to the letter; that was the first and last time he paid any attention to the author.

"In making *Just Gold* I began to seek after atmosphere and effects," he
said, "and the clue to causes. If I have had a measure of success, possibly
that effort was responsible largely, for it started me in the right direction.

"It was in making a picture with Mary Pickford that I believe she first
met Owen Moore.[2] It seems to me the title of the picture was *The Red
Man*, or something like it.

"At any rate it was in this we perfected the fade-in and the fade-out
effect, after a lot of experimenting.

"This received most severe criticism, which continued as late as my
Judith [of Bethulia] picture. That was made, I think, about three years ago,
and now that method is being used probably to excess.

"Mary Pickford's romance was reflected in her acting, which made
the picture; it became in heavy demand and thereby proved my contention on the new effects.

"*Ingomar* [released as *The Barbarian, Ingomar*, October 13, 1908] with
Florence Lawrence followed soon, and that went far toward sustaining
all my ideas which had been used in its making. As I recall Miss Lawrence

also had a romance created from that picture and married Harry Salter, who became quiet as distinguished as a director as she was as an actress.

"I could tell countless love affairs that developed into matrimony in those early days, but everyone had to work so hard, and so long, that it is difficult to understand how time was found for sentimental incidents.

"Those were the days of the half-reels; we made two pictures a week. It was something of a struggle to get them out, especially at the time when everyone was calling me crazy, and not only calling, but believing I was crazy. Or worse, a simple fool.

"Why, often we have got a picture completed in two days. Now we take that much time or more just to decide on the costumes we will use.

"Of course it hurts my sense of modesty to admit the fact, but it is true that in a few months Biograph pictures were considered far away the best.

"Newspapers began to notice them voluntarily, as a matter of general interest; the Biograph was quickly taken in by the General Film Company, which meant the largest organization and most profitable before or since.

"In 1911 the Motion Picture Patents Company, an adjunct of the General Film Company, earned 1,700 percent on its capital stock, according to certified reports.

"A few two-reel pictures began to be seen; under that regime we would make one reel a week and the other the next week. This was possibly the beginning of the serial idea of pictures.

"My largest picture with the Biograph was *Judith* [*of Bethulia*], a four-reel picture which I thought immense at that time. I made that with Blanche Sweet. She with Mary Pickford, in fact all the picture actresses of note, then came to the screen from the stage.

"One of my early pictures I did was *Pippa Passes* [more correctly *Pippa Passes or, The Song of Conscience* released October 4, 1909]. We put that on in three days; considerably less time, I fancy, than Browning used in writing the poem. We had to do everything at once.

"Then came *Enoch Arden* [a two-reeler, released in two parts on June 12 and June 15, 1911], *A Blot on the 'Scutcheon* [released January 29, 1912], *Taming of the Shrew* [released November 10, 1908], *Lines of White on a Sullen Sea* [released October 28, 1909], and others; these were all one-reels, and all were made before *Judith*."

Probably these titles mark the difference between Griffith and other producers.

Usually, then, scenario writers were employed by producers to evolve their own ideas in some form of sweet sentimentalism, with the blowsy, inevitable "Happy Ending"; few of the stories if written in story form would be bought for publication by the cheapest magazines; the result in the effect on the public is evident.

That Browning, or Shakespeare, or Tennyson, could write a better story for the screen than John Smith, street car conductor, or Tom Brown, cub reporter, and that the public does prefer real art to bunk, is a lesson than was long difficult for the get-rich-quicker producers to learn.

Some quite noted ones haven't learned it yet.

Griffith learned it before he began; those pictures were the first to invite Art to the screen; it was then called "attacking Art"; possibly that was in a measure true; at any rate Griffith shot his arrow at a star, and it hit the shining target.

Judith [*of Bethulia*] was his last effort with the Biograph, and he quit that concern in 1913 to go with Reliance-Majestic.

Of all the financing he went through, I know nothing; the story is best told by his pictures—the ones he made himself, untrammeled by any control.

How about Paul Armstrong? may be asked; did Griffith keep seeking among the illuminati for his material?

If he did not keep gathering from the illuminati, he illuminated the other sort, on whom he drew for subjects.

He did use Paul Armstrong's *The Escape* for his own first and one of his most impressive pictures, and Armstrong made $2,500 in royalties from the picture, which is thought to be much more than he ever made from the play. It only had a brief run in Los Angeles, where it was produced first by Oliver Morosco; Armstrong himself produced it in New York—with disaster.

There was a tip-top theme for a play, but Armstrong did not quiet hit the right angle. He tried too much for the curves.

In this picture Griffith did hit the angles, all of them; the film had much more "punch" than even the master of "punch," the hard-hitting Armstrong, had put into the play; some of it was fascinatingly repulsive, so much so that people were irresistibly drawn to see it again and again.

And it had the best fight ever put on the screen to that time; one which William Farnum has hardly excelled in his numerous exhilarating examples of white-hope acting.[3]

Strange to say, Armstrong and Griffith had no quarrel.

De mortuis nil nisi but forgetfulness of their regrettable traits. Armstrong, however, had such a prevailing insistence on quarreling with his friends that it is not indecent to recognize that fact, now that he is gone.[4]

"No, I had no difference at any time with Paul," says Griffith of this incident, "but I fancy that was because he had nothing to do with me, nor I with him, in the making of *The Escape*. He wrote to me suggesting its being made into a picture and sent me the 'script'; I read it, and thought it would do, and did it.

"He never saw it in the making, and, as far as I remember, he made something like $2,500 out of the venture.

"He did have some differences later, of a passing kind, with some of our business men, but it was all satisfactorily arranged."

The Battle of the Sexes followed quickly, and then came his center shot, *The Birth of a Nation*.

Probably one of the poorest plays ever put out was *The Clansman*, Thomas Dixon's novel dramatized. The novel was a best seller, and a cause for controversy.

The play was not a best seller; one manager told me, some time ago, that he paid a dollar apiece to ten negroes in San Francisco to form an Afro-American League which was to institute legal proceedings to stop the performance of the play. If I recall correctly it was Sam Friedman, the ever alert youthful theatrical expert, who tried this big business trick.

He paid for the filing of the injunction papers and hired lawyers to defend his side, meanwhile supplying the League with po'k chops and cigarette money.

Friedman won his case against himself, and the League paraded in sorrow before the theater, where the intake that night was something less than $100. Not enough, anyway, Sam said, to pay for the meal tickets he had bought.

Ask any theatrical man how much *The Birth of a Nation* has made, and he will immediately make a record elevation flight among the millions.

Admitting that Mr. Dixon did a fairly good piece of work in writing the story, you will have to admit that Griffith did a masterpiece in his treatment of the book.

It is very like the comparing of the original, forgotten, Italian tale of Romeo and Juliet with what the Bard did with it.

The story of the first showing of *The Birth of a Nation* in Los Angeles and of Griffith's surprise at what he had done, has been told.

Clune's Auditorium was packed to the fire limits that night, for much gossip had circulated; the racial excitement had either been artificially or naturally aroused; the city councilmen with a "close-up" of the negro vote before their imagination had at one time decided to stop the production, and a lot of lawyers had to be retained, and to some extent the word got about that the picture was an incendiary, dangerous affair.

There were coveys, even flocks, of policemen on hand with riot sticks; but the only riot was that of recognition of a great piece of work.

A number of negroes filled portions of the house; whether they liked the picture or not they said nothing, and very wisely kept their and everyone's peace.

It was my fortune to see several scenes of that picture in the making. That one where Booth leaps from the President's box to the stage of Ford's theater was rehearsed something like fifteen or twenty times with the camera.

All of those I saw were gone over and over, with very slightly differing "business"; there was enough film thrown away to make scores of thirteen-reel pictures.

A favorite story at the studios is of the horror of a man interested in the making of *The Birth of a Nation*, who saw Griffith throw out seventeen thousand feet of film and take the scenes over again!

He was one of the later fellows who thought D. W. G. crazy.

I asked Griffith: "What has made the Biograph go down in value since you left it?"

"I can't tell you," he said with a laugh; "I'd hate to say it about myself."

And then he talked about the reissues of the old pictures; pictures that he would like to have forgotten, just as Browning shuddered at the revival of his early efforts.

"I understand they are billing those old affairs as 'Griffith Masterpieces,'" he said, "and I can tell you they seem very bad affairs to me now.

"I used to think they were rather good pictures; but everything has changed since then, acting, effects, methods, photography—everything.

"Those pictures are my children, I admit, but their very existence is justification for my disowning them."

And now he has been nearly two years on his next picture, *The Mother and the Law*.

Who is the author of the scenario? For part, at least, a poet who five thousand years ago wrote an epic in the cuneiform characters.

Griffith can quote beautiful passages from the cuneiform, and, odd to say, they sound something like a futurist effort; they particularly look futuristic when read in the pasturistic original.

This master of the lens has been often three thousand years ahead of his rivals; in this, his latest ambitious picture, he has gone back five thousand years for a good portion of his story.

Notes

1. *Just Gold* is the title of a Biograph film, released on May 23, 1913. Griffith's next film as director after *The Adventures of Dollie* is *The Fight for Freedom*, released on July 17, 1908, followed by *The Tavern-Keeper's Daughter*, released on July 24, 1918, and *The Redman and the Child*, released on July 28, 1908.

2. Both Owen Moore and Mary Pickford were certainly at Biograph in 1908.

3. Presumably a reference to William Farnum's climatic fight scene with actor Thomas Santschi in the first, 1914, screen adaptation of *The Spoilers*, a fight which was declared the most realistic and violent ever shown on film.

4. Paul Armstrong died in 1915.

The Story of David Wark Griffith: Part Five

Henry Stephen Gordon/1916

From *Photoplay*, October 1916, 90–94. This interview is adapted from part five of Gordon's six-part series, "The Story of David Wark Griffith." Part Six of the series appeared under the title "The Real Story of *Intolerance*." The page numbers given above relate to this adaptation; the full citation reads pp. 86–94.

In recording the history of this picture [*The Birth of a Nation*], [story editor] Frank Woods again takes the center of the stage as the moving movie, Impulse.

It was in 1913 that Mr. Woods suggested to Mr. Griffith the value of the [Thomas] Dixon book as a feature picture.

A year or so before, based on a scenario by Mr. Wood, the Kinemacolor people had made what was called a "Clansman" film.

But the picture was so bad, from the difficulties of photography, and lack of discriminating direction, that it was never assembled for exhibition.

Griffith inclined to the idea and re-read the book and—but here is his own little story of the undertaking.

"When Mr. Woods suggested *The Clansman* to me as a subject it hit me hard; I hoped at once that it could be done, for the story of the South had been absorbed into the very fibre of my being.

"Mr. Dixon wrote to me suggesting the project, and I re-read the book at once.

"There had been a picture made by another concern, but this had been a failure; as the theme developed in my mind, it fascinated me until I arrived at the point where I had to make the picture; if I had known that the result would mean disaster I do not think it would have mattered to me; truly I never was sure that the result would be a success; that

58

first night showing at the [Clune's] Auditorium, if anyone had offered me just a shade over what it had cost, I would have taken the money just as quickly as I could reach for it.

"There were several months lost in the negotiations for the rights, as by that time other producers had gained the same idea, like myself, undeterred by one failure already having been made.

"As I studied the book, stronger and stronger came to work the traditions I had learned as a child; all that my father had told me. That sword I told you about became a flashing vision. Gradually came back to my memory the stories a cousin, one Thurston Griffith, had told me of the 'Ku Klux Klan,' and that regional impulse that comes to all men from the earth where they had their being stirred potently at my imagination.

"But there was nothing of personal exhilaration required to make a picture out of that theme; few others like it in subject and power can be found, for it had all the deep incisive emotionalism of the highest patriotic sentiment.

"I couldn't say that the story part of the picture can ever be excelled, but as for the picture itself, there will be others made that will make it appear archaic in comparison.

"For the feature play has just begun to come into its own; my personal idea is that the minor pictures have had their day; the two and three and four reel ones are passing, if not gone.

"As I worked the commercial side of the venture was lost to my view; I felt driven to tell the story—the truth about the South, touched by its eternal romance which I had learned to know so well.

"I may be pardoned for saying that now I believe I did succeed in measure in accomplishing that ambition.

"It all grew as we went! I had no scenario, and never looked again at some few notes I made as I read the book, and which I read to my company before we began. Naturally the whole story was firmly in my mind, and possibly the personal exuberance of which I have told you enabled me to amplify and to implant in the scenes something of the deep feeling I experienced in that epoch that had meant everything; and then had left nothing to my nearest, my kin, and those about me.

"There was not a stage star in my company; 'Little Colonel' [Henry B.] Walthall had been out with Henry Miller, and had achieved some reputation, thought by no means of stellar sort. Possibly he felt a bit of the impulse of locality, for his father was a Confederate colonel.

"Miriam Cooper, the elder Cameron sister, was a perfect type of the beauty prevalent below the Mason and Dixon line, and Mae Marsh was from the same part of the Union, while Spottiswoode Aitken—'Dr. Cameron'—was related to a large group of distinguished Southern families.

"Those people were not picked because of place of birth or of their personal feeling about the story; still it was a fortunate incident that they were what they were; it is hard to figure exactly how far what is bred in the bone will shine through the mind.

"The casting frankly was all done by types; Miss Cooper, for instance, I kept in the company for all the months between the idea that I might make the picture until the work began, because I knew she would be an exact 'Cameron' girl.

"Everyone of the cast proved to be exactly what was required.

"When I chose Lillian Gish as Stoneman's daughter, she seemed as ideal for the role as she actually proved herself to be in her acting. Mae Marsh had driven her quality so thoroughly into the estimation of the public in *The Escape* that I felt absolutely sure of her results. It was the same with Robert Harron and Elmer Clifton, for Stoneman's sons, and Ralph Lewis as Stoneman lived exactly up to what his personality promised when he was selected. And there were George Siegmann, the mulatto Lieutenant Governor, and Walter Long as the awful negro Gus, and Mary Alden, Stoneman's mulatto housekeeper.

"There has been question as to why I did not pick real negroes or mulattos for those three roles.

"The matter was given consideration, and on careful weighing of every detail concerned, the decision was to have no black blood among the principals; it was only in the legislative scene that negroes were used, and then only as 'extra people.'

"There were six weeks of rehearsals before we really began. I think it took something like six months to make the picture—that is, the actual photography; but in all I put in a year and a half.

"It was a big venture in numbers at that time; I suppose from the first to the last we used from 30,000 to 35,000 people.

"That seemed immense at that era, but now, in the piece we temporarily call *The Mother and the Law* (Mr. Griffith's huge new feature, just completed, and named *Intolerance*), we have used since the first of January about fifteen thousand people a month (this statement was made in the latter part of April), and I cannot see even the beginning of the end as yet.

"With *The Clansman* it was not alone the first expense, but the incessant fighting we had to do to keep the picture going that cost.

"We spent over $250,000 the first six months, combating stupid persecution brought against the picture by ill-minded censors and politicians who were playing for the negro vote.

"Lawyers had to be retained at every place we took the picture, and we paid out enough in rents for theaters where we were not allowed to show the picture to make an average film profitable.

"But we finally won.

"Now we are showing the picture with no hindrance, and most of those who opposed us at first, are now either admirers of the picture or quiescent.

"While on this censorship, this drooling travesty of sense, I want to say something that I have said before, but which is essential to a right understanding of my purposes and work.

"The foremost educators of the country have urged upon moving picture producers to put away the slapstick comedies, the ridiculous sentimental 'mush' stories, the imitation of the fiction of the cheap magazines and go into the fields of history for our subjects.

"They have told us repeatedly that the motion picture can impress upon a people as much of the truth of history in an evening as many months of study will accomplish. As one eminent divine said of pictures, 'They teach history by lightning!'

"We would very much like to do this, but the very reason for the slapstick and the worst that is in pictures is censorship. Let those who tell us to uplift our art, invest money in the production of a history play of the life of Christ. They will find that this cannot be staged without incurring the wrath of a certain part of our people. 'The Massacre of St. Bartholomew,' if reproduced,[1] will cut off the toes of another part of our people.

"I was considering the production in pictures of the history of the American people. This got into the papers. From all over the country I was strongly advised that this was not the time for a picture on the American revolution, because the English and their sympathizers would not take kindly to the part the English played in the wars of the American revolution, and that the pro-Germans would not care to see the Hessians enact their harsh roles in the narrative of our freedom.

"[George] Bernard Shaw spoke fatefully and factually when he said: 'The danger of the cinema is not the danger of immorality, but of morality; people who like myself frequent the cinemas testify to their desolating romantic morality.'"

"Do you anticipate a similar fight when your *Mother and the Law* picture is produced?" Griffith was asked.

"That depends upon what degree of success I achieve in my efforts to portray Truth in the picture."

That remark sounds as if it had been made by Columbus, Socrates, Christ, Galileo, Robert Emmett, Joan of Arc, Guttenberg, and the others of the holy and noble army of martyrs of sodden, stupid, blear-eyed disgust at Truth, inevitably frowned [on] at first by the mass of human kind.

After all Mr. Griffith only uttered a commonplace.

Try it yourself! If you have a glimmer of a great fact, if you can prove that a certain line of thought or action has been wrong, pitch your truth to the world and then turn tail and run like hell fire, or you will be immersed in that very same!

"If I approach success in what I am trying to do in my coming picture," continued the creator. "I expect a persecution even greater than that which met *The Birth of a Nation*."

Out and about Los Angeles, people still talk about the making of *The Clansman*.

Some of Griffith's stockholders also still talk and mourn over his exactitude—and its cost.

Something over 150,000 feet of negative was exposed in the making of this, and of this about 30,000 was "assembled for the making of the thirteen reels," from which the final production—less than 12,000 feet—was selected.

All the technical science used was Griffith's own devising. A new feature was the taking of battle scenes at night by the use of deftly placed artificial lights. These scenes look simple enough in the picture, but they were the object of repeated experiments and they caused all manner of excitement; the light illuminated the skies, and the explosions were the basis for many interesting rumors of foreign fleets attacking the California coast.

Note

1. As, of course, it is in *Intolerance*.

The Real Story of *Intolerance*

Henry Stephen Gordon/1916

From *Photoplay*, November 1916, 34, 35–40. This interview is adapted from the final episode of Henry Stephen Gordon's "The Story of David Wark Griffith," published under the title given here. The page numbers given above relate to this adaptation; the full citation reads pp. 27–40.

"Is this truly to be your last picture?" Griffith was asked.

"It is," he replied; "intolerance that I have met with and fought with in my other picture made it impossible to ask investment of the tremendous sums of money required for a real feature film with the result dependent on the whim or the lack of brains of a captain of police."

At that "runoff" showing, after the four spectators of fishy capacity for emotion had found their feet again firmly fastened in the clay of the commonplace, one said, "You've made a wonderful picture but you did have to pull the 'old stuff' to send 'em away with a good taste in their mouth.

"You're plucky but you didn't dare finish the picture true to life, and have The Boy executed, as he would have been in real life; Carlyle might well have written your scenario up [to] that finale; but there you allowed the Despot of the stage to rule and you saved The Boy simply to satisfy the lust for comfort which audiences demand."

"You're one of the fellows who would have stood up and answered Pilate's question, 'What is Truth?'" said Griffith.

"That finale *is* Truth, and because it is a comfortable truth you thought it false.

"If you had read the newspapers as much as you've written for them, you would know about the Stielow case in New York[1]; Stielow was convicted of a murder and sentenced to die; four times he was prepared for the chair, four times he and his family suffered every agony save the final swish of that current.

"What saved him was exactly what saved 'The Boy' in my picture; the murderer confessed, the final reprieve arrived just as the man was ready to be placed in the chair, his trousers' leg already slit for the electrode."

And picking up the copy of the New York paper containing the account, Griffith read former president Taft's sentence of the criminal law, "The administration of criminal law in this country is a disgrace to civilization."

The man who objected to the conventionally happy finale did it because he fancied himself just a bit more cultured than most, and believed that Art was only true in being disagreeable. . . .

Years ago, when he [Griffith] was in a road company with Wilfred Lucas the two were walking one day when Lucas saw a woman rocking a cradle.

He called the scene to Griffith's attention and quoted the Walt Whitman lines:

". . . . . endlessly rocks the cradle,

"Uniter of Here and Hereafter."

"Who wrote that?" asked Griffith.

"That's Walt Whitman," said Lucas, "you'll find it somewhere in his 'Leaves of Grass.'"

Griffith said nothing but darted away and found a book store, bought a copy of Whitman, and it happened as he opened the book the leaves parted at that very passage.

That was twelve or fifteen years ago.

But when the idea of *Intolerance* came to his mind Griffith recalled those lines, imagined the picture of the eternal cradle, and there you have Walt Whitman's thought photographed.

This chronicler is far from being a hero worshipper; I have been on much too intimate terms with far too many heroes to fondle any illusions about them; they often wear patent leather shoes with spats, and sometimes they bandoline their hair, and often they are careless about marriage vows and going to church, and paying debts, and occasionally I've met the best of them who can adroitly eat peas with his knife, and a lot of them wear wristwatches, and some use perfumery, but when a man can make a camera fasten to a negative film Walt Whitman's intellect he is none of these types but a man hero, and I kow-tow to him as being no less a poet than Whitman himself.

Beyond argument the measure of achievement today is that of money.

How much did it cost? will be the prime question about this work of beauty.

I know exactly and I will tell you exactly.

His picture of *Intolerance* cost five times as much as *The Birth of a Nation*. But what the latter cost no one but those who paid the cost know.

The press agents concerned claimed all manner of figures from $250,000 up to half a million.

An estimate from a number of those expert in judging, places the expenditure for *The Birth of a Nation* close to $100,000, some going as high as $200,000, none going below the first figure.

This last picture has been two years in the actual making, and work on the preparatory stages was begun over three years ago; considerably more than sixty thousand people were engaged at one time or another in the acting, and more in the various forms of effect outside of the acting.

I do happen to know authoritatively that much over three hundred thousand feet of film was used in the making and that this was cut in the "assembling" to the present limit of the picture of between twelve thousand and thirteen thousand.

As for carefulness, it is a fact that the captions have been set and changed close to two thousand times.

As for Griffith himself, he has put his heart's substance into the labor.

I saw him the day before he left for New York; he was brave, even gay mentally, jesting and debonair; but he was gaunt and excited though in thorough self command.

I asked him, "Now that your work is over what is your idea of your future? What is your next ambition?"

He looked frankly at me and said unsmilingly, "My idea of life now is a tremendously large bed in some place where no telephone, no messenger boy, no telegram, no voice, can reach me, and to sleep for a solid week, only waking very occasionally long enough to eat a good dinner, and then roll over and again sleep."

"What will you do if *Intolerance* fails?" I asked.

Blandly smiling, he said, "I'll seek the Jersey coast and try to find one of those man-eating sharks."

"And what if it wins?"

"I have told you before that this will be my last picture.

"That is as true as anything can be which the future holds."

"The speaking stage, producing drama?"

"I have told you before that such was my desire; if the picture succeeds it will not, it cannot, make the money that in fabulous fashion pictures are credited with making; the theaters cannot hold as much money as some newspapers say pictures make.

"The matter of the money to be made is very like the fellow blowing the bassoon in the orchestra who was told to blow louder 'That's all very well,' he replied, 'but where is the wind to come from?'"

He says he intends to take up the stage next as a means of finding expression unhampered, but when asked what he would do, and how, he side-stepped.

"There will never be any combination of the speaking and the photo drama," he added with a tang of satire, "not if audiences can help it.

"The stage is perfect now, to my mind, because it enables us to make moving pictures so much easier than it might.

"I'm sorry that [Richard] Mansfield, that [Augustin] Daly, that [Henry] Irving are dead, but as a moving picture man I am glad, for the movies sake, that they are gone. If those men were now alive, we of the movies would have to work harder than we do, and I don't know how that could be done, for I figure that now we work fourteen and fifteen hours a day, but if the stage were different we would have to work thirty-six hours in the twenty-four; so we are glad that competition with the stage is not fiercer than it is."

"Don't you regard the modern part of your pictures as an attack on the courts, on judges?"

"I certainly do not, because it is not.

"That Stielow case in New York is exactly like the murder case in the story; only reality goes the picture three better in the way of reprieves. Stielow and his family faced death-suffering four times, and three times the reprieve came at the very last minute.

"If I had shown scenes like that on the screen it would have made the public laugh as impossible, but the people should not laugh at the courts; judges do not make the laws, you, I, everyone are responsible for the laws.

"I have met several judges and have always found them very nice and often wonderful men. Real gentlemen, in fact.

"What has seemed peculiar to me about the law is that after so prolonged an experiment with the principles of Christianity we still find as was found through all the ages that justice demands if a man kills another he in turn should be murdered.

"No, I am far from attacking the courts or judges, for the only thing that has stood between the pictures and the censors and thereby prevented the pictures from utter extinction, has been the courts."

Here are his reasons as dictated by himself, for making no more feature pictures:

"It appears that henceforth there will be no middle ground in the pictures; there will be the ten, twenty, and thirty cent pictures, and the big two dollar ones.

"The first classification does not attract me, and the second offers too many stupid, cruel, costly, and apparently unpredictable offensives.

"Of necessity the stage must tell the truth more freely than any other method of expression. It is the only means existing today of even attempting to portray the truth.

"I do not mean the drama as it is known to Broadway, but the drama as it is known to dramatists.

"I have tried to tell the truth in my new picture.

"But I find that what we call the Movies are less free now than ever, and are more and more dependent on the censor, and on that account I feel inclined to stop.

"There are but a few means of conveying what we believe to be truth; the college is seriously handicapped, as too many of the universities are endowed by a few rich men whose brain power has been used only to acquire wealth; these have little or no knowledge beyond their immediate needs; they have never taken the time to gain knowledge of human nature in the little nor in the mass; they have their own ideas of life and deride everything foreign to their own little circles; they know little of the present and less of the past.

"There is very little doubt that most college professors' opinions on morals, politics, and even of history, are very different in their private and their public capacities.

"Who can believe that a man dependent on a university will have an opinion for the public which is not more or less sicklied with the pale cast of thought about the men who put up the money for the institution?

"The world can hope for no boldness of verity from the colleges.

"The preacher of today is as always swayed to some extent by the majority of the sect to which he belongs; he can seldom speak as an individual, and of necessity he cannot launch what may seem a new truth that infringes on what was an old truth, and remain in his denomination.

"I wondered recently at the daring of a certain professor of Assyriology who said in a little-read magazine that the average normal being of today would find himself with more decent associates and in happier surrounding in Babylon, or ancient Egypt, than in any intervening period of the world's history, up to the eighteenth century.

"The newspaper and magazine appeal to a certain clientele which they must please, and are forced to listen as a rule to the hydra-headed monster called Public Clamor, more than to her gentler sister, Public Opinion.

"But the producer of a feature picture depends on a much larger audience than any of these means; he does not have to defer to what Mrs. Smith thinks, or what Mr. Jones believes, for he has a million Mrs. Smiths and a million of Mr. Jones, and he is far more certain to get a fair hearing, or he would be if it were not for the censor.

"Isn't the folly of it all palpable? Because a new idea is expressed people are not forced to accept it. But certainly in this country there should be no objection to the discussion of all subjects.

"What kind of people, what sort of race, can continue to exist that is afraid of discussion?

"The politics of the world if founded on so much hypocrisy that everything is done for what is right nor even against what is wrong, but for the effect on a majority of the people.

"That is why all Europe is slaughtering.

"That is why 'Christian' nations will murder Turks and crucify pagans and slay with zest 'foreigners.'

"A 'foreigner' is always a man with a head so dense that he will not think as we think.

"The story for Truth as we see it has become barred from the pictures, so that anyone who has a real idea to express should not look to the moving picture as a means, but if he has enough money, to the stage.

"We of the moving picture craft admit our defeat; it is impossible for us to take any big subject of interest without the fear of the autocrats above us taking away our property.

"I now contemplate turning to the stage in making an attempt to find freedom of expression."

This ends what I have to tell about David W. Griffith.

Note

1. Because of its similarity to sequences in the Modern story of *Intolerance*, it is often assumed that Griffith borrowed details for this case, which involved the double murder of a Claude Phelps and his housekeeper in West Shelby, New York, on March 22, 1915. Charlie Stielow was accused of the crime, found guilty, and sentenced to be executed in Sing Sing Prison on September 5, 1916. Shortly before the execution, an ex-con and a peddler admitted to the killings, but they retracted their confessions, and Stielow was

again scheduled to die, on December 11, 1916. Governor Whitman of New York believed Stielow to be innocent, and commuted the man's sentence and had him released from prison. Because of the conflicting dates, it seems unlikely that Griffith based any of his story on the Stielow case, although he does cite it here a couple of times. The Stielow case is the subject of *Slaughter on a Snowy Morn* by Colin Evans (Icon, 2010), which makes no reference either to Griffith or *Intolerance*.

The Making of a Masterpiece

Edward Weitzel/1916

From the *Moving Picture World*, September 30, 1916, 2084.

After the curtain has descended upon the last scene of D. W. Griffith's colossal spectacle, now being shown at the Liberty Theatre, New York City, and the mighty palaces of Babylon, the terrible massacre of St. Bartholomew, the tragedy on Calvary, the impressive story of a modern day, and all the wizardry of a master producer's art is locked up in the small tin boxes that a man may carry away under his arm, the theater of Forty-Second Street becomes the scenes of long continued and exacting labors. The chief laborer is D. W. Griffith. Since the opening performance of his great picture he has been at the theater from eight in the morning until two the next morning busily at work. Counting the house attachés, one hundred and thirty-five people are required to give an exhibition of *Intolerance*. When this is over, the orchestra begins rehearsing new music or the producer and his staff of electricians and photographic experts try different lighting effects by the use of colored "foots" or "borders," the rapidly changing scenes on the screen being lit up with the same care given a performance on the spoken stage. Between orders and suggestions to his "crews," after the matinee one afternoon last week, the tireless but never ruffled director gave the writer some information as to how he came to conceive his wonderful photoplay. The remark, "You seem to be a very busy man, Mr. Griffith," brought the smiling reply, "Oh, yes, I'm a day-and-night laborer. This is the first duty of a director— to be always on the job."

"How did you come to conceive *Intolerance*?"

"That is a hard question to answer. It just growed—like Topsy. I didn't want to make it, principally on account of the expense. It cost four and half times more than *The Birth of a Nation*, and I felt that, after that achievement, someone else should experiment with such costly productions; but the subject took possession of me, and I thought it out. No scenario was ever made for it, you know."

"Do you mean that you carried all the scenes in your head?"

"Oh, no. I jotted down a general plan and followed it—at times."

"You are not a believer in the perfect scenario, then? The working plans, in which every scene, incident, and detail of production have been thought out and written down?"

The director's eyes lighted up with an amused smile, as he shook his head. "Hardly, the human equation renders that an impossibility. It is only when the director gets to handling his humans, singly or en masse, that he knows what he wants—or doesn't want. The unconscious expression on the face of an actor, a gesture by the leading lady, may give him a new and greatly improved train of thought."

"How did you dare attempt so revolutionary a scheme as running four parallel plots in the same picture?"

"Perhaps because it was revolutionary. I felt that we have not begun to realize the possibilities of the moving picture art, and such a radical departure from the old rules promised novel effects, at least. By the way, have you discovered the secret of how we keep from confusing the four plots in the mind of a spectator? It's by telling such a short portion of each story at a time and by running them all at the same tempo. The rate of speed at which the reel is unwound is a very important factor in showing a picture, you know. Heywood Broun, in his notice in the [New York] Tribune, remarked how the racing chariot of the mountain girl of ancient Babylon and the rushing train and speeding automobile of to-day seemed to be very close to each other. The characters are all on the same errand, and human hearts have been alike in all ages; only the garments that cover the body differ. Here again, the same tempo helped to bridge the long lapse of time. To return to the question of expense. One of the most costly scenes is the dance of the female slaves on the steps of the palace in Babylon. We had Ruth St. Denis teaching the movements to the large ballet for days, yet on the screen the scene lasts only a few seconds. Even a close-up often requires hours of work, the right expression being difficult to catch."

"How long were you in getting ready for the Babylonian scenes?"

"We had over three hundred workmen on the job from July to the following April. The buildings were made of staff, the same material as that used at the San Francisco exposition. In preparing the Euphrates, we damned up a river in California, and planted reeds and palm trees on its banks. You would hardly suspect that the scene of the onrush of the army of Cyrus is not far from Los Angeles. Excuse me for a moment." Mr. Griffith cast a critical look at the stage. "Those lights won't do, Bob, they are throwing shadows in the corners of the screen. Try a different color."

There was no impatience or indication of worry as the order was given. Mr. Griffith had been at the same work for days, but his smile was as pleasant and his self-control as complete as ever. The secret of his success in handling men and women lies very close to this fact.

"In preparing for *Intolerance*, Mr. Griffith, did you follow the method of Sir Henry Irving and call in a number of famous antiquarians and painters of ancient historical objects?"

"Not in the flesh. The scenes and incidents are all authentic, but our information was obtained from the writing of the different wise men. The legends of Creation, the Fall, and the Deluge are all found in the cuneiform writings of Bal, the High Priest, who betrayed Belshazzar and his city to Cyrus, you are aware, of course?"

"What are you going to produce next, Mr. Griffith? Another supreme effort?"

Again the maker of masterpieces smiled that amused smile of his. "I hope not. I'm willing that someone else should try the experiment. I prefer to make some simple five-reel pictures; they do not tie up large sums of money."

"What about the future of the motion picture?"

"We are only at the beginning of this thing. New and important improvements are bound to be discovered and the farther we attempt to get away from the art of the spoken stage, the more pronounced will be our advancement. Returning to *Intolerance*, we are attracting all kinds and conditions of men. The other evening a well known priest of this city came to me, between the acts, and said: 'I must tell you, Mr. Griffith, that I had serious doubts about the propriety of coming here. I was afraid the scenes from the life of the Savior might shock me, but they have been handled with due reverence. As for the rest of the picture, it has made me feel like God, as if I had the power to look down upon all humanity.' At the end of the performance a pugilistic friend of mine stopped me in the lobby to say: 'I'm comin' ag'in tomorrer night, Grif! I don't know much 'bout all yer high brow stuff, but there's somethin' 'bout th' show that's got me on me ear!'"

It was long after dinner time when the writer bade Mr. Griffith good-bye, and the last words which came through the closing door of the theater were: "That is still the wrong shade, Bob; try another color in your border lights." A boundless capacity for work and rubber-tired efficiency are important assets in the makeup of David W. Griffith.

The Film World's Greatest Achievement

Pictures and the Picturegoer/1917

From *Pictures and the Picturegoer* [London], April 28–May 5, 1917, 102–4.

[No author is given, but the interview is signed with the initials M. O. B. Spellings have been Americanized.]

Griffith the maker of *Intolerance* has pushed Griffith the maker of *The Birth of a Nation* off the map. In the latter film spectacle he produced a story which made the whole world believe that the last word in motion-pictures had been said; in the former he is one of the towering geniuses of the world, the creator of one of the greatest works of art ever known in any shape or form, and certainly the biggest achievement ever presented in any theatrical line.

To materialize his poet's vision of the force of bigotry operating in every age and clime and stifling the freedom of the human spirit, the producer of *Intolerance* has picturized four parallel themes—one ancient, one sacred, one medieval, and one modern—each depicting the consequence of this world-old evil. In the ancient theme he depicts the fall of Babylon, the collapse of one of the greatest civilizations of the world through intolerance. In the medieval we see the destruction of the kingdom of France—again the result of intolerance—in the time of Charles II. In the sacred theme are shown the developments which led to the Crucifixion of the Christ through intolerance. In the modern an entirely personal story is presented, showing the disaster brought upon a group of toilers—and one family in particular—through the intolerance of a band of social uplifters seeking notoriety.

A Mile of Festivity

As you may already have seen for yourself at Drury Lane Theatre [the Theatre Royal, Drury Lane, where the film had its U.K. premiere on April 7, 1917], some of the spectacular themes of *Intolerance* are stupendous. For instance, the Feast of Belshazzar, in one of the Babylonian scenes, is held in a mile-long hall, which was built at a cost exceeding that of the entire expense of any production ever made, including *The Birth of a Nation*—an erection which makes one marvel at the art and luxury of a vanished race. Then, in the Fall of Babylon, we see the most gripping and realistic war scenes ever conceived. With the massacre of the Huguenots in France there is more work which beggars description, whilst some of the Biblical scenes are remarkable for their delicate beauty.

But even with such spectacular magnificence Mr. Griffith has not overlooked the personal touches for which he is so famous. They are everywhere all through the picture, and are largely responsible for the way in which the moral of this greatest sermon ever preached comes home to one's own conscience. It was chiefly these little sympathetic but unique human touches which compelled me to follow up my first visit to *The Birth of a Nation* with some half a dozen more, and I was delighted beyond measure to find that several of the players who thus charmed me then were in this super-production. Chief among these is Mae Marsh, who played a strong role in the modern period of the picture. Other principals are Robert Harron, Josephine Crowell, Frank Bennett, Constance Talmadge, Margery Wilson, Walter Long, Eugene Pallette, Alfred Paget, Elmer Lincoln, Seena Owen, Miriam Cooper, Lillian Gish, Bessie Love, Howard Gaye, Fred Turner, Sam de Grasse, Vera Lewis, Ralph Lewis, Spottiswoode Aitken, Ruth Handforth, Joseph Henabery, Tully Marshall, and George Siegmann.

The Cinema King at Work

I was lucky enough to be present at the "dress rehearsal" of *Intolerance*, and spent one of the most interesting times of my life as a spectator of the final trial production of the picture, and Griffith's masterly direction of the orchestra and chorus. [The writer is referring to the dress rehearsal for the London premiere not the actual filming of *Intolerance*.] That glimpse of the "cinema king" at work gave me an understanding of the power of his personality and almost magnetic influence which fifty interviews would never have revealed. All the same, it was with the greatest eagerness that afterwards I seized an opportunity of a chat with him. At first it seemed almost impossible to interview Griffith. It was like trying to chain down a sunray or to grasp the fresh air. He is as free and individual that the cut-and-dried, hard-and-fast queries with which the interviewer must always bombard his victim literally dried up in my mouth. But he has a gift of getting quickly into touch with folk—a gift which must have stood him in good stead in his close business relationship with vast numbers of people of all types and classes and races—and it was not long before I felt thoroughly "at home" with him as, resigned with a good grace to his fate, he basked in the warmth of a theatre radiator in a mood of utmost good humor. He is a big, athletic-looking man, with a somewhat aggressive mouth and dogged chin, the hardness of which is mitigated by kindly, humorous eyes and flashing smile. Somehow I liked the carelessness—almost shabbiness—of his appearance; it was eloquent of the Griffith who produces out West in his shirt-sleeves, and eyes shaded by a shocking old Mexican hat.

"A few years ago—which is a long while in the motion-picture business—I produced a picture for Biograph called *The Reformers*,"[1] he began in reply to my query as to the origin of *Intolerance*. "In that two-reel subject I gave vent to some of my feelings on the matter of bigotry and carelessness of the true wellbeing of one's fellow-creatures. The picture did not in any way resemble *Intolerance* except in basic principles, but if you want the history of my new production you must go right back there, for ever since then I have been consciously and unconsciously collecting material for a portrayal, on as comprehensive a scale as possible, of the evil of intolerance. I have spent the last three years in the actual production of the picture. Of course much of the time has been taken up with historical research, for I am a great stickler for fidelity to fact in even the smallest details. Then there is the selection of a cast, which in its way is almost as big a thing as the actual production."

A Maker of Stars!

"I have decided ideas about types," he confessed, "and if the story calls for a particular kind of person I can't be satisfied until I have found that one. I would rather spend a week coaching up a young, inexperienced girl who knows nothing of picture acting but who looks the part, than spend ten minutes reading 'business' to an experienced stage actress. Why? Simply because looking the part is half the battle, and an intelligent girl with dramatic ability will quickly learn to be imaginative and expressive; it's only a matter of throwing off everyday superficialities; whereas the stage actress must almost necessarily be a matured woman, seeing that a stage training is a matter of years of hard work."

"That, of course, accounts for the tremendous number of people whom you have placed on the ladder of fame?"

Mr. Griffith shrugged his big shoulders carelessly, but I began to tick off the names on my fingers: "See, there's Mary Pickford, Blanche Sweet, Lillian and Dorothy Gish, Arthur Johnson, Owen Moore, Mae Marsh, Henry [B.] Walthall, Donald Crisp—"

"Flora Finch,"[2] he put in falling into the trap. "Charles Murray, Lionel Barrymore, Wilfred Lucas, Francis Grandon. Oh, more than I can think of at the moment. I have dismissed fewer actors and actresses than any other producer of big companies, and all with whom I have worked happily are my friends for life. When prominent or promising artistes leave some companies they are virtually placed on their black books; but I am never displeased with an actor who leaves me for better work. By the way, it may interest you to know that Charles Chaplin was once my assistant."[3] He went on to talk of the great little comedian, and interested though I was in his fresh, individual ideas and amusing stories, my conscience smote me that I was letting duty take care of itself. He was in a skittish mood—if I may use the word for so big a personality—and though he had suppressed it with real good nature for the sake of my "copy" it was beginning to break out and to infect me badly. His companionship was peculiarly entertaining, and I have to confess that I enjoyed a good fifteen minutes of idle chat and laughter with him before I exerted my will and begged him to talk about himself.

"Well, what do you want to know about me?" with mock resignation.

Producing from a Balloon

"To begin with, it is true that you produce without any sort of script?"

"Absolutely. I carry the whole scheme and the smallest detail of production in my mind. The only time I was ever at a loss was when I was producing one of the Babylonian war scenes—bloodcurdling, aren't they!—from a balloon. Something went wrong with the works, and we nearly came down to earth on top of a fallen siege tower. I confess that rather dazed me for a moment, and I shouldn't have minded a few notes to keep things going while I recovered my imagination."

"And I haven't asked you any of the sort of things I ought to have done," I lamented. 'Where were you born?' and all the rest of the things that our readers are longing to know."

"Oh, tell them—"

"No, no, Mr. Griffith," I threatened warned by the twinkle in his keen eyes, "It must be the truth, please!"

"Very well; let's be quick and get it over. I was born in Louisville, Kentucky, and I'm Southern all through."

"I really doubted that you were an American by birth," I interrupted; "your voice is deceptive—it is more that of an Englishman who has lived for awhile in America and picked up the accent than that of a native."

"Well, my mother was Scotch[4]—that may make a little difference. I was very Scotchly brought up, never even seeing a play of any kind until I was sixteen. Then came the red-letter day of my life—when Henry Irving and Ellen Terry visited the town. My parents were bitterly opposed to the stage and its connections, and it was decidedly against their wishes that I visited the theatre then. No sooner had I seen Irving, however, than I knew that I could follow no other profession than that of the stage. Shortly after that I began writing plays. I drifted to New York, and there, when reduced to a state of hardupshipness through devoting too much time to the writing of one of them, I gladly accepted work as an extra with the Biograph Company. I had already done some work on the legitimate stage, playing leading man for a time with Nance O'Neil [1905–1906]. How did I become a producer? By the providential absence of my own producer. I am afraid I rather startled the company with some queer ideas and innovations of my own. But I think, too, that they rather liked being made to gasp. It was a novel sensation. They were clearly appreciative of the 'close-ups' and 'cut-backs,' which I may say I originated. In 1914 I assumed charge of Reliance-Majestic Studios for Mutual. A year later I became producer for Triangle, and then general manager for Fine Arts. Lately I have been producing independently and releasing through Fine Arts. You probably know that I have now severed my connection with them."

The Mystery of His Future

"When you started producing did you feel you could improve upon the pictures as they were then?"

"Well, I certainly did not think I could do worse," was his amusing reply.

"And do you still feel there is room for improvement?" I persisted.

"Certainly I do."

"Then you have still bigger schemes in your mind? Will you tell me something concerning them?"

"There is nothing to tell." He tantalizes me.

"Oh, *please*! Is it true that you are going to produce in England? There is a rumor to that effect."

"Yes, some day, I hope."

"Then you may resume your work in California for the present?"

"Quite possibly. But I have made no plans. I haven't the faintest idea what I am going to do. At the moment I am in the happy, care-free state of a man without a future. Why won't you believe me?"

"You took too wicked," I declared; "you've something big up your sleeve!" Again I made my appeal. "I must tell *Pictures* something; they are longing to know what you are going to do, and they'll expect me to tell them."

"You can tell them anything else you like," he said, evasively. "Tell them this is my first visit to England; that I'm charmed with the country, the scenery, the people; that I mean to produce in England some day, chiefly because you have quaint old places that can never be faithfully and successfully copied. Tell them I want to produce in Spain, too. But that apart from that the future is blank."

"Very well, but they won't believe it; they'll think as I do, that there's some reason why you can't yet reveal your plans. I shall tell them that your future is 'wropt in myst'ry.'"

Notes

1. More correctly *The Reformers, of The Lost Art of Minding One's Business*, released on August 9, 1913.

2. More closely associated with the Vitagraph Company, which partnered her with comedian John Bunny, but Flora Finch did work for D. W. Griffith at the Biograph Company in 1908 and 1909.

3. There is no record that Griffith and Chaplin ever worked together until they co-founded United Artists Corporation in 1919.

4. Griffith's mother, Mary Oglesby, was born in the American South; this is perhaps the only reference to her Scottish ancestry.

D. W. Griffith Champions England's Natural Light

Moving Picture World/1917

From the *Moving Picture World*, September 15, 1917, 1678.

At various times we have either read or heard it said, that the natural light in England was poor for producing purposes. Now no less an authority than D. W. Griffith explodes the statement, as is shown by the following paragraphs from a recent interview which appeared in the *Weekly Dispatch* of London, England:

"There is nothing to compare with the variety of color in an English landscape. You have old walls of between three hundred and four hundred years old which only time could have painted. The winding lanes have unexpected lines and changing beauty. In the new country, the houses are all exactly like each other; in the old country, in the villages, there are so many different shapes and styles of houses that you wonder how it is possible for them to have been invented. Let the people in the United States see moving pictures of your English country life—the pastoral sympathy of the villages.

"It is absolute nonsense to say that your lighting here is a handicap. Some of the pictures we have already taken [for *Hearts of the World*] are the most beautiful we have made anywhere. The light is as good as in the States, and, what is more important, it lasts longer. In the States we have to stop at six o'clock; it gets darker much sooner. Over here we have taken pictures as late as nine o'clock in the evening. Here, too, we can get much more artistic effects because of your long, varying twilight. It is the most beautiful twilight imaginable."

Took Scenes in the Trenches

New York Times/1917

From the *New York Times*, October 16, 1917, 11.

David W. Griffith, an American motion picture producer, who has been in France for seven months, taking scenes of real warfare at the front, returned yesterday to an Atlantic port, accompanied by the sisters Dorothy and Lillian Gish, who took part in the realistic drama [*Hearts of the World*] that will be produced in this country.

"Thanks to the assistance of the British officers," Mr. Griffith said, "we caught actual scenes in the first line trenches and the surrounding panorama which was often a view forty miles long and ten to fifteen miles deep. By the aid of the new French lenses, with their fourteen-inch depths, one is able to show a charge along a two or three miles front and also to picture the grim work in the mudholes called trenches close enough to depict men actually wounded at their work, while others are tossing hand grenades over the ridge at the enemy's lines fifty yards away.

"There were number of Americans fighting in the Canadian ranks and in the French Army. On one occasion near Ypres a shell burst close beside one of our big cameras and knocked it to pieces. Another shell which fell a little distance away killed eleven men who were mending a hole in the road."

With regard to life in the trenches, Mr. Griffith said: "The soldiers do not get used to it. They bear it because there is no other place to go. When a barrage is moving slowly across a field you have to watch and see it is coming your way. If you lose your head and become nervous it means that you run into the curtain of fire and are killed instantly."

The Misses Gish said that they were not nearly so affected by the artillery fire at the front as they were in London during the six air raids which occurred in one week. The hotel where they were staying was struck three times, but not badly damaged.

Griffith Returns from the Front with Official Pictures Made under Fire—Will Use Them in a Film Spectacle of War

Exhibitors Trade Review/1917

From *Exhibitors Trade Review*, October 27, 1917, 1644.

D. W. Griffith, who has been abroad for seven months co-operating with the British War Office in securing film records of events on the French and Belgian battlefields, arrived at an American port October 15.

Mr. Griffith modestly admits that he has brought back with him some official war pictures which are to be woven into a spectacle of the world conflict [*Hearts of the World*] and that he is indebted to the English government for its great aid in making it possible for him to get up to the front line of the trenches with his cameraman, but asked to be excused from commenting upon this phase of his work until it is completed. He is to add an American finish to his story of the great war.

Mr. Griffith looked none the worse for his dozen or more trips up to the front or the several nights of aeroplane raids on London. Asked for some description of the battles he saw about Ypres, the director who has guided thousands of mimic warriors in his past spectacles said that any effort at personal description would be as futile as attempting to brush back the sea with a fan.

"Shakespeare, Hugo, Zola, in fact, all the great descriptive writers of wars that have gone in the past, would be unequal to the task of giving one an accurate idea of the things that daily happen 'out there,'" said Mr. Griffith. "You came away from it all with an imperishable recollection of depths of mud and vermin, of decay and stench and horror piled on horror, but also inspired by deeds that attain such heights of bravery and fortitude and heroic devotion to a cause that you wish everybody could know it and understand the spirit that is maintained behind those long lines. If this message could get through to every fireside there would be no question about the success of our Liberty Loans or our concerted efforts to see this war through to a finish. Every man, woman, and child who cannot get over to the front would want to do his bit to succor those who are doing this heroic work."

"Were you able to get pictures of actual battle scenes and their attendant details as you describe them?" he was asked.

"We got some wonderful scenes, but whether our camera caught the spirit and the message of it all depends upon how our story turns out," was Mr. Griffith's reply. "You cannot work there without striving for this effect, however. Thanks to the assistance of the British officers at the front we caught actual scenes in the first line trenches and the surrounding panorama which often covered a view forty miles long and from ten to fifteen miles in depth. This is where the motion picture camera is going to be important in writing the history of this war. It is not within the limit of human possibility for a dozen pairs of eyes to grasp half of what takes place in a modern battle. No one man, not even the general in command, can see a tithe of it. But the camera has been perfected to such an extent that it possesses a thousand eyes and reaches out in every direction so that it can catch the grand panorama one instant and the next it can disclose a minute detail of the most illuminative and atmospheric 'close-up.'"

"What modern improvements did you find that assisted most in this work?"

"The new French lenses with their fourteen-inch depths come first," was his reply. "You see they help materially in getting what are technically known as 'long shots' in motion picture work. Then also comes the gyroscope, a miniature combination of the aeroplane and box kite which is controlled by an electric wire from the field and which can be sent up a considerable height and get bird's-eye effects which a short time back would have escaped the most painstaking camera expert.

"In this way," he continued, "one is able to show a charge along a two or three-mile front and also to picture the grim work in the mud holes called trenches close enough to reveal men actually wounded at their work, or to see groups of two or three straining to toss hand grenades over the ridge to the opposite German line, but fifty yards removed, or to take a chance rifle shot through a three-inch aperture in the soggy wall—and all the time they are wondering how soon they can go forward to that obstructing wall of steel and fire and death only a few yards away. But they are ever going forward.

"It was wonderful work and more exciting than any drama you ever read or dreamed of. I suppose because I am an American I was struck most by the unusual number of American boys I saw in the thickest of these frays.

"An amusing bit of by-play happened on the St. Julian road just beyond Ypres. There was a view I particularly wanted to sight through one of the trench periscopes, so I crept along the ridge and got up to a first line trench just in time to hear in unmistakable accents a stirring song being sung by a husky veteran operating a Lewis gun who was on sentry duty. The song wound up its refrain, 'Take me back to Boston, Mass.' There was all the din of battle about us, but I was compelled to smile.

"We got our camera up to this point, but later fell back to a dug-out near the road and were clicking away when a shell burst just behind and all but smashed the instrument. That camera is now on exhibition in London. Some workmen were rebuilding a demolished dug-out apparently secure in the thought that shells, like lightning, never strike in the same place, but this was a perverse shell. A few minutes later they took eleven dead out of that one hole. It was one of the worst days along the St. Julian road, but I can truthfully say that it appeared to me that for every shell they dropped over the Allied lines I could count from eight to ten that were hurled in their direction from the artillery bases several hundred yards in our rear.

"The air was strident with these shell songs of death whining funeral chants in many different keys. It was like a testing ground for the souls of mankind. When you are up there and see human beings being put to the test of the last fibre of the least infinitesimal nerve, you come to understand why the ancients always were sure their departed comrades went to heaven. Such testing makes you understand that anyone's soul would be purged in such a fire. Surely this purging will burn the dross from all humanity and leave a world wherein to build a new brotherhood. And what a brotherhood it must be! As modern war is carried on, the need of brotherhood becomes more apparent. Each fellow is to a very great extent dependent upon the fellow next to him. You see infantrymen shoulder to shoulder with bomb throwers. As individuals caught in these terrific charges they are almost certain to meet death, but if there are two or three of them they are more liable to escape. So you see one is both helpless and hopeless without his brother. I have often wondered since seeing these things if we are not welding a greater tie of universal brotherhood which is to outlast the lives of these men who are so heroically finding new truths in the great struggle for the cause of democracy."

Mr. Griffith was asked if he saw the arrival of the first American forces under General Pershing's command.

"Yes and it would have done your heart good to see the reception accorded our boys. They are getting a different idea of America in England and France since we came in and I am sure that our effort there will strengthen these ideas."

[With one or two minor changes, this interview also appeared in the British publication, *Pictures and the Picturegoer*, November 14–December 1, 1917, 659, under the title of "Griffith Returns to America," and in *Motography*, November 3, 1917, 923, under the title of "Griffith Has European War in Films." *Motography*, October 27, 1916, 873, contains a four paragraph item, in which Griffith announces that "only a camera can see war." It does not constitute an interview, per se, and is not included here.]

Griffith—and the Great War

Paul H. Dowling/1918

From *Picture-Play Magazine*, March 1918, 23–31.

The massive walls of the lath-and-plaster Babylon were crumbling away slowly or being razed to the ground by scores of workmen. A fighting tower, swayed by the combined strength of half a hundred arms, bearing away at tackles and pulleys, toppled and crumbled into bits on the brown fields of stubble, raising into the clear air a cloud of dust and plaster and fine-chopped splinters. Babylon had fallen for the last time.

In the shadow of a city wall, where men had fallen in the battles of *Intolerance*, a small band of players were enacting a scene from a great drama. There were only a few in the group, and they—already hidden away as if in a corner of the ruins of some old Pompeii, were further protected from the gaze of the curious by canvas reflectors. There I found David W. Griffith, shortly after his return from Europe's battlefields, directing a scene in the shadow of Babylon's wall. With him were Lillian and Dorothy Gish, apparently none the worse in youthful sweetness, health and charm for their experiences in bomb-frightened London and amid the shattered ruins of Belgium and France, and with them Bobby Harron, camera-genius [Billy] Bitzer, George Siegmann, and others. It was just a small particle of a scene; but the production of which it was a part is expected to be greater than the story of Babylon, greater than *The Birth of a Nation*, for it was a bit of Griffith's forthcoming production [*Hearts of the World*] based on the most stupendous drama of all history—the present war.

After eight months spent at the front, after hours and days in the very frontline trenches, Mr. Griffith returned to Los Angeles a few weeks ago to complete his undertaking. He was a more rugged Griffith than the man who went over to London nearly two years ago to stage *Intolerance* there. He was more serious. Having done what he modestly calls his "bit," Mr. Griffith came home, bringing with him the precious prize of eighty thousand feet of film, the only motion pictures taken at the fronts with the exception of the official war pictures taken by the allied governments and preserved for a permanent record of the events of the struggle. Mr. Griffith went to England to stage his *Intolerance* with no thought of the work he finally undertook. It was at the request of titled personages who saw *Intolerance* and suggested that he might do something to aid in the world's charity work that turned his attention from private business, and, armed with unheard-of passports to the front, set forth on his greatest venture.

Not primarily for personal gain were those pictures taken. They will form the background of a great photo drama—or perhaps several photo dramas, a part of the proceeds of which are to be donated to the allied relief funds.

"The man who sees the war at first hand," declared Mr. Griffith, "forgets that he ever had any petty ambitions of his own. He feels that this is the one great thing which is going on in the whole world. Beside that, nothing much matters now."

It is, in fact, with great difficulty that one can get the noted film director to speak of his own work, in which he is now so engrossed. It developed, withal, that he was the first American to get into the first-line trenches in France.

"I was within fifty yards of the boches on the Ypres front at one time," he said. "How did I feel? Well, I was so frightened I didn't realize what was happening. Yes, I was actually under fire, and men were killed within a few feet of me. At one time we were inside a dugout with a big gun, and even as we were leaving the long range guns were trained on the spot, and the gun was shot to pieces in a few minutes. One of our own cameras, in fact, was standing in a position exposed to fire when a shell exploded, and—but that is a story which will be told later. I wore the gas helmet and the gas mask, for we were within reach of the poison-gas grenades of the enemy. We witnessed and barely missed personal contact with the horrors of liquid fire; we passed hours among bursting shells, and had on eight occasions experienced the dangers of German aerial raids in London. Four of these times we were caught in the street in great peril of the rain of fire. Only a few weeks ago I was on the firing line in Flanders, where the bloodiest of the recent furious fighting took place, and it will give you some idea of the intensity of the contest to know that in the short space of time since I left it is estimated that in the small sector where my headquarters were established there have been between sixty and a hundred thousand casualties.

"It is very difficult getting into the front line trenches, not so much from physical as from official obstacles. But letters from the great ones in England to the great ones in France made our path comparatively smooth."

Mr. Griffith had the honor of being summoned to appear before the King and Queen of England, but he was in the midst of operations in France at the time and could not leave. On his return to England, however, he was presented to the queen. Mr. Griffith's position in England was unusual. He was given the assistance of the British government in making his pictures, and he and his camera man were permitted in territory denied to all correspondents. In London, he had the cooperation of the most distinguished women of King George's court, many of whom have played an active part in his big charity production. Such notables as Lady Diana Manners, daughter of the Duchess of Rutland; Miss Elizabeth Asquith, daughter of the prime minister, and the Princess of Monaco are all seen frequently in the film [subsequently released as *The Great Love*], their work gladly offered because the ultimate purpose of the film was for war relief funds.

Mr. Griffith's own perspective, after seeing so much of the actualities of war, includes both the awful elements and the hopeful significances which are to arise. But let him give his impressions of the throbbing march of events in his own words:

"Vimy Ridge in the spring, Ypres on that memorable September 19, Arras—I saw those. What I saw in detail I cannot tell, for my pledged word forbids. Without that restriction, I would not want to tell.

"My 'close-up' of the war front is a blur of conflict, horrors, heroism, terror, sublimity—and promise. When you see the physically half dead, the mentally obscured thousands of men from the cities and slums who are shortly transformed into real men with real minds by the process of discipline and the implanting of the consuming lesson of devotion, courage, and true patriotism, you see that the war is not all unblessed. This war will, in many ways, liberate the world from itself—its worst self.

"Speaking of the salvage of war, we may consider the fact that the death rate is now five per cent. What then of the ninety-five per cent of the men who return home? These are the men who have been through the fusing process of the melting pot of trench life. We may expect these men to return to their homes and their governments demanding a more sensible world, and being big and strong enough to make their demands respected."

In the film production which he has made in the past, Mr. Griffith has proven to be a master of dramatic technique, which includes the handling of that difficult attribute—suspense. It is extremely fitting, therefore, that he should realize the dramatic values of this, the greatest drama which has yet happened. "It is a drama at the front," he said, "for suspense is the keynote of all dramas, and the suspense at the front makes it the drama of dramas. It gives you a dry, nervous choking; you are taught, strung tight with intricate emotions, your whole being involved at every move."

The producer described with picturesque vividness an experience on one of the fronts where he had journeyed to take pictures: "There was a shell-broken forest where we were to meet some men at the edge of the woods. We went by the sixteen-inch guns; then the nine-inch, the six-inch, and the eighteen-pounders, the latter, of course, the nearest to the front line. Over our heads was a British plane, and the batteries were going like the furies of hell. As the day passed, we saw countless thousands of men spread over the fields as thick as the grass would have been had there been any grass. Suddenly where the men were there were no men; they had disappeared in the trenches and communications.

"We advanced to a position where there had been a crossroads and farm, but now all was obliterated in a mass of shell holes, bricks and dust. As the shells fell, and we made slow time, there came an awful feeling of fear and a desire to go back. But no one went back, for that would have required even greater courage. On the other side of the wood, a party, including our friends, advanced. When the shells came faster, we broke for an old pill box. It was hit, and some of our party were hurt, but the shelter held.

"Then a shell broke back of the other group. A rain of shrapnel came down, and the little group divided for greater safety. We had a desire to shout at our friends to go back, but a shout could not be heard amid the awful scream of the shells. The men in the little party continued to advance. Half a dozen big shells broke, and suddenly men and battery were all obliterated. The rest was like a nightmare, with the awful sickening feeling of death near at hand. We mourned our two men.

"When we had returned later to the rear, the discovery was made that our two men had been warned against going out with the party. An old war-worn captain exclaimed: 'I told you this morning that your people should not have gone into that wood. The boches do not like any one to walk in that wood.'"

After Mr. Griffith had talked of the war, his party moved to a little house across the street from the *Intolerance* settings, where the producer, together with several Frenchmen, Austrians, and Germans, who of necessity are engaged in completing the war productions, poured over hundreds of war photographs taken by a Los Angeles correspondent who had spent much time in Germany, Poland, and Russia during the early periods of the war. This study of the enemy is of extreme importance, in view of the matter of costuming of accurate details of rank, and a thousand and one other things which must be taken into consideration in the completion of a tremendous spectacle of gripping realism such as the material of this conflict must furnish.

Then the party again took up its work of making pictures, this time at a pretty little garden exterior, constructed on one of the gently sloping hills a hundred yards back of the Babylonian elephants and tottering walls. A crew of carpenters and scenic artists were removing from the vast wreckage of the time-worn settings bits of plastered boards and canvas and fastening them up to complete the exterior of what might pass for a charming little country house in Belgium. Here Dorothy and Lillian Gish shortly appeared to sit down on the sunburned slope of the hill and wait for their scenes, which were to match up with pictures made in a ruined city of Flanders.

Dorothy sighed a sigh of complete peace and relaxation as she sat with her sister and the mother of the celebrated actresses, Mrs. M. R. Gish. "Oh, isn't it good to be back here again!" the little lady exclaimed with a genuineness of expression which revealed her true feelings at being able to sit down, safe and sound, on a sunny hillside in California and never have to go back again to the terrifying air raids in London and the pitiful sights in the towns of Belgium and France. "I want to settle down on a farm in Southern California," was Dorothy's heartfelt wish.

Lillian spoke up and told of Dorothy's fright during the air raids in London. "We were on the third floor of a family hotel," said Lillian, and every time there was an unusual commotion outside or in the hotel, the people in the adjoining apartments declared they could hear Dorothy's knees shaking above the din and clatter of the bombing.

"No book that I have read," declared Lillian, "has portrayed the full horror of war. It would take a superhuman writer to picture it.

"The English did nothing but three-cheer the American boys who first arrived, from start to finish. Naturally, as we were among the few Americans in London at this time, we were wildly excited, but those English folks showed every bit as much excitement as we did. We were in London on the day of a parade by the first contingent of American soldiers, and the feeling displayed by the English people disproved all that has ever been told of the staid and unsentimental English."

"It was that way in Paris, too," Mr. Griffith added. "While a year ago Paris was a gloomy place, filled with mourners, yet at the time of our later visit, the arrival of the American soldiers had had the effect of making every one cheerful again."

"London displays considerably more of a war spirit than does Paris," Lillian continued. "In both cities, however, it is considered rather poor taste to wear fine clothes, or to display luxury. We did not see a really well-gowned woman throughout all our travels in Europe. In Paris, every third woman wears mourning, while in London nearly every man is in uniform. They are using men that you would think had passed the age for military service. These middle-aged men, of course, are not sent to the trenches. The only amusement in London is the theater. There are no dances or society dinners."

Dorothy Gish described the return of their party on a camouflaged ship; one, she says, "daubed with every color of paint you could think of. Several times on the return trip over the Atlantic we were ordered to dress and adjust life belts, but nothing happened in the way of a U-boat attack. Of course the very thought of submarines was terrible, but after going through the air raids in London nothing was as bad, even being within range of the guns, as it was in Belgium."

Lillian Gish, with a far-away and wistful look in her eyes, expressed her sympathy for the soldiers of America and the Allies who are now going into those shell-torn areas which she saw on the French and Belgian front. "I never thought or dreamed of the actuality of warfare, and I hold the hope, so often expressed by the English people, that America's entry into the war spells an early victory."

While the scenes were in preparation, Mr. Griffith moved about among the ruins of *Intolerance*, not unlike the devastated cities of Belgium and France, and again reflected over his experiences of the past ten months. "My most dangerous moment," he said, "was at a time when I was under the guidance of a young British officer who was extremely proud of the lacquer on his boots. He wanted to avoid the mud in the trenches, so we walked outside, and ultimately had occasion to examine a map of the district we were in. This evidently attracted the attention of the Germans, who supposed we were deciding upon a site for a gun, for they at once began 'strafing' us. A 'dud'—that is, a shell which doesn't explode—dropped within five feet of us, and then the rattle of artillery came with deafening proximity until we found our way back to the trenches and rolled in, boots and all, glad to seek safety in the mud."

Though Mr. Griffith did not disclose the exact nature of the films which are being completed, it is evident that they will furnish a valuable record; for they will contain views of every kind of mechanical device used in the present war. The spectator will know everything there is to know about the fighting devices of this war; aeroplanes, tanks, blimps, and trenches. Every position of danger, every vantage of attack, will be presented in the first production, which is to be for charity. A part of the proceeds, by the way, will go to blind solders and to sailors injured in the trawlers, who, Mr. Griffith declares, have one of the nastiest, meanest jobs of the whole war, taking their lives in their hands every time they venture half a mile from shore, and seldom receiving relief money for their wounded.

While the work of completing the film spectacles goes on at the romantic old spot where Babylon fell, the film producer walks among the ruins which recall those of the actual fighting front. And he is glad to have returned. But there is ever present a spirit of abstraction—a thought of what is going on over there, and a dream of what is going to come of it all.

"There can be but one result," he asserted, with intense earnestness. "It may be a long war. It promises to be a long war. But the Germans are defeated now, and will ultimately be conquered. It will be the beginning of the birth of a new world."

Griffith, Maker of Battle Scenes, Sees Real War

Harry C. Carr/1918

From *Photoplay*, March 1918, 23–28, 119.

It was in the ruins of the Court of Belshazzar. A decayed and very tough-looking lion who once graced the Imperial throne of Babylon looked down with a dizzy smile. One of the beast's majestic hoofs had been chipped off and some graceless iconoclast, with no respect for art, royalty, or lions, had thrust the decapitated member in the lion's mouth. And you know that none of us could look our best with an amputated foot in our mouth.

And the lion saw—what he saw.

In the middle of Belshazzar's court stood a small stage and at the edge of the stage stood a tall man with a straw sombrero punched full of holes. There was never another hat like this in motion pictures. David Wark Griffith, maker of canned wars and mimic battles, having looked upon a real war at very close range and having been in the midst of a very real battle, is back on the job again—making another war picture in the midst of the studio where *Intolerance* was filmed.

Of all the interesting events of this great war, not the least interesting was the visit of Griffith to the front line trenches.

I have met men who have seen the great battles of Europe face to face and I have never been able to get anything satisfactory out of them. I went to Europe as a newspaper correspondent myself and saw one of the greatest battles of the war; and I never could get anything out of myself.

For months I have been waiting anxiously to hear what Griffith, maker of battles, would have to say.

The question that naturally rises in every one's mind is this: "Was the real thing like the battles of his imagining?" And that question is naturally followed by another. "Now that Griffith has seen a real war, what use will he make of the material?"

I asked him and he threw up his hands and laughed.

"There was a man once," he said, "who contended that fiction was a good deal stranger than fact and a darned sight more interesting. He had some grounds for his contention."

And then he went on to explain. "Viewed as a drama, the war is in some ways disappointing. As an engine it is terrific

"I found myself saying to my inner consciousness all the time, 'Why this is old stuff. I have put that scene on myself so many times. Why didn't they get something new? Do you catch what I mean?

"It was exactly as I had imagined war in many particulars. I saw, for instance, many troop trains moving away to the front. I saw wives parting from husbands they were never to see again. I saw wounded men returning to their families. I saw women coming away from the government offices, stunned with grief, a little paper in their hands to tell that the worst had happened.

"All these things were so exactly as we had been putting them on in the pictures for years and years that I found myself sometimes absently wondering who was staging the scene. Everything happened just as I would have put it on myself—in fact I have put on such scenes time and time again.

"By rare good luck I was able to get into the front line trenches. This honor was never before accorded to any American motion picture man.

"The Misses Gish, Robert Harron and the others of my company were permitted to go to one of the ruined French villages and we made the greater part of the picture that I am now finishing here in the Studio.[1]

"The conditions under which these girls worked were exceedingly dangerous. The town was under shell fire all the time. We all feel that, as we shared their dangers, we would like to give the proceeds to alleviating the hardships of those who were left behind and have to face it through to the end. The entire proceeds of this picture will go to some war charity—probably for the benefit of mine sweepers whose lives are sacrificed to make the seas safe for the rest of us to travel."

I asked Griffith what the battle looked like when he got into the front line trenches. He looked at me narrowly.

"*You* saw a battle; what did it look like?" he countered.

"It looked like a meadow with two ditches in it and some white puffs of smoke and no signs of human life anywhere."

Griffith laughed. "It looked something like that to me," he said.

I said that many of the battles of the war made me think of our own motion pictures; but not the battles—not the battles.

"A modern war is neither romantic nor picturesque. The courier who dashed up on a foam-covered charger now uses a desk telephone in a dug out. Sheridan wouldn't bother to dash in from Winchester twenty miles away. He would sit in front of a huge map of Winchester and rally his troops by telling two draftsmen how to arrange the figures on the scale map while a man in a corner at the phone exchange with a phone head piece would send out the orders over the wire.

"Every one is hidden away in ditches. As you look out across No Man's Land, there is literally nothing that meets the eye but an aching desolation of nothingness—of torn trees, ruined barbed wire fence, and shell holes.

"At first you are horribly disappointed. There is nothing but filth and dirt and the most sickening smells. The soldiers are standing sometimes almost up to their hips in ice cold mud. The dash and thrill of wars of other days is no longer there.

"It is too colossal to be dramatic. No one can describe it. You might as well try to describe the ocean or the Milky Way. The war correspondents of today are staggered almost into silence. A very great writer could describe Waterloo. Many fine writers witnessed the charge of Pickett's army at Gettysburg and left wonderful descriptions. But who could describe the advance of [chief of expeditionary forces in France Douglas] Haig. No one saw it. No one saw a thousandth part of it.

"Back somewhere in the rear there was a quiet Scotchman with a desk telephone and a war map who knew what was going on. No one else did.

"A curious thing that everybody remarks who has seen a modern war is that the closer you get to the front, the less you know what is going on.

"I know a war correspondent who was with the Austrians when they retreated before the Russians in the Carpathian Mountains in the spring of 1915. I asked him to tell me just what the rout of a modern army looked like. My friend looked sheepish and finally told me he would kill me if I ever told but—'The truth is,' he said, 'I didn't know they were retreating until I got back to London three months afterward and read about it in the files of a newspaper.'

"The most interesting and dramatic place in a modern battle is four or five miles back of the line. Back there you get something of the stir and thrill of the movie battle. Artillery is moving, ambulances come tearing down the roads with the dying screaming as they take their last ride. Streams of prisoners are marching in tatters and dejection back to the bases; wounded soldiers are making their own way. Motorcycle messengers go tearing to and fro. Strange engines of war covered with camouflage are trundling by on their way to some threatened point.

"It is back there that you begin to catch the meaning of this terrific machinery of battle.

"You begin to realize that, after all, you are face to face with a drama more thrilling than any human mind could conjure up.

"The drama that is in modern machinery is not at first realized. The world of art used to bewail the passing of the picturesque old phases of life and the coming in of machinery. It took a [etcher and illustrator of industrial war activities Joseph] Pennell to see the wonderful artistry of machinery.

"Just so it finally comes to you that the real drama of the war lies in the engulfment of human soldiers in these terrible war monsters men have built in work shops.

"Promoters often boast of having made motion pictures for which the settings and actors cost a million dollars. The settings of the picture I took cost several billion dollars.

"When you see the picture you will see what I mean. I thought in my mimic war pictures I was somewhat prodigal for instance in the use of cannon. In my picture made at the French front, I made one scene showing thirty-six big guns standing almost wheel to wheel firing as fast as the gunner could load and fire.

"I think I will be able to make good the claim that I will use the most expensive stage settings that ever have been or ever will be used in the making of a picture."

Griffith smiled and declined to state his plans for the use of this war material.

"This first picture is for charity," he said. "After that I will go on making Artcraft pictures."

Motion picture people are looking for another spectacle from him. *Intolerance* proved to be a big hit in London and Paris and has practically paid for itself over there, without counting the receipts on this side. In the older culture of Europe, the story of Babylon was better understood and better appreciated.

In fact, it was *Intolerance* that got Griffith the rare boon of a pass to the front line trenches. His previous spectacle also made a great sensation abroad. *The Birth of a Nation* happened to go to London for the first time when the Battle of Loos was in progress [September-October 1915].

It translated the war for the Londoner into terms that the human mind could comprehend. As I have said before, no one can comprehend a modern battle any more than any human mind can comprehend the real significance of a billion dollars.

You can look at a dollar and dimly realize what a billion of them mean. So they needed an epitomized battle to make them comprehend the conflict in which their husbands and sons were dying. They found this in *The Birth of a Nation*. It gave them a better idea of a battle than any one could tell; in fact a better idea than as though they had seen the real battle.

Although Griffith speaks of it lightly, he had a very narrow escape from being killed in the battle that he saw. In fact it may be said to have been a little private battle for him.

A British officer had been detailed to take him into the trenches. He had a new pair of boots and was unwilling to drag those gorgeous foot coverings into the filthy muck of the trenches. When Griffith insisted upon going into the front line, the officer started to walk along the top of the trench. Griffith had no choice but to follow him. It happened that the Britisher was carrying a map case that was very shiny. It caught the gleam of the sun and the other end of that gleam evidently hit a German artilleryman in the eye. At any rate, there came the peculiar whining howl that tells you that a shell is on its way.

There was a good marksman at the breech of that distant .77. The shell struck not a dozen yards away and threw up a shower of mud. It happened to be a "dud" and did not explode. Otherwise there would have been no Griffith left to tell the story.

They both made a dive into the trench. It was one of the old Hindenberg trenches that [had been taken over by the English.][2]

Hardly had they taken refuge before the storm began.

Griffith crouched down behind a cement pillar that had been part of the old German fortifications. Then it began. Shrapnel and explosive shell came like a terrific storm around them. The noise was beyond all human description. Every shell that came near threw up torrents of mud and slime.

In the middle of it, a British officer appeared on the scene and looked with astonishment at this lone civilian crouching down behind a hunk of cement while the shells rained all around him.

"What are you doing here?" he demanded.

"I'm trying to keep out of sight," said Griffith.

The officer was standing at the window of a shell proof [shelter] that faced the other way. "I shall have to arrest you," he said sternly.

"Oh thank you; pray do," said Griffith gratefully seeing a chance to get into the shell proof [shelter]. As the British officer would have been obliged to come around in plain sight of the German to "pinch" the intruder, he evidently thought better of it and closed the aperture.

Griffith had to stay there, squatting in the mud until night came and the shelling stopped. The British officers said afterward that they had never seen a fiercer artillery display than this little private battle between Griffith and the German artillery.

Since he has come home, he is the adored of all the war veterans in Los Angeles. And already there are scores of men who have done their bit and are home again from the war.

A natty young Italian aviator with a war badge and a soldier from the French Foreign Legion form the first line trenches of his board of consultation.

As one snap shot photograph gives a better idea of the trenches than all the words in the dictionary can possibly tell, it will not be surprising if the most accurate and comprehensive idea of this war will be given to the generation to come, not by the pages of written books but in the motion picture films that will be left by David Wark Griffith.

The banging of those German guns will be crystallized in a message that millions will see. It is not the man who describes what actually happens who best tells history. It is the genius who symbolizes it for us; who puts it into doses we can take without mentally choking.

[In a photograph that appears with this interview, Griffith is shown pointing at the desolate Babylonian set of *Intolerance,* remarking, "These ruins are more impressive,—to me at least, than anything I saw in wartorn France and Belgium."]

Notes

1. There is extreme doubt that either the Gish sisters or Robert Harron ever set foot in France at this time.

2. The published text is incomplete at this point, and the editor has assumed what the missing words must have been.

Pictures and Projectiles

New York Times/1918

From the *New York Times*, April 14, 1918, X9.

A number of the scenes in *Hearts of the World*, now showing at the Forty-Fourth Street Theatre, give the impression that D. W. Griffith and his company often worked dangerously near the center of the war, and, according to Mr. Griffith, they were actually exposed to considerably more than interesting excitement on several occasions. In relating yesterday some of his experiences and observations while making the picture, Mr. Griffith said:

"We crossed the Channel to France and moved behind the firing line into the vicinity of the present fighting. I am not permitted to give the names of the different villages which figured in many of our scenes, but I may say that for a long time our headquarters were Ham [a village on the Somme where Joan of Arc was once imprisoned]. In the party with me were Lillian and Dorothy Gish, their mother, Robert Harron, George Fawcett, George Siegmann, Little Ben Alexander and his mother, my cameraman Billy Bitzer, and several assistants. Two British officers were detailed to accompany us whenever we went near any of the battlefields or within the zone of fire. On three occasions our little party was caught unexpectedly in a bombardment, and on one occasion we had to spend four hours in a cellar.

"That four hours underground was about the most nerve-racking experience I have ever had. It was not for myself alone that I worried, but I felt that I had taken my associates into a dangerous position and it was necessary for me to get them out again safely. The sound of the shells bursting nearby was terrific, and we were glad when the British officers came to tell us it would be safe to retire behind the lines.

"On another occasion the little town in which we were taking some quiet scenes, at least twenty miles from the firing line, became the object of an air raid. A great bomb fell within thirty yards of the inn in the courtyard of which we were working. Once more we took refuse in the cyclone cellar.

"I don't mind adding, now that it is all over, that Mrs. Gish worried so much about her two daughters' safety that she lost thirty pounds during her stay in France, and that Lillian herself faded away until she was fifteen pounds lighter. The only one who did not lose weight was Dorothy.

"In the course of my trip I had many experiences which upset my previous idea of things. One thing I discovered was that a real hero always ducks his head or runs when a sudden shot or an unexpected attack comes. It is a tradition of the drama that the hero or heroine in time of peril or surprise should move with calmness, almost contemptuous deliberation and composure. Of the tens of thousands of persons I saw in London during the air raids, and in France at the battlefront and in the villages exposed to cannonade, I never saw one person remain motionless when danger came. There was always movement, facial, body, or both.

"The first, and therefore most elemental, instinct seems to be to duck the head, and then comes the urge for greater action. Persons grimace, clench their hands, clutch at their legs, jump about, if only in a circle, and the majority run. They seem to care not where or why. For instance, I never saw but one person who remained quiet during an air raid in London. It was a woman who was in the street when the alarm came. She slowly sank to the pavement and remained unconscious all during the raid. But she was the only human being that didn't move.

Mr. Griffith said that all of the members of the *Hearts of the World* company had returned to America safely last November. He added that on the occasion of a previous trip to Europe before America entered the war he had been wounded in the arm by a shrapnel bullet while in a British trench.

Life and the Photodrama

Harry C. Carr/1918

From *Motion Picture Classic*, December 1918, 16–17, 70.

The sun had gone on a little vacation behind the great Babylonian god-
dess Ishtar, and the camera had to stop. So Griffith came over and we sat
down on one of the battlements of the weather-beaten *Intolerance* set,
which still stands in ghostly glory out Hollywood way.

With tufts of his dark hair sticking out of the peek-holes in the funny
old Mexican straw sombrero which "D. W." always likes to wear when
directing, he spoke of many things. Unlike the famous walrus, he did
not confine his attention to shoes and ships and sealing-wax or cabbages
and kings. But he did speak at length of Motion Pictures.

Griffith is a fascinating talker. Out of the depths of a philosophical
mind, fed with worldly experience and wide reading, he talks. I only
wish I could remember all that he said.

I remember that the subject of plots came up.

"Plots?" he said. And then he added with a grin, "Go ahead and say
the rest of the patter—anti-climaxes, dramatic unities, etc., etc."

He took off the old dilapidated head-gear and surveyed the holes with
critical interest. "I'll tell you a typical motion picture play," he said. "A
gallant young officer, going over the top, encounters a Hun in No Man's
Land. They fight with bayonets, and our gallant young hero jabs a bayo-
net thru the gizzard of the German, thereby killing him to some extent.
The Hun's gas-mask is torn off, and our hero discovers that he has killed
his long-lost brother."

"What's the matter with the story?" I asked. "I think it's a beautiful
story." To tell the truth, it sounded very much like one or two masterly
screen dramas with which I myself was preparing to enlighten the world
and uplift the screen.

"Mush!" said Griffith, briefly. "All these dramatic rules don't matter.

Such little tricks are not real drama. Any one can conjure a series of peculiar coincidences. But if you examine these so-called stirring dramatic effects by the cold light of logic, you must come to the conclusion that the more 'dramatic' they are the farther are they really away from the true drama.

"Some day pictures must attain the height of true drama. And only those earnest workers who are trying to that end will survive.

"The true drama is life. The so-called 'dramatic effects' are not life. They are isolated life conditions shuffled together. The process of getting up these situations is not unlike the ancient industry of manipulating three walnut-shells and an innocent green pea."

"Sounds darned interesting to me," I protested weakly, "that stuff about killing his brother in the gas-mask."

"Peeling an onion is darned sad by the same standards," parodied Mr. Griffith.

"Then what is real drama?"

"Real drama is life, and life is yourself," said Mr. Griffith.

"There is only one subject in which every person is genuinely interested. Man is a self-centered beast. I don't know why we are all put here, but we have a hard row to hoe. The hoeing of it absorbs our whole thought and effort.

"It is literally true that our whole existence is a battle with fear. Our first emotion is fear, or hunger, which is only a fear that we may not get the means of sustaining life. We fear and we hope, which is the reverse side of fear. This struggle to get on absorbs our whole effort. We are not sincerely interested in anything else.

"When we go to the play or when we read a book, we merely look into a mirror. We are interested in the characters only as they reflect ourselves.

"The boy looks at the heroine of the movie drama and he thinks of himself. He says, 'gee, I wisht I had a girl like that.' And the mother sees herself. She says, 'I hope my daughter will be like that.' And the father sees himself and the little girl sees herself.

"To the exact ratio that people see themselves is dramatic or literary work a success or a failure. There are occasional great works of literature in which the whole world—every one in the world can see the reflection of himself.

"I remember being very much amused when Mr. J. M. Barrie's *Sentimental Tommy* came out. About every man of my acquaintance confided in me that he was exactly like Tommy, but he didn't see how Barrie could have written him up, as he was positively sure he had never met Barrie. In other words, Mr. Barrie was writing of the man who is in every man's inside.

"In a way, the early primitive works of literature were the truest. There was nothing artificial about the old sagas of the Norsemen. One old wandering minstrel after another added to them until the finished result was the poured-out heart of the Norsemen.

"*Beowulf* was a great work of art, because in it every swashbuckling old two-handed sword-wielder saw himself as he wished to be—killing dragons and demons and spilling blood all over the map. It was the daydream of the primitive killer set to words.

"Just so *Siegfried* was the echo of the thoughts of the rough old Germans of that day. Both of these works are immortal because they register the heart-throbs of the people of that time. There were no little tricks of plot in those great folk stories.

"The so-called dramatic situation which in plain terms really means a shuffling of coincident, as I have already said, cannot be the real stuff for two reasons:

"The dramatic coincidence does not happen to enough people to give it the universal appeal.

"It is by its very nature physical, not mental or mortal."

"I am not sure that I get you," I said. D. W. was wading into water too deep for me.

"Well, here," he said. "There are twenty million or more men fighting in this war. They all have folks at home; they all know fear and hope and despair. They all know pain and suffering. These are the universal emotions. How many of that number have killed brothers by mistake? Possibly two or three. Do you think the twenty millions would be more interested in a drama that truly reflected their own emotions and perhaps helped them solve their own problems, or in a drama that touched upon the experience of the one or two men of the twenty million who killed their brothers?"

"I think they would be interested in the story," I said stoutly.

"So do I," said Mr. Griffith. "They would be interested in it not because of the brothers in the gas-masks, but because out of it they got a glint of the horror that they translated into other terms and applied to their own cases."

"Then what's the answer?" I asked.

"The answer," said Griffith, "is the drama of human character without too much worry about situations, climaxes, and plots. The answer is the drama of realities—of situations that do happen, not those that don't happen.

"*Vanity Fair* is one of the supreme masterpieces of literature, yet you couldn't tell me the plot of the story. But Becky Sharp stands out so clearly that she is a part of your life, a part of the world. Becky Sharp plays more part in your life and my life than the Statue of Liberty and the city of London. Becky is everywhere. We meet her every day. We learn to govern our lives and control our judgments because we have known her. So with *Hamlet*, with *Oliver Twist*. It is an axiom of the theater that all the great masterpieces of literature are difficult to dramatize because they can't find a plot."

"And then . . ." I suggested.

"Camera!" said Mr. Griffith, abruptly, for the sun had stopped flirting with Ishtar and had come out again.

How Griffith Picks His Leading Women

Harry C. Carr/1918

From *Photoplay*, December 1918, 24–26.

When the editor of *Photoplay* asked me to write a story about the methods that lie behind the visible work of David Wark Griffith, and the reasons for those methods, I simply answered: "Why don't you send me to Great General Headquarters behind the German lines for a nice little advance announcement of Ludendorff's plans for next Spring? I feel that will be much easier to get than the Griffith stuff you want."

Nevertheless, both the subject and the difficulty of it were fascinating.

Mr. Griffith is not only remarkable because he remains year after year the supreme creator of the motion picture business; he is about the only director in it who doesn't accompany himself to work with a jazz band and a drum-major. He is not impolite to reporters. On the contrary, he is probably the most courteous host who ever welcomed one on a lot. But he has that adroitly irritating faculty of some captains of industry: when you are sent to Pierpoint Broadanwall's office to ask him why he put up New York Central as a stake in a poker game you are astounded to be greeted by the great man himself, you get a comfortable chair, a cigar, whatever you want to drink, a talk about the weather, three funny stories—and while you're still laughing at the last one you wake up to find yourself on the asphalt without one grain of information. Hundreds of reporters interview Griffith and vote him a great fellow, as, indeed he is; but what have they gotten for their publics?

Mr. Griffith says quite frankly that a man should be judged by his work; not by his own talk about it. Theoretically he is absolutely correct,

but he doesn't take into account the great human frailties of hero-wor-
ship and curiosity. When a man becomes as extraordinary in his kind
as Mr. Griffith he is, in the public mind, a superman, and a superman
has—to quote Mr. [humorist and journalist Irving S.] Cobb—no more
privacy than a goldfish.

If the myriad questions which Mr. Griffith's public would like to ask
him could be put to an individual vote, I think the winning candidate
would be this one: "How do you pick your leading women?"

It was this interrogative forlorn hope that I led out to the Sunset Boulevard studio on a bright September morning.

I had already picked a soft place to fall, but I ventured to tell him that
the man who had first upborne Mary Pickford, made Blanche Sweet
great, discovered the forlorn pathos of Mae Marsh, unveiled the gentle
melancholy of Miriam Cooper and the bright white beauty of Seena
Owen, found Constance Talmadge and developed the shy elusive talents
of the Gishes was to most women the most interesting man in the world;
that while no one expected him to publish the formulas of his labora-
tory he might at least get acquainted . . . give them a general idea . . .
speak at least a few words to people who had been imploring a word for
many years.

It was no talent of mine that made him talk. I think he spoke, rather,
to defend himself from being flatulently acclaimed a genius of selection.
He seemed to feel that impending.

"The art of acting is at once very simple—and altogether impossible,"
he said.

"It isn't what you do with your face or your hands. *It's the light within.*

"If you have that light, it doesn't matter much just what you do before
the camera. If you haven't it—well, then it doesn't matter just what you
do, either.

"Before you give, you must have something to give. This applies to
emotions as well as money.

"All art is the same. The orator, the sculptor, the painter, the writer,
and the actor all deal with the same divine fluid. The only difference is
the mechanical mould by which they express it One pours it into one
mould; one into another.

"I am not sure but what the concrete expression of art is about the
same, too. Athletes tell me that all games of physical skill depend on an
instinctive knowledge of time and distance. The aviator, the boxer, the
runner, the fencer, the baseball player—even the jockey—succeed or fail

in exact proportion as they have this instinct. So I dare say that the individual artist is one in whom this strange instinct is combined with the inward illumination.

"Now, you have asked me about women:

"Certainly there are a few mechanical characteristics that have a certain importance. For instance, deep lines on the face of a girl are almost fatal to good screening, for on the screen her face is magnified twenty times, and every wrinkle assumes the proportions of the Panama Canal. It is important that her face have smooth, soft outline.

"So with the eyes. Every other physical characteristic is of insignificant importance compared with the eyes. It they are the windows of your soul, your soul must have a window it can see through. The farther motion picture art progresses the more important does this become. In the early days, screen actors put over effects with elaborate and exaggerated gestures. Every year the tendency is more subdued in this regard. Actors make less and less fuss with their hands, and tell more and more with their eyes.

"But a good pair of eyes and a smooth face of proper contour will not suffice to make a motion picture actress.

"There are plenty of horses with legs for derby winners who are pulling milk wagons. They have the legs, but they haven't the fighting heart.

"In other words, they lack the inward illumination.

"History has one very striking instance of a light that went out. Napoleon had an instinct for mathematics that made him a great artillery officer. He had the divine vision for strategy and logistics. But what made him the transcendent military genius of all time was the feeling within his heart that nothing could beat him. After his divorce from Josephine, and the Russian campaign, the light flickered and went out. He still had the same instinct for strategy, the same genius for artillery fire. But he became a second-rate general. When the time came in which he lost faith in himself his military science availed him nothing. *His* light had gone out.

"I don't pretend to know what it is, but you either have it, or you haven't it. If you have it, you can polish up the tools and make them more effective, but if you haven't it no amount of study will bring this queer illuminative elf to you.

"Any director can squirt glycerin tears over a pretty face and tip over a few chairs, break up a table or two and have some sort of imitation tragedy. That isn't real. Real tears aren't always real, if you get my meaning. It is the feeling behind the tears that can open the beholder's heart.

"Now don't understand me to say that a girl is born a heaven-sent genius or a predestined failure. Nothing could be a more ghastly untruth.

"Remember what I said about having something to give, as a preliminary necessity for giving?

"*The only woman with a real future is the woman who can think real thoughts.*

"Some get these thoughts by reading and study; others by instinct. Sometimes deep analytical thought seems born in one."

Presently we went onto the set and Griffith went to work. His first subject was Ben Alexander, the tiny boy in *Hearts of the World*.

They made him a bed of straw over in the corner of the little French dug-out. The lights were low, and the shadows were playing queer gaunt tricks as the wind caught the candle-flame. Outside there came a muffled roar of artillery that re-echoed dully against the studio walls.

The megaphone was at Griffith's lips. "Now, Baby," he said, quietly.

Little Ben sat up rubbing his eyes.

"You're frightened," said D. W.

Abject terror spread over the baby features, as though someone had lowered a dark curtain over his face.

"Now sleepy again." The terror faded. The little head dropped back to the straw.

Griffith turned to the little group behind the camera. "Gentlemen," he said, "the forgotten art of tragedy. You have just seen a very fine example of it."

"But a great deal of it was not the baby, but Griffith," I suggested.

"On the contrary," resumed the director, "nobody told the baby what to do. I told him he was frightened, and that look of terror came into his eyes. When he grows up he may be able to add certain mechanical tricks, but he will never really do any better acting, at seven or seventy.[1]

"I daresay our friends the theosophists would say that personalities like this baby have old souls that have been on earth before, and are drawing upon the subconscious experiences of their previous lives.

"I don't know anything about that. But I am sure that this little soul-light is usually born with the child. Some feed it into a lambent flame; others let it die into gray ashes."

Note

1. Ben Alexander (1911–1969) continued to act on screen through into the 1950s, when he had his best-known role, that of Jack Webb's partner, Frank Smith, on television's *Dragnet* (1953–1959).

Humanity's Language

New York Times/1919

From the *New York Times*, May 18, 1919, 52.

D. W. Griffith was talking. The writer had gone to see him on business—the business of setting up an interview. But Mr. Griffith, producer of pictures, is not a producer of interviews, ready-made or made-to-order while you wait. Apparently he does not keep a stock of assorted statements and pithy sayings pigeon-holed and indexed in his mind to be drawn from for purposes of public education and self-advertising as occasion may require—or unguardedly permit. But he is a sociable man and talks, as one person does when he meets another, about whatever happens to come up as a subject of discussion. He was talking to two friends when the writer came in. The principal effect of the writer's entrance seemed to be simply the addition of another individual in the conversation—for it was a conversation, Mr. Griffith being as ready to listen as to talk.

All of those present being identified with the screen in one way or another it was natural that moving pictures, particularly photoplays and pictorial effects should be mentioned. And it was when Mr. Griffith began to tell of some of his studio experiences that the writer picked up the trail of the interview he was looking for. But Mr. Griffith apparently did not keep in mind the fact that here was a newspaper man present with an ulterior motive. And the newspaper man himself forgot this fact—while Mr. Griffith talked.

"The most difficult thing in making photoplays," he said, "is to get the human touch into pictures. A little scene with human beings in it is harder to make than the biggest spectacle ever staged."

"This from the man whose spectacles are famous," thought the writer.

"Recently we worked for hours trying to get a girl's smile," Mr. Griffith went on. "We wanted just a simple, human smile, and yet, no matter what we did, it seemed to elude us. Finally we thought we had it, and quit. But a few minutes later, as I was walking down the street, I saw a real girl smile—and I knew we had missed it.

"Getting humanness on the screen—that's the difficult thing, and the important thing. No one has succeeded in doing it to his satisfaction yet, but there has been an approach to success in this picture and that, and we are always trying and improving. Therefore we are hopeful. We know the screen can be human."

It became evident in a moment that the idea of humanness on the screen meant more to Mr. Griffith than just the representation of life for the idle entertainment of the movie-going public. More intently he kept talking without changing the subject, that is, not changing it as it presented itself to him, but developing it comprehensively to its full importance.

"The common humanity of all men and women is what people fail to realize," he said. "They are not impressed with the fact that all men are human beings, with like characteristics, instincts, virtues, vices. Many talk of the brotherhood of man and do not seem to be aware that intrinsically all men are brothers, separated by barriers of selfishness, prejudice, and ignorance. They fail to appreciate the fact those barriers between men of different countries and of the same country must be broken down before there can be any real brotherhood. A company of estimable gentlemen in Paris form a League of Nations—while families in New York gather at their dinner tables and fight over the steak or the coffee. They can't even have a working league in the family. The nations, through their dignified representatives, agree to become friends—while to the people of any country, to us in America say, the Italian is a wop, the Frenchman is a frog-eater, and the Chinese is a chink. What vital force can a League of Nations have so long as persons in the same family, the same community, the same country, or the same world remain potentially or actively hostile toward each other. Men everywhere have got to realize their own faults, the virtues of others, and the common humanity of all before they can really co-operate in a world community. Their mental attitudes must be the result of this realization.

"Don't think I'm getting away from the subject we started with," Mr. Griffith put in. "I'm not. For it is in helping to bring men and women together in a universal understanding of their essential brotherhood that the screen can do its greatest work. To the family or the small group in which people rub elbows and step on each other's corns, the screen has something to say. It can show men and women to themselves. In it they can see themselves as others see them. They can see their little meannesses and mighty offenses mirrored, from bad table manners to acts of selfishness that destroy the well-being of others, and the seeing may make them uncomfortably self-conscious of themselves as they really are. And when a man becomes uncomfortably self-conscious of himself, he may find comfort in improving himself.

"To the people of different nations and races the screen can emphasize the common human character of all. A mother in Italy who sees a moving picture of a mother in Russia nursing her baby may grasp the meaning of the fact that mother law is universal. The love of a man and a woman humanly represented on the screen has meaning for spectators in every theatre in the world and establishes a common bond between the human being in France and the human being in China.

"The people of the world have different languages. They cannot, so far as the masses are concerned, read each other's books and understand each other's speech. But they can understand each other in the language of moving pictures. In the screen the world has a universal language that does not need to be translated for any one anywhere. A reel of film can go around the world telling the same story, taking the same humanity, to every one in every land. It may have the human touch in comedy or tragedy, seriously or frivolously. The man in Japan who laughed at Charlie Chaplin's feet is closer to America in his heart than if he had not seen the little comedian."

Mr. Griffith's idea seemed to be similar to the idea of those who work for an international language of words like Esperanto. But he has the advantage because his language of moving pictures does not need to be learned with labor, and it has already been universally accepted, being universally intelligible. It is waiting only to be developed. It needs only a vocabulary sufficient for the use to which it should be put. This thought seemed to be in Mr. Griffith's mind, for he went back to his starting point and said:

"You see why I regard the putting of humanness on the screen of such prime importance. That girl's smile must be the real smile of a real girl anywhere if it is to have a human appeal for every one."

The writer thought of the rural scenes in *A Romance of Happy Valley*, the German mother and her son in *The Girl Who Stayed at Home*, and the little disturber in *Hearts of the World*, so unusual and yet so human. And while he watched "the chink and the child" in *Broken Blossoms* he thought again of what Mr. Griffith had said.

Griffith Points Out Need of Tragedy on the Screen; Likes San Francisco

Moving Picture World/1919

From the *Moving Picture World*, July 20, 1919, 1800.

David Wark Griffith paid a high tribute to San Francisco when he selected this city for the premier Pacific Coast presentation of *Broken Blossoms*, now being shown at the Curran Theatre. "I was governed in my choice of San Francisco for the first coast presentation of *Broken Blossoms*," he said recently in an interview, "primarily because of the reception the people of your city gave *The First Born* when that one act play was produced here for the first time by David Belasco a number of years ago.[1] That is harking back rather but, but I felt that a people who could understand and appreciate Mr. Belasco's *The First Born* would understand and appreciate *Broken Blossoms*, for the former, which I consider the most artistic one-act play ever written by an American, was a radical departure from the then usually accepted playlet, just as is *Broken Blossoms* decidedly a departure from the ordinary film drama of today.

"There is no gainsaying that *Broken Blossoms* is a 'different' picture; I mean thematically different. It shatters all from drama precedent. The characters do not find gold and happiness at the end of the rainbow. They find grim death."

Film Needs Tragedy

"The picture is tragic and purposely tragic, for I believe that there is absolute need for tragedy on the screen. And it is because of this belief that I determined to produce *Broken Blossoms*. I am convinced that the constant reiteration of stories in which ease and wealth, requited love and happy endings, as pictured in the usual film dramas is not for people.

It makes the average persons dissatisfied with their lot. They leave the theatre with the feeling that all is not well with the world.

"On the other hand, photoplays in which life, with its trials and disappointments, are pictured, where grim tragedy stalks through the lives of the characters, where the end of the story is the end of all things, even life itself, cause the beholders, I maintain, to take up the thread of their existence after leaving the playhouse with the feeling that the old world in so far as he or she is concerned, at least, is not such a drear place, after all. *Broken Blossoms* was intended as an experiment along this line. It was an expensive experiment, I admit, but it has proved an extremely successful one, and opens up an entirely new field in photodramatic production."

Likes San Francisco

Mr. Griffith paid a high compliment to the mild climate and scene attractions of San Francisco from the standpoint of the producer. "Think of it," he said, "here I sit during the middle of August with a light overcoat on, while down south in the studios they are actually suffering with the heat. You cannot imagine, unless you have had the experience, how disagreeable it is working under the heat of the intense studio lights during hot weather. I do not see why some of us do not come up here. San Francisco is certainly better suited to our needs than is the south. But you see we motion picture people are a good deal like sheep. Some of us went to Los Angeles and the rest of us followed. I am absolutely sure that if San Francisco could secure one of the big producers, many of the others would follow. There is an ever growing feeling of dissatisfaction with things as they are in Los Angeles, and a break might assume the proportions of a stampede."

Note

1. *The First Born*, written by Francis Powers, is a tragic sketch of character and life in the Chinese quarter of San Francisco, first produced by David Belasco's brother, Frederick, at the Alcazar Theatre in San Francisco, in 1897.

The Poet-Philosopher of the Photoplay

Hazel Simpson Naylor/1919

From *Motion Picture Magazine*, September 1919, 28–30, 102.

Tuning a pen to the melody of the poet of the photoplay is a pleasant but difficult essay.

For the melody of David Wark Griffith's mentality is so entrancing that words are as empty of feeling in comparison; as a beautiful woman is without a soul.

David Wark Griffith does not impress you as being superhuman or godlike. His very naturalness, simplicity and lack of pose are a few of the qualities which convince one that he is a great man. For it is an axiom that upon casual acquaintance, one cannot differentiate between a true genius and the ordinary run of human beings, except that the great man is more likely to be genuine, and natural, and less of a poseur, than the waiter who brings you your coffee, or the sales "lady" who sells you your shoes. The mediocre person, the would-be, the man desirous-of-genius, alone adopts a greater-than-thou attitude.

Griffith is a genius of countless possibilities. Not only is this true, but every press and person of any consequence throughout the world has recognized him as such. So that he himself cannot be unaware of the world's favor.

And yet when I met him the day after his most loudly trumpeted success, when all New York was bowing down before him thru the medium of the press, the mails, and the wires—in other words, the morning after the opening of *Broken Blossoms*, I found a man of natural poise, boyish eagerness, and a perfectly human concern over a bad cough.

"How did you like the picture?" he greeted me early, a bit anxiously and altogether unaffectedly.

Thus one finds the mainspring of D. W.'s existence, his interest and love for his work.

He creates artistic poems in celluloid—far above the prose pictures of other producers, because, added to his innate ability, he produces, not for money, nor for fame—although he appreciates these desirable adjuncts when he attains them—but for the *love* of the doing.

"After all is said and done," said Griffith, gazing dreamily down from his office window upon the hurrying throngs of New York's restless streams of humanity, "work alone will satisfy. The only real joy there is in life comes from the delightful struggle, from incessant endeavor. To be happy, one must have something to strive for. Oh, the delights of discontent! The search for success! The only true happiness that a mortal finds comes not from the goal, but from the game. Show me a man who can no longer find anything to strive for, to work for, and I can only pity him in his prison of deadness.

"Discontent is what makes the world go round. Congenial work alone furnishes a bottomless well of happiness."

"How about love?" I queried, for it was June, and you know the old saying about "In the spring."

"Love," said Griffith, swinging his office chair at attention and speaking in the rich, low tones that are so characteristic of him, "love is very fine—but it is a will-o'-the-wisp, here today, gone tomorrow. Work we always have."

"Then you don't believe that love ever lasts?"

"Ah, I could scarcely make so broad a statement as that. I only know that I feel an infinite pity for the average sweet things who think themselves in love. For a few weeks, life is surrounded by a roseate glow. They tread upon the clouds and live on milk and honey. They marry and then they wake up. The black night of reality curtains love's rosy dawning— and there follows an existence of pained endurance—or divorce. Oh, yes, I feel sorry for young things in love—the awakening is so sad."

"But surely you, with all your knowledge of human nature, must believe that love lasts. What would there be without it?"

"Work," smiled Griffith, tenderly, and then, "Yes, love sometimes lasts, but only when tended by a master gardener. Love is the most powerful seed in the world and bears the most beautiful bud of any plant. But the trouble is that most people wish love to stay in the delightful blush-pink blossom stage. That is impossible. The bud must bloom, become full-blown, and in turn become seed to produce more blossoms. Most loves are incapable of bringing this growth. The few that do are the lasting loves. The law of change is the law of life. Show me a woman, who by the depth of her understanding of man's weaknesses (we are all children and weak), by her ability to progress with the man, by her patience, sweetness, and constant endeavor, has held a man's love throughout his life, and I'll show you the greatest life-work that any woman can accomplish. Yes, it has been done! But it takes good gardeners; the plant of love must be tenderly and patiently cared for."

Having settled life's greatest problem, we turned instinctively to the photoplay.

"Why," I asked, "has the silent drama ceased to advance?

"Because," answered the foremost producer, "of the enormous manufacturing cost. It is too expensive to experiment with the picture of today. A feature production costs from $40,000 to $200,000, and very few firms can afford to try new paths at that price. The consequence has been that pictures continue to be produced according to the pattern of proven popularity. In the old days it was a different proposition. A two-reeler could then be made for a few thousand. One was willing to try out new ideas at that price. But you will admit one hates to place a life's fortune on one little advancement that may mean the loss of the whole! You can't very well blame the manufacturer. He has to live. Take, for instance, my experience. *The Birth of a Nation* made a fortune, but I sunk it trying out new ideas with *Intolerance*. Then I had to turn to making program pictures for a living. These had to be made according to a set rule of what the public wanted. I tried to inject a little of what *I* wanted to do, as, for instance, the realism of the small-town stuff in the first reels of *A Romance of Happy Valley*, just to see how it would go—but in order to have my pictures accepted by the releasing company, I had to complete the picture with the elements of action they considered necessary to satisfy public tastes. I no sooner received the money for my program pictures than I sunk it in *Broken Blossoms*. I reckon *I* am the Broken Blossom," he added whimsically.

"Why?" I asked.

"Because," he said, "*Broken Blossoms* will break me, unless it is a financial success, and I fear it will never be a financial success because the majority of the people won't understand or enjoy it."

"I have more belief in the masses than that," I interrupted. "I am sure they will appreciate *Broken Blossoms*, the most beautiful picture ever produced."

"And yet," said Griffith, with an expression which must have been similar to that of the disciples when the way seemed hard, "for every person who marvels at the beauty of a sunset, there are thousands who will stop to admire an electric sign on the hot street."

And it is because D. W. Griffith can see beyond the hum of our hurried business marts, because he can hear the pulse of the universe, can sympathize with the joys and sorrows, the cares and tribulations of humanity, because even in the most sordid life he can find something beautiful, something to be admired, that he and he alone is a pioneer in the advance of the photoplay.

It is because he has the courage to ride ahead and trample down prejudice, take chances with the very wherewithal of his existence, that he has made the advance he has.

He works for the joy of it, and his twin tools are enthusiasm and an ability to hear the call of temple bells among the most humble.

Exhibitor Is a Co-Artist, Says D. W. Griffith, Returns from Los Angeles to Open Eastern Studio

Exhibitors Trade Review/1919

From *Exhibitors Trade Review*, October 18, 1919, 17–21.

The presentation of a motion picture by the exhibitor is as important and as vital to the success of that picture as is the careful and painstaking efforts of the director by whom it is produced. The exhibitor today must be an artist. This is particularly true of the exhibitors of the larger cities of the country, for upon his judgment depends hundreds of exhibitors who cannot spare the time nor money viewing trade showings at the exchanges.

But David W. Griffith, director of such remarkable picture plays as *The Birth of a Nation*, *The Fall of Babylon*, *Hearts of the World*, *Broken Blossoms*, and others, who arrived in New York from Los Angeles on October 6, did not terminate his statement on the importance of the exhibitor to the motion picture industry with the foregoing paragraph.

On the contrary, Mr. Griffith has further praise—praise that places the exhibitor on equal footing with the producer.

This "master man of the films" was interviewed by a representative of *Exhibitor's Trade Review*—and confined his remarks, as much as possible, to the industry as viewed from the exhibitor's angle. Mr. Griffith's opinion of the theatre man is so laudatory that it would make the modest exhibitor blush for the want of words with which to return the compliment.

But lest we ramble on forgetting Mr. Griffith's mission be it understood that he is in New York preparing the way for taking over the studio erected for him at Mamaroneck, which he will open on October 20, though the new structure, said to be the most elaborate in the East, will be ready for occupancy October 15. However, Mr. Griffith is an industrious individual and according to his own admission, "is playing when working hardest." Therefore, it was with no wonder that the writer received his announcement that for a time he will confine his efforts to turning out short picture plays for the First National.

But the exhibitor—that's the fellow who interested Mr. Griffith. Anyway, that was the trend of his remarks. With Mr. Griffith any individual connected or concerned with motion pictures is either an artist or a failure. And when Mr. Griffith used the word "artist" he meant the exhibitor, as well as the star, producer, director, and cameraman.

"The word exhibitor," he said, "is improper. What will I say—it—it, well, it's a bad word. The man who shows the picture today should be called a co-artist. He is a co-artist and with the producer is starred, because a picture needs an artist to properly present it. And proper presentation of a picture by an artist (I mean exhibitor) should be on a par with the artist producing the picture."

Mr. Griffith added, "Directors today realize that pictures must be realistic; that they must concern the everyday life of those who see the pictures. Take *Broken Blossoms*, for instance. It portrays life as it is and paves the way for better plays. Not until we place the motion pictures on equal standing with music and art can we sit back and console ourselves with having done something big.

"It is a fact that motion pictures constitute an art—an institution as necessary to the everyday life of Americans as art, literature, and the press. Today the efforts of the conscientious director are not toward breaking box office records but to giving the public an artistic presentation. We all, some time or other, scramble for the mighty dollar; but there are times when we forget the greenbacks and labor for an ideal.

"In all my pictures I try to inject art and turn out the best pictures possible. I work as hard and as energetically with the shorter subjects as I do with the big feature productions in which thousands of people are handled.

"The exhibitor? *Yes, your publication is the exhibitor's bible.* I have been working with the exhibitor for many years. You have probably been told that the exhibitor isn't an appreciative fellow. On the contrary, I have found him a very appreciative gentleman. The exhibitor and producer should be thankful for the ever-increasing number of better theaters—all our effort's towards the highest and the best.

"In the showing of a picture the exhibitor is as important to the success of that picture as is the careful and painstaking director by whom it is produced. I always bear the exhibitor in mind when I make a picture. That is one reason why I select my own musical scores for the pictures. I do this because the exhibitor is too busy to look around for appropriate music consistent with the theme of the picture.

"Advertising means a great deal, and I am glad to say that the leading exhibitors of the country are paying as much attention to their newspaper displays as they are to lobby displays.

"We've got away from the battlefields and have gone to a more important scene—the battleground to reach the *human heart*. That is what the exhibitor wants today—pictures that reach the heart. That is what I am striving at.

"In *Broken Blossoms* I confined my efforts to so presenting scenes that they will touch the heart.

"The new type of co-artist exhibitor would naturally call attention first to the scene settings of this picture, then the theme, the realistic characters, and the music—for music is as important to pictures like *Broken Blossoms* as to the Winter Garden or Ziegfeld shows. The exhibitor cannot pay too much attention to the music. The music must be consistent with the theme—consistent with the ever changing scenic settings and atmosphere.

"In other words, there is no greater artist in motion pictures than the man exhibiting the pictures.

"There are various ways of entertaining the public. There are times when these means and vehicles of entertainment have, through necessity or an unforeseen change, to be altered. Today the public is entertained only when it is made to take a picture play seriously; only when it is real and when he feels the thrills of certain occurrences.

"The days of invention have gone, never to return—for the screen play, anyway. Today the public demands the real thing, or pretty close to it.

"The public has had altogether too much war stuff, and that class of pictures will meet with a cold reception. The public today wants pictures that take questions—domestic questions—questions confronting them or with which they are forced to contend as a small part of this great wheel we call civilization—into consideration. It wants to see these questions, tangled, wrangled, and finally answered. But the working out of these questions must be natural; there must be no superfluous characters; there must be no exaggeration or leanings toward the impossible—it must be true, and presented in such a manner that it will make the 'fan' believe that he is seeing the real thing.

"The exhibitor who makes a study of his patrons is usually the most successful of his lot. The exhibitor who gives his patrons what *he* likes or what he can get for a cut price is usually the fellow you will find kicking and snarling at the business. The public is the big factor in show business. It's the public you must satisfy. And it's the exhibitors' job, as showman, to give his public what it wants.

"The motion picture public today constitutes all classes—something that is not true of any other American vocation, industry, or institution. But this is all the more reason why the exhibitor should make a special and careful study of his patrons. The exhibitor, you see, is a very important factor in the industry, for the very good reason that the motion picture producers and directors have to depend upon him for information as to the wants of the market, for he is the fellow nearest to the public.

"There should be a closer cooperation between exhibitor and producer. They should work together, for the failure or success of both depends upon their cooperative efforts. An incompetent, uninformed exhibitor can kill a good picture by poor handling. Many an exhibitor has 'made' poor pictures go for producers by intelligent and artistic handling.

"So you see the exhibitor is as important to the industry as either producer, director, or star. He can either 'do' or undo a picture. The fact is that the welfare and future of the industry is in the hands of the exhibitor.

"I have conferred with exhibitors. I have also studied the motion picture public, and my deductions led me to believe that what it wants today is pictures that tell a story that will make it think.

"To illustrate what I mean I will give you an example. A young woman and man see a murder or robbery committed in the street. They are thrilled; whether through fear or something else, the fact remains they are thrilled. And yet, when the same thing has happened on the screen, no one seems to mind it. What I am aiming at is to make these screen incidents so real they will give the same impression when they appear in the pictures that they would were they being enacted on the public street in real life."

The Filming of *Way Down East*

Charles Gatchell/1920

From *Picture-Play Magazine*, August 1920, 27–30, 82.

On the north shore of Long Island Sound, not far from New York City, there is an estate of sloping lawns shaded by giant elms, on which Henry M. Flagler, the former Florida railroad magnate, once planned to have erected what he hoped would be the most beautiful country house in America. It was to have been a monument to the success of a multi-millionaire, as distinctively the last word in dwellings of its kind as the Woolworth Building and tower was the last word in its type of city architecture.

On this same estate, D. W. Griffith is now completing a film production which I believe will be, in its way, a monumental work, the last word in a certain phase through which motion pictures are passing; a phase which is marked by the purchase at fabulous prices of the great stage successes of former days, and of their transformation by amazing expenditures of time and care and money into plays for the screen.

The play in question is *Way Down East*, a vehicle well chosen to such an endeavor, for the record of its phenomenal run still stands unbeaten by any similar stage production, and the purchase price of $175,000 for the screen rights stands, at this writing, as the top figure for such a transaction. Impressive as this figure is, the story of its filming is, to me, even more impressive. I shall not attempt to tell the entire story of this undertaking, but I am going to endeavor to show something of the infinite pains with which the work is being done by the impressions of a single day spent at the Griffith studio.

It was a day set apart for work on interior scenes, which were to be filmed on the set representing the dining room and kitchen in the old New England home of the Bartlett family.

The set, which stood in the center of the spacious studio, was, to all appearances, complete to the last finishing touch. The fire-stained pots and kettles hung above the charred logs that lay across the andirons. All the rustic properties from the Seth Thomas clock to the farmer's almanac had been carefully put in place as indicated on the detailed sketch. Twelve of these sketches had been made from which but one was to be chosen; twelve finished pieces of work, each a different design, combining, together, all of the most characteristic bits of home atmosphere which Mr. Griffith's art director, an Oxford-trained authority on architecture and design, had found in a trip through New England. I was later to learn that before this set finally had been decided upon as satisfactory, four other sets previously had been built and torn down.

Anyone accustomed to the methods of other producers would have concluded, from the appearance of the studio, that everything was ready for action. From overhead, the set was bathed in the diffused light of the Kliegs. Through the open doorway at the right entrance came a flood of yellow sunshine thrown by that marvelous invention, the sun-ray arc, whose beams reproduce so literally those from which they take their name that if they shine upon you for long you will be burned as you would be by midsummer sunshine.

Standing in place, ready for the long interior shots, were the two motion-picture cameras, manned by the cameramen and their assistants, while nearby was stationed the "still" photographer with his big bellows camera.

As a final indication that all was in readiness for action, Mr. Griffith, who was personally directing the production, had taken his position in the open space between the cameras and the front end of the set—a distinctive figure—his rugged height accentuated by the short raincoat which hung, cape-wise, over his broad shoulders, and by the large derby hat which, tipped far back on his head, vaguely suggested the pictures of the Mad Hatter in *Alice in Wonderland*.

But no command was given to the waiting cameramen. There was no expectant hush, as when a conductor mounts the dais before an orchestra. The members of the cast, fully costumed and made up, knowing the methods of their chief, stood or sat about in little groups, as they had for several days, patiently waiting. The studio orchestra, for no particular reason, was softly playing "Turkey in the Straw," to which Martha Perkins, a prim and severe-looking New England spinster, was executing, with grotesque solemnity, a very creditable, though strangely incongruous, buck-and-wing shuffle. The atmosphere of the entire studio was that of a highly trained organization, ready to spring to instant action, but resigned to await the order, forever, if need be.

"I don't quite like that door," said Griffith, suddenly breaking the silence he had maintained for several minutes. He called for the decorators.

"It looks too new," he explained. "The edge of it, don't you know, in a house like this, would be worn down, and the paint darkened near the knob by years of use."

The decorator nodded understandingly and started for his tools.

"Be careful not to batter it up any," Griffith called after him. "I don't want anything to look mistreated, but to have just the appearance of long years of careful use.

"Now, how about those chairs?" he went on, addressing the art director this time.

He walked on to the set, seated himself in a rocker, rose, and returned. "That chair's comfortable enough, but it doesn't *look* comfortable enough for the effect I want. I want this room to radiate from every last touch the feeling of being homelike—a home of comfort and welcome and coziness. Let's get some cushions for the backs of the chairs."

The art director groaned.

"A hundred dollars' more time to be charged up while we put them on," he began. "But we'll do it," he added hastily, as Griffith gave him a look that said, "Huh—a lot I care about a hundred dollars' worth of time, or ten thousand dollars' worth, if I get the result I'm after."

"Now, let's see," he went on. "There's something lacking—something—I know. It's flowers! Oh, Miss Gish, how does the idea of having some flowers on the table or the mantelpiece strike your feminine taste?"

Lillian Gish, who has had some experience of her own as a director,[1] looked thoughtful for a moment, and then voiced her approval.

By this time several decorators were at work again on the set, making the changes that had been suggested. But Griffith was not yet satisfied. I am not going to attempt the tedious task of recounting in detail the suggestions that followed, but for the rest of the morning—the work had begun at about ten o'clock—one thing after another was criticized, discussed, and debated; scarcely a detail of the set was overlooked. The floor, it was decided, was a shade too light, and the painters were set to work on it again. The bunches of seed corn were taken down from the ceiling beam on which they had hung, and were tried in almost every possible place from which they could be suspended. The pots in the broad fireplace were rearranged. The figured tablecloth was removed and replaced by a plain white one. And not until the technical staff had received enough instructions to last them until late into the afternoon did Griffith consent to consider the work as even temporarily completed.

"This business of getting the exact pictorial effect is of the greatest importance," he said when at last he left off, and walked over to where I had stood watching him work. "And it might interest you to know that I believe that to be a matter to which the average dramatic critic who is sent out to review pictures is somewhat blind.

"Your dramatic critic obviously doesn't pay much attention to stage pictures," he went on, speaking earnestly and with emphasis. "In the spoken drama the pictures are only incidental. At the best they are poor reproductions of nature, mere backgrounds which may even be dispensed with. So your critic devotes his attention—and rightly so—to the play—the drama—the *story*, if you will.

"But a moving-picture production is a different thing. It lack the chief element of the stage play—the spoken word. It is—or should be—as its very name implies, a series of wonderful *moving pictures*. The values you see are completely reversed. But does your dramatic critic recognize that? Usually he does not. He comes and views our work with but one of his two eyes. He looks upon it from the same point of view from which he considers a stage play.

"Take, for example, my picture, *The Idol Dancer*." There was a note of impatience in his voice. "We went to such *great* trouble and expense to reproduce a certain phase of nature and of life, and I think we succeeded in our attempt. But the reviewers, many of them, dismissed that succession of beautiful screen paintings with a word, and spoke disparagingly of the story. Perhaps the story was not unusual, perhaps it was slight. Should they, on that account, dismiss the entire production as of little consequence?"

Moved by the eloquence of the Griffith argument, I shook my head in mute agreement—though I could not help thinking, at the same time, that I had heard a good many persons who were *not* dramatic critics speak disparagingly of *The Idol Dancer* and many another production, finely wrought from a pictorial standpoint, because the story had not satisfied them. But I was of no mind to argue the matter; moreover, I felt, at least, respectfully inclined toward this point of view, which, it occurred to me, I had never given much consideration.

"For myself," Griffith went on, after a moment's pause, "I hold that if we but reproduce beautifully one single effect of the movement of the wind upon the water, the swaying branches of a tree, or even an etching on the screen of the wrinkled face of an old man in the shadows, we have done something which, in itself, is an artistic achievement.

"I do not mean to disparage in the least the value of a good story," he added, "I merely offer a protest against the ignoring of every phase of a production by some of our reviewers. Do I make myself clear?" he concluded abruptly, with a smile and a whimsical bow, as though apologizing for having delivered so serious a lecture.

I replied that he did, and it occurred to me that what he had said was worth setting down and remembering, as a means of understanding better what Griffith is striving to attain in the making of a picture.

"While we're waiting for the set I am going to hold a rehearsal, and if you care to see it—" Griffith said, with the courtesy and cordiality which is shared by the entire personnel of his studio.

A Griffith rehearsal was something which I had wanted to see for some time, and I followed him and the members of the cast into the old Flagler home, which would not be standing today, had its former owner's dream materialized. This rambling old mansion connects with the studio proper; it is used for dressing rooms, and by the executive and scenario staffs.

The rehearsal was to be held in the former state dining room of the late magnate, a magnificent room overlooking the sparkling water of the Sound, its massive walls hung with dark, rich, hand-tooled leather, and its ceiling decorated by carved beams brought from Europe. And there, where groups of men representing the wealth of the nation had often gathered to dine, a company of actors ranged themselves about an imaginary table, prepared to enact a dinner scene in a humble, old-fashioned country home.

They were far from being humble folk, though, these actors. Lillian Gish and Richard Barthelmess, two of the regular Griffith players who have the principal role, on the completion of this production are to begin separate starring engagements, with salaries that will place them in the first rank of featured screen players. Creighton Hale, who plays a character part, has been a well-known star. And the other members of the cast who were engaged solely for this production, had been chosen with more care than the furnishings of the famous room in which they had gathered. Accustomed as I was by this time to the convincing evidence of the infinite pains which were being taken in this production, it hardly seemed credible—though I was assured of this by Mr. Griffith's personal aid—that a list of nearly one hundred actors had been considered in the selection of the man who was to play the part of Lennox Sanderson, the villain of the piece, and that before the part had finally been given to Lowell Sherman—who is playing a similar role in *The Sign on the Door*, an all-year Broadway stage success[2]—twenty-eight other actors had actually been tried out.

The rehearsal was but a variation of the Griffith method which I had previously seen applied to re-arranging the details of the set in order to heighten the desired effect, or feeling. This time the action, which the players evidently had rehearsed many times before, was criticized and altered in as minute detail with the same object in view. Each bit of business, each expression, each gesture was done over, time after time, to give everything its proper relative value and emphasis in perfecting the effect, the feeling, which Griffith had in mind, and toward which he was patiently striving. He was like a composer who, having written a piece of music, was going over the score, indicating the accents, the tempo, the mood of expression.

"I want this scene to be played smoothly—smoothly—smoothly," he said to Barthelmess and Miss Gish, as they were working over a tiny bit of action. And I felt that I was beginning to understand, better than I ever had before, how, through his shadow plays, he is able so skillfully to play upon the emotions, the feelings, of an audience.

Luncheon followed the rehearsal. It was a leisurely sort of "family affair," quite in keeping with the general atmosphere of the studio. I should like to visit the Griffith studio often, just to join the company at luncheon.

I sat at a small table with Mr. Griffith's personal aid and listened to a recital of incidents and figures concerning the filming of *Way Down East*, which would be almost unbelievable were they not backed up by the knowledge of Griffith's former undertakings.

"This picture," said my host, "is Mr. Griffith's first personal production for United Artists, and, of course, we hope to see it mark another step in the development of motion pictures, as so many of Mr. Griffith's pictures have done in the past—though, of course, the proof of the pudding is in the eating," he added hastily, as he laid down his fork, and solemnly knocked on the underside of the table.

"But if effort counts for anything—" He paused for a moment. "No one not intimately connected with this production can really appreciate the effort that is being expended on it; yet, perhaps I can give you a tabloid impression of the mere hugeness of the undertaking.

"Already more time has elapsed since we began in January than was spent on any Griffith production since *Hearts of the World,* and even more time than on that one if you eliminate the months spent on the battlefields of France. Yet the picture is by no means near completion. It will not be finished before mid-summer."

He paused while I gulped that impressive statement down with a swallow of coffee.

"Our vouchers show," he went on, "that scouts traveled six thousand miles in the mere preliminary work of obtaining photographs of New England life. Pictures of every sort were taken, including photographs of about four hundred New England homes.

"I've no idea how many scenes will appear in the completed production, but for the interior scenes alone forty-four different sets will be used. There were three, you may recall, in the stage version.

"Up to date two hundred and ten reels of film have been exposed, and the greatest number of times that any one scene has been taken is only thirty-one." He said this as though it were a mere commonplace to photograph one scene thirty-one times. "But none of the really important close-ups have been taken yet," he added. "Those always require much more patient effort in order to get a perfect result."

"And the cost?" I inquired feebly.

"Oh, $650,000, according to the present budget," he replied, as though that were the least important item.

Luncheon finished, we returned to the studio. But the alterations on the dining-room set were not nearly completed, so, after watching Dorothy Gish work in another part of the studio for a while, I came back and chatted with Lillian, who is as ethereal and appealing in person as she is in shadow.

"I hope," she said, "that the snow scenes will be worth the suffering they cost us. I don't think I ever experienced anything as severe as what we went through. Some days it was so cold that the cameras froze, and we had to stop work. We were out in blizzards for hours until, some nights, it was hours and hours before I felt really warm, though I was home early in the evening."

She was interrupted by another call for the company to assemble. The workmen had finished the alterations. But the call did not include the cameramen. The scenes which had been worked over so painstakingly in the rehearsal room now were to be rehearsed again—a dress rehearsal, as it were. And, as a bus was just leaving for the station, I thought it best to start back for New York.

I shall be interested in seeing *Way Down East,* interested in seeing what the reviewers say about it, and even more interested in seeing whether or not it will take its place as another of the Griffith milestones along the march of progress of the motion picture.

For in predicting that it will be a monumental work, I do not mean to prophesy that it will mark a distinct step in picture making as did *The Birth of a Nation* and *Broken Blossoms*. That remains to be seen.

But it must be obvious to anyone who has read this account, that as an example of the present phase of frenzied scrambling and high bidding for popular plays and novels, to be turned into lavishly produced and sensationally exploited pictures, this production of *Way Down East* must tower above most, if not all similar endeavors, at least as a huge undertaking.

A strange undertaking, in a way, too; strange that such an attempt should be made to make a monumental thing out of this simple homely play; it seems almost as incongruous as though someone were to try develop *The Old Oaken Bucket* into a grand opera.

But there is something splendidly audacious about these big undertakings of Griffith, about every one of them. He is a very canny combination of showman and artist combined. He knows pretty well what type of thing will catch and hold the public interest at any given time, and I have a shrewd idea that he had his hand on the pulse of the moviegoing public when he chose this vehicle for the first of his new series, and decided to "go the limit" on it. So, without having seen a foot of the finished film, I shall venture one more prophesy—that *Way Down East* in its revival on the screen will repeat the wonderful record which it made on the stage, two decades ago.

Notes

1. She had directed *Remodelling Her Husband*, starring sister Dorothy, and released in 1920, at the Mamaroneck studio, as well as a screen test of Mary Astor.

2. *The Sign on the Door*, written by Channing Pollock, featured Lowell Sherman as Frank Devereaux; it opened at the Republic Theatre, New York, on December 19, 1919.

The Moral and the Immoral Photoplay

Frederick James Smith/1920

From *Shadowland*, September 1920, 55, 81.

David Wark Griffith sat on the edge of a camera platform in his Mamaroneck, N.Y., studios. He had been experimenting for hours with lights for close-ups of *Way Down East*, and Billy Bitzer, his famous camera man, was "shooting" at the very moment.

Griffith, like all unusual people, is a man of moods. An interview with him has to be caught at just the right moment. And this was obviously one of those moments, for he launched directly and abruptly into modern photoplay making. Someone has described Griffith by saying that he seldom emerges from silence, but, when he does, he illuminates his point like a blinding lightning flash.

"The screen at this moment is shackled by a relentless practicability," he began. "One often hears discussions of the commercial and the artistic as applied to the theater and to films. Unfortunately—and there is no getting away from the fact—it is the commercial which reaps the reward. Once, in those rare instances which occur as a phenomenon, both the commercial and the artistic are welded. Then you have the perfect contribution to art.

"You have only to look about to have the truth that commercialism pays, driven home to you. Consider recent stage successes. Take *East Is West*.[1] A claptrap conglomeration of every stage trick ever pulled. And in its third year on Broadway! On the other hand consider an excellent drama like Eugene O'Neill's *Beyond the Horizon*. Its appeal is to a limited and discerning few.

"Let me point out that the stage can take chances where the photoplay can no longer do so. It still only costs around $10,000 to stage a footlight drama. The total loss of that amount will not entail financial disaster.

"But nowadays the production of a feature photoplay costs half a million or more. A director cannot afford to take chances, for failure means bankruptcy and personal disaster. Today a photoplay is a colossus of endeavor, and nowhere can you wholly live up to your ideals without facing possible failure. Stop to realize what it means when a director is confronted with the knowledge that he is spending other people's money—and that this money belongs to people who have placed every iota of faith in him. . . . Then the intellectual critic arises to declare that ideals are being sacrificed to commercialism.

"It was different in the old days of the photoplay. When I was producing for Biograph I did such things as Browning's 'Pippa Passes'[2] and 'A Blot on the 'Scutcheon.'[3] Production cost little then, while the market was tied up in such a way that production was limited and exhibitors were forced to take your pictures. All this resulted in a far higher artistic level than now exists. Imagine announcing to exhibitors today that you intended to film a Browning poem!"

Mr. Griffith paused for a moment. "I firmly believe that the mental age of the average audience is about nine years. An audience demands primitive emotions; it insists upon seeing life reflected on the stage and screen according to its own thinking. In a sentence, it insists upon going on receiving the same old distorted and diluted stuff as a commentary upon life. Hence the success of *East Is West* and of many present day film plays.

"So the camera goes on exaggerating life to suit the mob. Now, untruth is the most immoral thing in the world. Photoplays, spoken dramas, and books which deliberately strive for mob success are aiming at downright immorality. Consider *Pollyanna*, for instance.[4] I think *Pollyanna* is the most immoral story ever produced on the screen. It teaches a false philosophy of gilded bunkum. Its reasoning, if applied to actual life conditions, will handicap its believers and leave then actually menaced.

"As long as we go on producing stories which show life to be the definite and invariable triumph of good and the sure defeat of evil, to instill the theory that people either are all good or all bad, to go on filling up people with a completely false theory of existence as it is, we are actually harming humanity. We often hear of the word immoral applied to something salacious, but the real menace of immorality is in an entirely different quarter.

"Now, it is all wrong to go on in this fashion, but what can we do? The making of photoplays has reached the point where pioneer work is well-nigh impossible, unless you throw your everything into the balance of chance. We have created a *Frankenstein*.

"The stage may be able to approach life if it is courageous, but only now and then will the photoplay be able to combine truth and success— or, if you wish, the commercial and the artistic."

Griffith turned abruptly to his *Way Down East* scene, the porch of a New England farmhouse standing stark in the glare of the studio Coo-per-Hewitts. He sighed. "Enough—we're talking in a circle."

[In March 1921, *Shadowland* published two lengthy responses to the interview. The first by W. D. McGuire, Jr., executive secretary of the National Board of Review of Motion Pictures, argued that directors with artistic aspirations should get together "and dictate to the powers that be below the financial deadline." (p. 66). The second by Wilton A. Barrett, review secretary of the National Board of Review of Motion Pictures, asked that Griffith free himself from "the clutch of a relentless practicality." He sought "A Griffith, to wit, who, if he could, might be the man we are looking for—the artist who will help toward a truer morality by putting truth on the screen in a human way and without believing that 'the production of a feature photoplay' must cost 'a half million or more'" (p. 68).]

Notes

1. A comedy in three acts and a prologue by Samuel Shipman and John B. Hymer, which opened at the Astor Theatre, New York, on December 25, 1918, and ran for 680 performances.

2. *Pippa Passes or, The Song of Conscience* was released on October 4, 1909.

3. The actual Robert Browning poem is "A Blot in the 'Scutcheon." The Biograph film was released on January 19, 1912.

4. A 1913 novel by Eleanor H. Porter and a 1916 play by Catherine Chisholm, but Griffith is obviously referring to the 1920 film, directed by Paul Powell, and starring Mary Pickford in the title role.

The Greatest Moving Picture Producer in the World

Mary B. Mullett/1921

From *American* magazine, April 1921, 34.

[This article does not constitute an interview. However, in a sidebar, Griffith is asked to comment upon what he thinks interests an audience when it goes to the movies. Those comments are reprinted here.]

"I think the greatest thing in the world is unselfish love. The love between a boy and a girl is beautiful, and I like to show it. But love, in its greatest sense, is much more than just that. It is loyalty and sacrifice, forgiveness and service. The one word which covers it all is unselfishness. An unselfish love, that trusts and strives, and, if necessary, forgives, but never fails—that is the great fundamental appeal. I believe that every human being, rich or poor, educated or ignorant, city-bred or country-bred, good or *bad*, responds to that appeal.

"Take the scene in *Way Down East*, where the hero leaps from one cake of ice to another, running, stumbling, slipping into the water, trying to rescue the unconscious girl, who is in instant danger of being crushed in the rush of the ice floe. It is a thrilling exhibition of courage and daring. But the big thing is the *motive*. He is not doing it for any commonplace end. He is not even trying to save his own life. He is risking his life to save the girl he loves. And it is because an unselfish love drives him to supreme courage that the scene lifts the spectators out of themselves."

Griffith Reveals Sartorial Secrets

Los Angeles Times/1921

From the *Los Angeles Times*, August 7, 1921, III3.

David W. Griffith was seated in the darkened auditorium of the theater, and on the screen before him was shown his production, *Way Down East*, now playing at Philharmonic Auditorium [formerly Clune's Auditorium, in downtown Los Angeles].

It was a sort of dress rehearsal with the men who manipulate the lights, the experts engaged in the creating of effects and all the members of the orchestra, benefiting by the occasional suggestion the producer made. The picture had not long been running, when there came into view the scenes of luxury that are in contrast with those of the main part of the story dealing with plain people of New England.

"You might think it strange," Mr. Griffith volunteered, "but it was in these scenes of frivolity that we had many of our difficulties. We wanted to show the contrast between the luxury-loving and the men and women who lead simple lives, and there came up the important matter of garb.

"It would not do, for instance, to have the women in the ballroom scenes attired in a conventional evening dress of the day. First of all, that would make the wearer appear just one of the crowd rather than an individual. Nor would inferior materials give the right effect of what sometimes is termed 'class.'

"So we had Lucile [fashion designer, Lady Duff Gordon] in consultation, and it was decided to have the women wear what are called 'period gowns,' such as those we designate Empire, Watteau, etc. Such gowns are really for any period, and they do not change with the years or seasons, save only in the adaptation of the original design to new conditions of life. The hoop skirt appears in support of nearly every dress, although modified in accordance with the mode. I am sure that the dresses that you see are typical, and yet not of any fashion that may be set down as of, say 1920, 1910, or any part of the 1800s.

"The people in the latter part of the picture are in many instances in their customary garb—for a number of them were New Englanders who just wanted to be seen; those who play the leading roles wear the clothes that people in the country wear. The contrast with those who are gorgeously arrayed is striking, and yet is not overdrawn."

D. W. Griffith's Screen Version of *The Two Orphans* Would Fill Its Author with Awe

Edward Weitzel/1921

From *Intimate Talks with Movie Stars* (New York: Dale Publishing, 1921), 63–70.

Strolling through the streets of old Paris, the Paris that saw the Revolution, and the head of Danton roll into the basket of the guillotine, I stopped and recalled the first time I witnessed the stage presentation of *The Two Orphans*, and I thought of the remark of the aristocratic Chevalier Vaudrey about having seen one of Beaumarchais' plays[1] that contained revolutionary sentiments which the police had forbidden, but the people took sides with the author, and the king was compelled to yield:

> De Presles—The king compelled to yield? If that is true, royalty has lowered its dignity.
>
> Vaudrey—No, marquis. It is the people who are asserting theirs.
>
> De Presles—Why, if this goes on they will not be satisfied until they suppress one's titles and privileges.
>
> Vaudrey—That would not at all surprise me. (Picard, the Chevalier's valet laughs.) Why, Picard, that seems to amuse you.
>
> Picard—Excuse me, sir, but that is as ridiculous as though you were to say that one of these days the Parisians would rise and demolish the Bastille.
>
> Vaudrey—Who knows?
>
> Picard—What? The Bastille? Well, when that time comes everything will be upside down. They won't even respect a nobleman's valet.
>
> Vaudrey—Nor a nobleman either.

Here all references to the tragic unrest that was to result in the French Revolution ends, so far as the play is concerned; but it is also into this momentous period of the world's history that the two orphan girls enter when they alight from the Normandy coach. And it is upon this hint that D. W. Griffith has seized the comprehensive scope of the screen and used the tragic episode of Danton's execution as part of the atmosphere in his silent version of the Dennery story. The long life and immense popularity of *The Two Orphans* would tempt any producer to put it on the screen, with its appealing story and the vigor and variety of its characters and incidents.

The City by the Seine which Griffith has built on the shores of Long Island Sound is an impressive collection of ancient structures, with the grim old Bastille facing the fountain in the center of the square and the keen knife of the guillotine gleaming in the sunlight at the lower end of the street, a sinister and repulsive object.

As I came through the lodge gate at the entrance of the studio grounds a hurrying crowd of French citizens were disappearing under an arch behind a rude cart in which rode a young girl, her arms bound behind her and a look of resignation on her face. By the time I reached the side of the arch the last of the excited mob was out of sight, but the voice of some one in authority could be heard urging everyone to remember that the girl in the cart was about to have her head chopped off and was not taking a ride for her health. It was not the voice of D. W. Griffith but that of his assistant. I stole around to the end of the set and glanced into the square. The famous director was standing on the camera platform, calmly smoking a cigar and giving an occasional order intended only for the ear of his second in command.

It is related of D. W. Griffith that when one of the biggest scenes in *Intolerance* was ready to be photographed word was brought to him that the engine which hurled the stones during the assault of the army of Cyrus on the walls of Babylon had broken down and must be repaired. Everything else was in readiness. The thousands of men and women were in their positions, the caldrons of oil lighted, and delay meant a serious expense. The situation would have driven most directors into a justifiable rage.

"How long will it take to fix the catapult?" asked Mr. Griffith.

"Half an hour," he was informed.

"Go ahead," was all he said. When the engine was fixed, work was resumed on the scene as though nothing had happened.

In the same unperturbed spirit he listens to criticism of himself and his pictures. Upon being told that one fault of a certain picture of his was its length he exhibited no resentment but replied smilingly: "That is said generally of my pictures. But pictures should not be restricted as to length. The development of character is the essential thing, and time should be taken to do this thoroughly. The moving picture," he concluded, "is becoming more and more like a story by Dickens. Not *Tale of Two Cities*, which is drama first of all; but like *David Copperfield*."

I walked over to the reverse side of the arch and presently the mob and the cart came trooping back through it and I got a smile of recognition and a wave of the hand from the blind Louise. The next instant sister Dorothy [playing Louise] hove into sight, and I was treated to another smile and a sample of her wicked little wink. There was a hurried right-about-face on the part of everyone, and then the cart went plunging ahead with its sad-faced victim; Henriette, pale and torn with anguish, and the frenzied mob bringing up the rear. It was a raw, bleak day, and just suited to the mood of the shouting mob and the tragic scene. Tragedy of this sort, deep and relentless, is where Griffith excels. *Broken Blossoms* is of the same order of story.

When the first three-dollar movie was shown at the George M. Cohan Theatre in New York, D. W. Griffith remarked to me:

"*Broken Blossoms* will do more for the moving picture than was accomplished by *The Birth of a Nation*. I didn't recognize this when the picture was finished, but since coming to New York and putting the matter to the test it is plainly evident. I did not think that a simple story told in picture form and running only an hour and a half would take such a firm hold on the public, but the opening night at the George M. Cohan Theatre showed how little a man can guess the amusement business. Out West they preferred *True Heart Susie*. Here in New York we have had a number of the more critical sort of amusement seekers in to see *Broken Blossoms* three and four times, and the house has been sold out every performance."

"So the public does not put the spectacle first after all, Mr. Griffith?"

"It certainly looks like it," was the reply.

"Please explain in what way *Broken Blossoms* will benefit the moving picture."

"It will help to classify it. There clearly is a demand for a form of screen drama that will attract a class of patrons who do not care for the regulation program. The price of admission does not weigh in the matter at all.

This portion of the public is now paying $3 to see *Broken Blossoms*. It is related closely to the public which attends such stage productions as the Barrymores in *The Jest* [1919, starring only John and Lionel].

"Have you ever thought, Mr. Griffith, that there are two forms of screen fiction—the photodrama and the photonovel?"

One secret of D. W. Griffith's success is his open mind.

"No, I never have," he said, "but it is a good idea."

"Would not the general acceptance of this fact enlarge the scope of the picture?" I asked.

"Very much so," was the reply. "Like every other form of art the screen is bound to develop the specialist, who will be known for his particular brand of picture."

"At present," he was reminded, "directors, in most cases, have no clearly defined school of their own. They see some new thing applied successfully to the making of a photoplay and they introduce it into their next picture without stopping to find out if it belongs there."

"We all have a great deal to learn about this profession of ours," remarked Mr. Griffith. "An entertainment which is completed at one sitting is not like a book which can be put down when the reader pleases and picked up again when he is ready to assume his reading, and it is this which had led to the preference for the straightaway story."

Another interested watcher that day was the Romanian poet and dramatist, Miss Adrio Val,[2] who was visiting the Griffith studio for the purpose of learning how motion pictures are made in America. When the march to the guillotine was finished, Lillian and Dorothy Gish came over to where Miss Val was standing and chatted with her, while a body of troops on horseback dashed across the square and straight up to the entrance of the Bastille, in a vain attempt to ride right into the prison before the massive doors could be closed. The scene was "shot" several times, but the shouts of the horsemen and the clatter of their horses' hoofs as they came tearing out of a side street and plunged straight ahead without slackening speed until within a few feet of the doors gave a fresh thrill to the scene every time it was repeated.

"What wonderful riders those soldiers are!" exclaimed Miss Adrio Val; "and the horses are wonderful, too: they seem to enjoy what they are doing."

"They are all cow ponies, and the men are cowboys and stunt riders," Lillian Gish explained.

Monte Blue, who is playing Danton, came hobbling up with the help of a cane, and something was said about a badly bruised knee, a souvenir of a nasty fall the day before, when there was also some wild riding and one of the horses slipped and threw his rider.

Mr. Griffith joined the party at this point and led the way into the studio, where there was a grateful sense of warmth, and workmen were rapidly demolishing the great hall in which Danton and Camille and their companions were condemned to die.

Danton! "With all his dross he was a man," Carlyle says of him: "fiery-zeal from the great fire-bosom of nature herself."

As for Monte Blue, I have Mr. Griffith's word for it that his Danton has the "wild revolutionary force and manhood" demanded of this farmer's son who at one time ruled France by force of his inflexible will. This day Monte was only half as impressive a Danton as he should have been. But there was a reason for it: His coat and hat and the lines of his face were those of the French leader of 1792, but his feet and legs belonged to the year 1921. Above his waist he was the famous head of the French Revolution; below his vest pockets and his Republican sash he wore the long trousers and laced shoes of the present. A time-saving sartorial arrangement popular with moving picture actors when there are only close-ups to be taken.

A walk about the studio disclosed several bits of local color in the nature of dens and parts of "The Reign of Terror" settings, not to be found in the original play. There isn't the slightest doubt that if Adolphe Dennery were alive today, the D. W. Griffith screen version of *The Two Orphans* would fill its author with amazement and awe.

Notes

1. Pierre Augustin Caron de Beaumarchais (1732–1799) is best remembered as the author of the inspirations for the operas, *The Barber of Seville* and *The Marriage of Figaro*. The quoted dialogue is from *The Two Orphans* by Adolphe Dennery and Eugene Cormon, the source material for *Orphans of the Storm*.

2. Born in Romania in 1897, educated in France and entered the United States in 1921. She authored plays, novels and poetry.

An Intimate Closeup of D. W. Griffith

Movie Weekly/1922

From *Movie Weekly*, January 7, 1922, 11.

[An argument might be made that this is not strictly speaking an interview. However, in that it provides such a good study of a day in Griffith's life, I feel it appropriate to include it here. No author is given, and the piece is signed "Anonymous."]

"D. W. Griffith is the Shakespeare of the motion pictures," a picture man propounded.

"The secret of his success," another declared, "is work, plus a human, vivid imagination."

Little or nothing has ever been printed about this master of screen artistry that has, to any extent, actually revealed the man more than the artist. Perhaps one reason is the difficulty to actually get to Mr. Griffith and have a few minutes alone. He is always busy.

He rises in the morning about 7:30 or 8 o'clock. Before having breakfast he goes for a swim, if it is the summer, or for a horseback jaunt, if it is winter, or a concentrated active period in the gym.

His house is almost adjacent to the studio in Mamaroneck, New York, thus facilitating and economizing on valuable time that would be spent in traveling from one place to another.

After his morning exercises, Griffith goes to his studio, where he holds a conference with his right hand man and assistant, Herbert Sutch, telling him what his plans are for the day, what players and how many extras he is going to work with, what the scenes will be—whether interior or exterior, and other production instructions.

Griffith then leaves matters in his assistant's capable hands and goes for a bite of breakfast. It is now about nine or nine thirty. He returns to the set, where the mechanical details and the assembling of the players has already been accomplished.

Griffith determines just where the cameras are to be set up, for this vital detail he leaves to no cameraman. Then work begins. If the scene is a very important one it is rehearsed seventeen times before the camera commences to grind. And even then, twelve or more shots of it are taken, but if they aren't exactly what D. W. wants he keeps on until he gets it.

Patience—patience personified. That's D. W. A man of beautiful patience. Which may partly explain that magnetic something about him that inspires every man, woman, and child who may at any time have come under his direction.

The "extras" who play in D. W.'s big scenes have been known to make three or four, perhaps more, changes of costume in one day. And this is not customary with them. They usually fight the producers and refuse to put themselves out to such an extent under the usual remunerative conditions. But they do it for Griffith.

Griffith never shows his principal players how to act a big scene. Seated in his chair, with his megaphone by his side, he says: "Now, let us talk it over." And they do, calmly, seriously, studiously. Then the principals give their interpretation of the situation. Over and over it they go. If it does not meet with the fundamental idea of D. W., he gets up and acts it himself.

But never does he intrude and overshadow the personalities of his players by his own. It is *their* individuality he wants, and he always strives to get it.

He is never in a rush to complete a certain number of scenes a day. Many is the time he has discontinued shooting to go to the projection room in his studio and see his own productions, *Broken Blossoms* and *Judith of Bethulia*, an old picture, run-off. Usually he has his cast with him. His purpose in re-viewing these pictures so many times a week is perplexing to the outsider. Perhaps he singles out certain scenes that explain in action better than can be explained in words the *idea* that he wants to have expressed, in pantomime.

D. W. never carries a script. He never carries any papers remotely connected with the story. It is all in his head. And his memory is positively prodigious. Months after the actual taking of a scene, he can recall it from his memory as living a thing as it was the very day he directed it.

While Griffith is primarily a dreamer, he is not a "sleepy" dreamer. His mind pivots on vitality and actions in a dream world of his own creation.

He is practical. He has the nervous energy to carry out his dreams. You would suspect such a person of being moody. Griffith is moody.

He is a man who, for the most part, lives with his own thoughts and his books and his work. His social activities are few. Not that his is the personality not sought after by society—from the Four Hundred denomination to the lesser lights. But with Griffith, work is his recreation.

The entire time he was working on *The Two Orphans* [*Orphans of the Storm*], Griffith studied the famous men of the French Revolution period—Danton, Robespierre, and the others. Returning home at two or three o'clock in the morning after a long and hard day's work, Griffith would, likely as not, read before retiring. Read everything about this period that he could get. Assembling the material of others and molding it to his conception, remaining faithful, at the same time, to history.

Indeed, before Griffith even began production on *The Two Orphans*, he knew as much about the characters as he did about himself. Which may sound slightly exaggerated, but, remember, D. W. is a complex individual.

If there is one man who understands "audience-psychology" it is Griffith. When he is making his pictures, he weaves his action in a way that will get across with greater effect to the audience. It is not "Do I like this?" but rather, "Will the audience get the full value of this?"

Griffith believes that fundamentally there is little difference between woman and woman, man and man. A woman who moves in the circles of Kings and Queens is fundamentally the same as she who struggles for a mere pittance in the worst of tenements. With D. W. Griffith there is no class distinction. People are human beings, expressing in the big, dramatic moments of life relatively the same reactions. It is this masterly ability to strip the veneer of class from his characters and make of them palpitating human beings that grips the heart and brings the quick, stinging tears to the eyes and the lump to the throat.

As you would naturally believe, Griffith is a lover of the Arts. You can see him oftener at the opera than elsewhere. He enjoys the theatre. Sculpture, painting, architecture—all come under the sweeping category of Art.

And this is a homely sketch of him who is said by many to be THE greatest master of cinematic art. Reiterating again: "D. W. Griffith is the Shakespeare of motion pictures." But his greatest strength lies in his prodigious love for work, which to him is recreation in itself.

Griffith: Maker of Pictures

Harry C. Carr/1922

From *Motion Picture Magazine*, August 1922, 21–25, 88–89.

It is said that no one knows anything about any woman who has not seen her before breakfast. After she is marcelled and lip sticked—or lip stuck—all you are going to know about her is what she wants you to know.

And that is just as true of directors. Especially D. W. Griffith.

There is a D. W. Griffith that the world sees at banquets and at the theater when his pictures have their formal openings—a most attractive and rather regal gentleman in evening dress. But the public doesn't know anything much about the real D. W.—the maker of pictures. So I am going to write about the real one.

Let us say it is early one Sunday morning—the beginning of a day late in autumn. Mr. Griffith has issued a call for his personal staff to meet him at his office in the Longacre Building at Broadway and Forty-second Street—the supposed hub of the theater universe. The old war-horse has sniffed the battle. D. W. is going to start another picture.

They drop in—the staff—all the way from ten minutes to half an hour late—secretaries, scenario writers, publicity men—all men and women who have been with him for years. They wait some more. D. W. is always late.

When he finally gets there he wants to talk about everything but the question before the house, which was story. He takes his publicity man off into another office and they fuss around with a lot of newspaper clippings. Then his secretary is called in and they dictate telegrams. One of Griffith's peculiarities is that he has never found out about the post-office. The only means that he knows of communication between human beings is the telegraph. It is absolutely useless to write him letters. He leaves them unopened in his overcoat pockets, on the back seat of his limousine, and all over the studio.

After a couple of hours' conference on other matters, Mr. Griffith suggests that, after all, the best place to talk story would be over at his rooms in the Claridge. So we all troop over there.

Books, books, scenarios, plays. They are scattered all over the place—books from hopeful authors, books from agents; they all want D. W. to film them. He hands them around to all of us and generally disappears into the other room of his suite.

An argument always starts. Somebody thinks he ought to put on Kipling and somebody else thinks he ought to put on a Revolutionary story.

Griffith seldom listens to this feast of reason. He spends most of his time trying to get the windows just open and just shut enough to suit him. Whenever he gets into the debate, it is usually to change the subject. He will cut into somebody' infuriated eloquence about Kipling's *Light That Failed* to say that the income tax is all wrong and something ought to be done about it. You can usually get a rise out of him by mention of a Revolutionary War story.

"They are out," he says. And tells a story.

When he was a young actor he was doing a vaudeville sketch—scene laid in the Revolutionary War.

"I tried being a Dutchman and an Irishman and a Frenchman," said D. W. "But it was no use. I sank all my money in the most beautiful costumes, but the audience was always bored to agony. I tried bouncing out of a grandfather's clock at the heroine; but the darn thing just wouldn't go. At last the old property man stopped me one day.

"'Well kid,' he said, 'your sketch ain't going very good.' I admitted it.

"'Well,' he said, 'Lemme give you a tip, kid. You won't never git nowhere with any play where the actors wear them damn wigs.'"

D. W. said that cured him of Revolutionary War plays forever [or at least until 1924 when he directed the Revolutionary War drama, *America*]. I know that the question of wigs "prevented him from giving *Two Orphans* [*Orphans of the Storm*]" for years.

At about this point in the proceedings he usually suggests that we ought to eat. So he orders up a gorgeous luncheon from the hotel dining room. D. W. is an epicure and a most wonderful and charming host.

Finally the telephone rings and he discovers that he has to go to a financial conference with his business managers—and so that's all for the day. He tells us to meet him at the hotel early next morning.

The next day begins with another wait. At last the limousine comes and we all pile in. D. W. is distrait and silent. We know from experience he is thinking about stories. Somebody has a copy of the *New York Times*. He picks it up and immediately begins talking about Lloyd George and English politics. Griffith is a wonderful talker—an extraordinary memory—an unusual point of view and brilliant glowing words. It's a wonderful auto ride but you don't make much progress getting a story.

His chauffeur is a wild man with a sardonic, inscrutable face; he was evidently trained to drive run-away fire engines. Usually he escapes arrest; but now and then the stern hand of the law reaches out for him. I remember one day he had to pull up to the police booth. The red-faced Irish sergeant took one look at Griffith and groaned to high Heaven. "Now, I'll get it," he said. "I've gone and pinched D. W. Griffith. Oh my, oh my, when I get home and tell my old woman I've pinched her wonderful D. W. Griffith who made *Broken Blossoms*, I'll get what's coming to me. Oh my, oh my."

Well, you don't get far finding a story that day.

Or the next.

This process is likely to go on for days. You have long discussions of books and plays and scenarios that you know he hasn't the slightest intention of putting on the screen. Then one day he suddenly grabs you into a side office of the back room of his hotel and swiftly outlines to you a story of which you have never heard, but which he has probably been thinking about from the first.

And that's the story that will stick.

It may be something he has read years before. A plot once read remains in his extraordinary, tenacious brain forever. He never forgets anything.

Rehearsals usually begin at once. D. W. never works from finished scenarios like other directors. He makes up his photo plays at rehearsals and then remembers. Without a scrap of paper he can remember every small, minute detail of the action in two or three thousand scenes.

But like W. R. Hearst and many other big men, D. W. has a disorderly mind. He has a wonderful studio out at Mamaroneck, but he couldn't think of rehearsing out there—anyhow not until he has selected the cast of characters. He gets the company crowded into hotel dining-rooms with the chairs piled on tables, or into hotel parlors into which guests of the hotel, losing their way, keep bobbing in, to look at the proceedings with dismay and retreat with apologies.

Picking out the actors for a Griffith play is an agonizing process. He tries them out by herds. He tried out nearly a hundred actors before he selected the villain of *Way Down East*. It is a painful process for the actors. They have to get up in the middle of the floor and pretend that two chairs and an overcoat are a stagecoach. And continue while a bunch of other candidates for the same part are sitting in a row on the side-lines, breathing their unfavorable scorn of his efforts.

Griffith has a few old stand-bys, actors who always rehearse all the parts at the first of these try-outs; they are like the old horses used to break in young colts to harness. There is Adolphe Lestina who "made up" Griffith for his first dramatic part on the stage and who shared his dressing-room in D. W.'s early actor days. And Kate Bruce who has played so many mother parts in Griffith pictures.

Sweet old Kate Bruce!

A never failing joke with Griffith is to have her rehearse rip-snorting bad lady parts in which she had to deceive husbands and so on. And comes Porter Strong who usually rehearses French counts in darky dialect. Porter always has a red hot tip on some distant horse race which itches him with emotion at all the morning rehearsals; and saddens him all the rest of the afternoon—after the race has been run.

The Gish girls are there faithfully and punctually. Dorothy is usually kidding the performance. I remember that she rehearsed most of the part of Louise the Blind Girl [in *Orphans of the Storm*], pretending to have hare-lip and cross-eyes. She is the infant terrible of the Griffith company.

But when it comes to a close decision between two actors—a decision which may mean the success or failure of the play—D. W. depends on Dorothy's opinion. She has a keen incisive mind and a fearless way of blurting out her opinion. Having been on the stage since she was two years old, she has had a wealth of experience.

Griffith is a great hand to ask advice. He needs the least and asks the most of anybody in the motion picture business. You can go to him in the middle of a huge mob scene, with two thousand extras on the set, a half dozen cameras clicking and a mob of assistant directors bellowing around, and he will stop everything to listen to your suggestions.

The rehearsals are interrupted from time to time by flying trips to Mamaroneck to make photographic tests of the actors. Some of the most superb pictures ever made are these tests, which will never be seen by the public, but are filed away in the studio vaults.

Finally the cast gets selected, and one day everybody moves out to the studio and real rehearsals begin in the room that was formerly the dining-room of the Standard Oil king, [Henry Morrison] Flagler.

Even then the cast is usually in doubt. Griffith dreads to turn away the actor who is unequal to the part. Sometimes he is paying salaries to three or four of them for the same part. But when he has to hand someone his walking papers, he always does the job in person; never hands the painful task to some assistant director. When the time comes when one of two or three contesting actors has to be thrown overboard, Griffith leads the victim to the end of the room or out into the hall and explains—and another heart is broken. But, for some reason or another, the victim always swears devotion to D. W. for the rest of his days. Such is the force of diplomacy.

I remember one young lady, aged nine, who went into hysterics and yelled bloody murder for two hours when she couldn't have a part. To soothe her grief, Griffith gave her twenty dollars and loaded her with all the dolls from the prop room that she could carry.

To see a Griffith rehearsal is a marvelous experience. It is to sound the most subtle depths of acting. Griffith goes over the play—over and over, until the actors are ready to commit suicide—but each time it grows a little under his hands. The gorgeous little touches of art which have been planned there in the old dining-room, with a couple of kitchen chairs for stagecoaches and a chalk-line for a mountain chasm, are among the masterpieces of American drama.

Every once in a while, D. W. Griffith will leave his chair by the little kitchen table and act one of the scenes himself. Sometimes he is a little, sixteen-year-old girl, screaming with fright; and again a maiden, fancy-free, flirting with her lover. But somehow it never seems grotesque or funny. That's how good an actor he is.

At last, one morning you go out and D. W. is walking in front of a new set, with Huck Wortmann. Huck is the man who built Babylon in *Intolerance*, and all the other marvels of Griffith pictures. Huck is a stocky, steel-eyed old stage carpenter. If you asked him to build an exact reproduction of heaven, he would merely take another chew of tobacco, and say, "All right; it'll be ready a week from Monday." Nobody would ever know how he found out; but the set would look just like the place.

And so the picture begins.

It is like watching a sculptor molding a beautiful statue to see Griffith directing. He has an arm-chair, raised on high legs, like stilts. There are no puttees in his young life. He always comes onto the set beautifully dressed—the perfect turnout of the best tailor in New York. Only as he works, his derby hat goes sliding back onto his head and an eye-shade comes down over his forehead. I don't know what power it is that he has over actors. He doesn't say much of anything to them. But somehow he catches them in the grip of his finely tuned sympathetic mind and lifts them over the bogs of artistry as though he were making a pair of wings. He is never impatient with their failures. He is always courtesy itself to his actors. I never remember to have seen him lose his temper over their stupidity, which used to make me long to lead a lynching party against them. An actor can be more kinds of stupid than other humans.

Griffith treats children just as he treats grown-ups. He never talks goo-goo talk to the child actors who have done such wonderful work for him. He treats them with the same grave, quiet courtesy that he does the grown people.

It gives you a thrill to see him directing Lillian Gish in her big scenes—as for instance, the baptism of the baby in *Way Down East*.

Dear, patient Lillian. I can see her now, waiting quietly for the lights while the cameramen are nervously fussing with the lenses. There is a tense feeling in the air, like waiting for a battle to begin.

"Are you ready?" says Griffith.

"Yes, sir," says the cameraman.

"Camera," says Griffith.

And Lillian begins. Scarcely a word is spoken. Once in a while, Griffith speaks a word of caution in a low voice. "Slower, slower." Then he will speak the lines for her—"My God, he is dead." She is like some wonderful sensitized instrument, vibrating to a master impulse.

"Cease," says D. W., at last; to the cameras. And he nearly always at such moments turns to the group around him with his eyes filled with tears. He is very easily affected, very easily driven to tears by art such as hers. It is only Lillian Gish who stands there, quietly waiting to do it again. Even the stage carpenters are frequently in tears.

D. W. sets great store by the opinion of "Blondy," a veteran stage carpenter who builds the sets.

"Blondy," said Griffith one day. "I wish you would come around here and give me your opinion of this scene."

"Who's doing it?" asked Blondy, pausing with hammer upraised.

"Miss Gish.

"Nope," said "Blondy." "No use my going over to see her. She's a mechanic. She knows her job. She does everything right."

At other times, however, "Blondy's" opinions have a frankness that is appalling.

And so the picture goes to the end.

Every night we all went to the projecting-room to see miles of film run off. Every scene for a Griffith picture is taken three or four times by three or four cameras. The consequence is, we would absolutely go to sleep from exhaustion looking at these "takes." Even now I can hear Griffith's voice coming to me across a chasm of sleep; I can drowsily make out what he is saying, "Do you like the second shot, or the fifth shot best?"

Griffith shot over eighty thousand feet of that ice scene in *Way Down East*, and used only twelve hundred feet.

Finally, the picture comes to an end; then we write the sub-titles. Griffith has the strength and endurance of a prize-fight champion. And, by the way, he is a very fine boxer and an all-around athlete. In these terrible days, at the end of a picture, he will shoot close-ups all morning, arrange music with a professional conductor all afternoon, have financial conferences all the early part of the evening, and write sub-titles all the rest of the night. These sub-title conferences take place over the length of a big table, formerly used by directors of the Standard Oil Company when they used to foregather at Flagler's.

D. W. smokes interminable cigarettes—that is to say, he lights millions of them, takes a puff and lights another one. At the end of a title conference the place looks like a jury room.

He never gets thru writing titles. I have seen him dictating them, sitting in the dark theater, two hours before the first performance was to begin.

The try-out of a Griffith picture is great fun. He gets his staff into a flock of automobiles and we go trundling up-state to some queer country town, where we fill the hotel. Wondering crowds stand around the street corners to see him pass. You scatter around thru the audience and hear what the people say. Then the local manager comes up, full of mysterious importance and we are all invited up to the Elks' Club to a midnight supper of lobster a la Newburgh—and other things.

And then we go trekking back to town again. When I think of these trips back in the auto, it makes me laugh, contrasting them with what a movie party in an auto is supposed to be. Our brand of ribald wickedness used to consist of teasing D. W. to talk about history.

With his wonderful memory, his sympathetic insight, his knowledge of drama, and his glowing power of words, he tells stories from history in a way that would put H. G. Wells to shame. I remember one day, riding back from Middletown, N.J., he talked all the way about the Empress Theodora. And another time he told us stories of Oliver Cromwell; we would never let him stop.

Coming back from the try-out, Griffith always proceeds to tear the picture all to pieces. He never gets thru taking a picture. Sometimes, months after it has appeared on Broadway, he is still taking new shots to be cut-in.

At last the big night—the Broadway opening—dress suits—critics—actors in boxes—personal appearances—a speech before the curtain—D. W. in a darkened box with a little row of electric buttons where he can signal to the orchestra leader or the stage hands.

Then at last at three or four o'clock in the morning—the society people and critics gone—D. W. and his little "gang," as he called us, with the morning papers still damp from the press, somewhere in a little soiled restaurant, eating scrambled eggs—talking it over.

The Genius of a Masterpiece

Shadowland/1922

From *Shadowland*, August 1922, 62. This piece is signed simply "The Prophet," and is probably the work of Frederick James Smith.

D. W. Griffith told a little story not so very long ago. It was about himself, and it possessed the qualities his pictures possess . . . whimsy and pain and laughter, intertwined. He told about himself as a little boy, living on a Kentucky farm, was—impoverished . . . but *home*. "A castle of freedom, it was," he said . . . He told how, among his many duties, he had to go at night and bring in the cows, and he told what peculiarly fearsome cows they were, and what a long distance it seemed to him he had to go for them . . . across a meadow . . . across a creek, thru a grove of ghostly sycamore trees . . . "Sometimes," said Mr. Griffith, "I would call my older brother and sometimes, only sometimes, he would go with me, and I cannot tell you what a relief it was to me to have him go along. It did not seem so dim and dreadful a way; the creek was not so remote and the sycamores did not seem to cast such shuddering shadows. Ah, I cannot tell you what a blessed thing it was to have a brother to whom I could call, knowing that he would respond. And so, someday, perhaps two thousand years from now, I hope to make a picture which will show a world where every man, adventuring thru the ghostly sycamores and distant creeks and many pitfalls which we call 'life,' will be able to raise his voice and call 'Brother!'—knowing an answer will come."

The Universal Brotherhood of Man . . . beautiful, beatic, tender, tremendous theme. The Photoplay of the Future . . . what more profound hope can it have than this . . . that it will bring the clasping of men's hands to pass.

Griffith Film Stirs Anger of Parisians

New York Times/1922

From the *New York Times*, September 17, 1922, 5.

Paris, Sept. 10—The disturbance caused last night in a Boulevard motion picture house during the first production [presentation] of D. W. Griffith's film *Orphans of the Storm*, although it was actually started by a handful of young royalists, whose ire was aroused by the manner in which the *Ancien Régime* was depicted, apparently has a wider significance than a mere demonstration by a few hot-headed, unbalanced youths. Their angry protests were supported by almost the whole body of spectators, the reason being that the American producer's idea of conditions under the old monarchy profoundly offends French pride and self-respect.

La Liberté, a paper which by no means supports royalist ideas, this afternoon, under the heading "A Scandalous Film," expresses sympathy with last night's demonstration.

"If we are to believe Mr. Griffith," it says, "the French nobility before 1789 took pleasure in crushing children under the wheels of its carriages, had peasants' veins opened in order to pour hot lead into them, violated young girls, and spent the rest of its time in orgies and debaucheries, of which he gives us a surfeit of pictures. It is inadmissible that a foreigner should take upon himself thus to travesty an epoch whose faults and qualities we know much better than he, and one must ask what the censors were thinking of to allow a film which denotes so unfriendly a spirit toward French history. Fortunately Parisians will know how to act as their own censors and avoid the picture theatres which make the mistake of showing this film."

Griffith Says He Followed Dickens

D. W. Griffith, the motion picture producer, expressed his amazement yesterday afternoon when informed of the receipt by the *New York Times* of a wireless dispatch describing the hostile demonstration provoked in a Paris motion picture house by the first showing in the French capital of his *Orphans of the Storm*. When the account of the hostile demonstration and the adverse newspaper criticism occasioned by the picture was read over the telephone to Mr. Griffith, who was at his studios at Mamaroneck, he said he had received only a brief "verbal report" of the reception of the picture in Paris, and that he understood the hostility to the film was manifested by a "small coterie of your men who probably were royalist or Bolshevist sympathizers."

In defense of the film Mr. Griffith said that it there were any ground for complaint on the part of the French people it was to be found in *A Tale of Two Cities*, and that complaint should have been lodged long ago "against Mr. Charles Dickens," from whose famous novel the incidents of the people largely were drawn.

Mr. Griffith maintained that the picture carried a great moral which must have been entirely apparent to the authorities of the French Government when they permitted the distribution of the film in their country—a moral which emphasized the danger of the overthrow of Government and letting the mob rule.

"No one has more love and respect for the French people than I," said the producer of *Orphans of the Storm*. "And no one is more astonished than I because a small group of Frenchmen apparently have taken exception to the manner in which we have undertaken to reproduce the historical incidents through the medium of the production. According to what the French say about me, they ought to have said something about Mr. Dickens, because he made it much stronger in *A Tale of Two Cities*. We had to modify the horrors of that period of French history, of course, for artistic purposes, but we could have gone a great deal further had we elected to give a more detailed version of the history of that period."

Mr. Griffith said that when he was in London he talked with French critics who had seen the picture at private showings, and he asserted that they spoke most enthusiastically about the film. He explained that, while the picture showed some of the crimes of the nobility, the real hero was a French nobleman. While the picture went into the excesses of the nobility, it also showed how much worse matters were when control passed into the hands of the mob.

"The French take everything so seriously that they forget to look at both sides of the picture," continued Mr. Griffith. "Those who may have taken exception to the picture of the nobility of that time did not consider how much worse was the picture of the mob which succeeded the nobility in control of the French Government.

"You see, the picture producer gets into a mighty poor position. He is assailed from all sides. When the same picture was exhibited in the United States we were berated by labor papers, who said that the picture was the work of royalist (meaning capitalist) sympathizers, because we undertook [a subject that][1] is really aimed more at mob rule during the French revolution.

"The picture to which the French object is really aimed more at mob rule and against the Bolshevicki as they are represented in the days of the French Revolution, than against any other group.

In justifying the picturing of some of the horrors recalled by the film, Mr. Griffith said that the incident of the child being run down by the carriage of a nobility [sic] was taken from [Thomas] Carlyle. He pointed out that this incident also was utilized by Dickens in *A Tale of Two Cities*.

Mr. Griffith then made it clear that it was practically beyond his power to do anything to appease the anger of the Frenchmen who took exception to the film. He said that its production [presentation] in France and elsewhere in Europe was a matter entirely in the hands of distributors who had contracted for it. At the moment, he said, he could not recall the names of the distributors.

Note

1. Some words appear to be missing from the printed interview at this point, and they have been provided by the editor.

Stereoscopic Films

New York Times/1922

From the *New York Times*, November 5, 1922, 98.

D. W. Griffith, who may be counted on to be interested in any new cinematographic development, whether he himself is responsible for it or not, has become interested in the possibility of motion pictures with three dimensions, and when asked to give his ideas on the subject, commented as followed:

"Motion pictures will never realize their ideal effectiveness until they are stereoscopic. In every art where there is an industrial feature to it, the industrial part develops more rapidly than the artistic. That is because we are an industrial nation and have more minds trained that way.

"With a real stereoscopic effect, however, motion pictures could be made so vivid that they would drive the audience from its seats. Our public is trained to the utmost resource of the voice. We can scream on the stage, explode weapons, shriek and agonize, and the audience is prepared. But if a powerful dramatic scene were put into a film with absolute stereoscope vividness, I don't believe an audience could stand it.

"For instance, suppose we were to show a dagger thrust driving into the very faces of the audience; what would happen? If we were to show some figure coming toward the audience a figure that we consider forceful with our present photography, it would be appalling.

"The true stereoscopic effect will add a mighty force to motion pictures. It will make them beyond any comparison the most powerful medium of expression of which any one has dreamed.

"We are, of course, in what will be called the experimental stage of such development. When the effect depends upon individual mechanism for each spectator, it is of course a complicated arrangement, and difficult to reduce from a novelty to popularity.

"And before the stereoscopic film is generally used, it will be necessary, it seems to me, to have a period of preparation for audiences, which will take many months, if not years."

Some of the pictures in Mr. Griffith's *One Exciting Night*, now at the Apollo, would surely shiver your timbers is they were stereoscopic. You don't exactly sit still watching them as it is.

In and Out of Focus: D. W. Griffith

Louella Parsons/1922

From the *Morning Telegraph*, November 26, 1922, Section 5, page 5. "In and Out of Focus" was the overall title of a series of weekly interviews with filmmakers and stars conducted by Louella Parsons.

What is the matter with the movies will be answered when some theatre owner invents a remedy for the present handicap in the theatre of permitting the public to see the last half of a picture before the first has been unreeled, David Wark Griffith says. He believes conditions in the film world will continue as black as some of our most erudite writers have pictured them in the recent scathing magazine articles, until this crying evil is overcome.

"How long could David Belasco hold his supremacy as the stage's most artistic producer," asked Mr. Griffith, "if his audiences straggled into his theatres all during the performance, some of them seeing the big dramatic climax before they had seen the events leading up to it. Brilliant as he is, he would be a lamentable failure if the public were permitted to see the surprises in his plays first; if the denouement was presented before the first act was seen, he could not possibly survive.

"The greatest dramatic producer in the world of any age could not have any appeal to his public if he had to plan his plays with the idea in the back of his mind that he must work out his plot step by step with the thought it could be seen backward as well as in its logical sequence of acts and scenes.

"Take my picture, *One Exciting Night* [1922]. It is full of unexpected moments. The audience is not supposed to know who murdered Johnson [played by Herbert Sutch]. The name of the arch villain who is constantly killing someone is not known. If the patrons of a theatre walk into the house and see the whole plot exposed with the murderer brought to justice and the reason for all this wild excitement, what is there left for him when the first scenes go on again? The picture is ruined. You could not expect anyone to find an evening's entertainment in a mystery play with the mystery explained in advance."

Mr. Griffith feels so keenly on the evil of continuous performances he believes it is as grave a problem as censorship.

"I talked with Mary Pickford and Douglas Fairbanks on the harm that has been wrought by this backward presentation," said Mr. Griffith. Mary talked for half an hour and agreed with me something should be done.

"If any theatre owner," said Mr. Griffith, "blazed the trail and announced he would show his features only at certain hours, he would probably lose money. His fellow exhibitors would laugh at him for his visionary plan, but he would be doing a big thing for the artistic future of motion pictures. A plan might be devised on Broadway," went on Mr. Griffith, "whereby no one would be seated after the feature had been on half an hour. If anyone arrived that late he would have to wait until the end of the photo-play. There are comfortable divans and commodious lobbies to take care of the late arriving patrons, but I am not sure this plan would be practical in the smaller towns, where the theatre owner has no way of taking care of his patrons outside of the theatre."

Mr. Griffith feels it is highly essential for some way to be devised for a picture to be seen as the producer intended it when he made it, that he is willing to award a prize to anyone who can work out a practical solution of the difficulty and offer some substitute for the haphazard plan that so upset the soul of those who are striving to give the world better pictures.

One Exciting Night is not the sole motive for prompting Mr. Griffith to make this plea, but every other production, he says, that has been made with a care and earnestness that gives its producer the right to expect a different presentation.

"We ask ourselves what is the matter with motion pictures. Why do some of our most brilliant minds ridicule the motion picture as cheap and ridiculous? Simply because many producers purposely make their pictures with an obvious theme. They figure if they try any subtlety it will be submerged when the films are run off with the last scenes first and the first scenes last.

"There must be some way to overcome this evil that is holding the motion picture down to a lower level and preventing it from attaining the place it was destined to reach," said Mr. Griffith. "Even the stumbling over pairs of feet in the dark is minor compared with the irreparable harm being done our finest productions by the vogue now existing in the theatres where the films are run off as quickly as the operator can operate the machine in order to seat as many people as possible."

Someone suggested to Mr. Griffith that a system might be evolved whereby the exhibitor would send out to his patrons postcards with the hour the feature would be shown, asking that the patrons try and get to the theatre at the time mentioned on the cards.

"Naturally the theatre owner wants to make as much money as he can," said Mr. Griffith. "No one blames him for that. The postcard might keep people away. He would not want to do anything that would work a hardship against his business. But I feel there is some brave soul somewhere who for the sake of what it means to motion pictures will try the experiment of not permitting his patrons to take their seats after the feature has been on for half an hour. He would be doing a great good and every producer would rise up and call him blessed."

Mr. Griffith says he will be happy to receive any suggestions either from men who are in the film business or from outsiders. He is confident there is some solution to this evil which threatens to be so disastrous to the finer productions and he asks that everyone who is sincerely interested in giving not only New York, but Keokuk, Iowa, or Oshkosh, Wis., the best in motion pictures try and help find the solution.

What is the matter with the movies, as [highly regarded entertainment journalist] Karl Kitchen and other writers have asked in articles in the various magazines, is not a desire on the part of the producers to make cheap films with tawdry subjects, but an inability to get away from these subjects so long as the films are presented backwards.

David Griffith always has something to say when he speaks, and we believe this is worthy of consideration. We should like to hear from someone else on the same subject.

What Are the Chances of a Beginner

Photoplay/1923

From *Photoplay*, August 1923, 35–36.

[This unsigned piece consists of a series of comments, beginning with D. W. Griffith, and continuing with Rex Ingram, Cecil B. DeMille, Allan Dwan, Marshall Neilan, John M. Stahl, Hobart Henry, Charles Maigne, and the following casting directors: L. M. Goodstadt (Lasky), Harry Kerr (Metro), Clarence Jay Elmer (Cosmopolitan), Robert B. McIntyre (Goldwyn), William Cohill (Paramount East Coast studios), and James Ryan (Fox East Coast studios).]

"There is always a good chance for the right sort of beginner. That applies to every field of human activity. Indeed, in making motion picture dramas I am inclined to favor beginners.

"They come untrammeled by so-called technique, by theories and by preconceived ideas.

"If you were to ask me what sort of beginner I liked best, I would say in brief: I prefer the young woman who has to support herself and possibly her mother. Of necessity, she will work hard. Again, I prefer the nervous type. I never engage a newcomer who applied for work without showing at least a sign or two of nervousness. If she is calm, she has no imagination. The imaginative type can picture the glamorous future with its possible great success—and is always nervous. Imagination—and nerves—are highly essential.

"To me, the ideal type for feminine stardom has nothing of the flesh, nothing of the note of sensuousness. My pictures reveal the type I mean. Commentators have called it the spirituelle [sic] type. But there is a method in my madness, as it were. The voluptuous type, blooming into the full blown rose, cannot endure. The years show their stamp too clearly. The other type—ah, that is different!

"When I consider a young woman as a stellar possibility I always ask myself: Does she come near suggesting the idealized heroine of life? Every living man has an ideal heroine of his dreams. Thus the girl, to have the real germ of stardom, must suggest—at least in a sketchy way—the vaguely formulated ideals of every man. Again, she must suggest—and this is equally important—the attributes most women desire. If she is lucky enough to have all these things, she may well look forward to popularity and success—if she has great determination."

D. W. Griffith Is Struggling to Pay His Debts

Sara Redway/1925

From *Motion Picture Classic*, October 1925, 39–40, 70, 77.

Virtue, alas, is often its own reward. I have heard of genius, dying undiscovered in an attic, but I have never heard of a moving picture director peddling matches on Christmas Eve. I hope I never shall. I would sooner see a realtor's lip quiver. Perhaps it is because genius doesn't go about in riding breeches with a megaphone.

No one with a megaphone could remain undiscovered. But I have seen a man who must be almost a genius, although being almost a genius is about the same as being almost an angel, so I will be milder with my words and say that I have met a man with a rare talent. He has had the talent to be a good director and to be a poor one.

He has no marble swimming pool, not even a modest marble bathtub; he has no Beverly Hills house, Spanish Style, nor a Long Island house, Dutch Colonial. I say "house" where I should say "home." Only poor people can afford the luxury of a plain house. He has no Renault, special body, nor has he engaged the Japanese army to wait on him.

This remarkable man is D. W. Griffith. I assure you that he has no more than you and I, except perhaps a little more fun. At the present time he is working for Famous Players for quite a comfortable salary. But every week his salary is signed over to pay his debts, which leaves Mr. Griffith on Saturday nights in the same financial condition he was on Monday morning. Lots of us are in the same boat, to be sure, but Saturday nights and Sundays are so pleasant, while all Mr. Griffith can do is add up on paper what he might have had—if things were different. I don't know why this had to be, but I do know that he will work this way for three years.

He seems to think that it has been a question of luck.

"When I work for someone else," he told me, "I always make money for them. When I back my own ideas, I am bound to lose. I borrowed the money to finance *Isn't Life Wonderful*. I am still paying it back. I suppose I could have gone bankrupt, but I didn't. I'd rather do it this way.

Gave Away His Ideas

"About two years ago, I realized that I could have patented an idea of mine that I had used thirteen years before. It would have made me a millionaire."

"What was the idea?" I asked.

"Well, I think it was in 1909, when I was making a picture with Mary Pickford and Owen Moore. The picture was the James Fenimore Cooper story *The Last of the Mohicans*.[1] When we came to the final love scene, it seemed a shame to cut it off abruptly. I wanted to have it gradually fade out, leaving a more lasting impression. I told the cameraman what I wanted, and he said he didn't see how it could be done. We talked about it for a while and decided to pass something slowly over the lens of the camera. The 'something' that we used was an old shoe box. It was the first fade-out. I put a piece of gauze over it to soften the effect.

"Now if I had patented that idea, I might have made some money, because it has been used ever since.

First to Use the Close-Up

"I think that I was the first person to use the close-up. I'm not sure of this, because it might have been used in foreign pictures without my knowledge. But I do remember that when I suggested it to the cameraman, he refused to take it. He claimed that you couldn't take pictures of peoples' faces and leave their bodies out. My answer was a trip to the art gallery. I saw plenty of paintings without bodies attached, and I won the argument. When the picture was shown in the theater, the audience stamped on the floor and hissed.

"I also believe I used the miniature first. I used one in *Intolerance*. No one knew it, so it must have been done pretty well."

"How does anyone get to be a director?" I asked. "I don't see how you could learn directing in the home very well. If you practiced on the wives and kiddies it might lead to complications. Do you begin on a small scale and work up, or do you stand around and look wistful until someone asks you to play?"

"I don't know what they do now," Mr. Griffith said. "I began writing stories and scenarios at fifteen dollars a story. Before that I had written stories and poem for magazines, also at ten and fifteen dollars per effort."

Once a Country Reporter

"My brother had a small newspaper in Kentucky and I wrote for it. I was the local reporter. You know the sort of thing; 'Bob Jones went to Louisville last week, and has come back with a new suit. How are you Bob?' or 'Ben Harkins buggy has been in seen in front of Susie Simpkins' house almost every week now. How about the wedding bells, Ben?'

"Quips like these were supposed to be very daring, real town-topics stuff. The subscriptions were paid for in farm produce mostly."

"What were the first pictures you ever made?"

"They were comedies, regular slapstick comedies. I made the first comedy chase, the kind where they all pile up in a ditch in the end, that had ever been made. Mack Sennett was working for me as an extra then. Later when I gave up the comedies, he took them over.

"I was surprised at the criticism of my new picture, *Sally of the Sawdust*. People seemed to think it funny that I had burst into low comedy. I didn't burst into it, it cropped out again."

"Do you like moving pictures, after all these years?" I asked.

"No," said Mr. Griffith, "I don't, and I'll be perfectly frank about telling you why."

Faults of Film Presentation

"Suppose you were to go to a theater. The play you go to see has been produced with care and with brilliance. When you get to your seat, the first two acts are over and the third is well under way. The climax is reached. A man and a woman are quarreling violently, but you don't know why they are, because you have missed the first part. No matter how well the actors are doing their parts, you naturally remain lukewarm. All the money, the art, the energy that the producer has lavished on the play, are wasted.

"It is the same way with moving pictures. If audiences are allowed to

enter a theater at any time during the film, the story falls flat. It is bound
to. Why should a climax be reached, why should the action build around
it, if it is the first thing you happen to see as you walk in the theater?

"I say that no story, no matter how good, can compete with the flim-
siest slapstick comedy. A comedy is a series of gags. It doesn't matter
which gag comes first. Why then spend $200,000 on a story that hasn't
a chance from the start.

"Why should an actor earnestly try to give you a character it you
aren't allowed to study that character from beginning to end?"

Gags Succeeding Stories

"A great actor like John Barrymore may succeed on the stage where he
could not possibly succeed in pictures. Harold Lloyd and Charlie Chaplin can. Barrymore may be many different people. He may be Hamlet,
Richard III, Dr. Jekyll, or Mr. Hyde, and you, in the audience, can't say,
'That's John Barrymore. I know what he's going to do.' You don't. To
know, you must see the picture from beginning to end, the same way you
would go to see a play.

"If you see Harold Lloyd, you know that he will be himself. No matter
what picture he is in, he wears the same clothes, and acts the same way.
He himself is the personality that you pay to see, not the part he takes.
The picture and plot are unimportant.

"I believe comedies are the best bet the way pictures are shown today.
To prove my point, it is a fact that pictures shown in regular theaters, as
stage plays, one performance an evening, can succeed there, and then
fail when they are shown in moving picture theaters.

"The critics have said that pictures made in Germany are good. They
are. In picture theaters there, the audience is admitted for the first fifteen minutes of the film. After that, they must wait until the next performance. A good picture has a chance to get across. *The Last Laugh* had
no subtitles. None were needed, provided you could see the picture from
beginning to end. I also hear that when it left New York the subtitles
were added. They probably had to be.

"In every subtitle in my pictures, I'm going to explain as much of the
plot as possible, in sheer self-protection. So long as audiences come in
later, I'll make everything clear. I don't think it's art, but I do think that
it is a necessity."

Should Show Pictures Properly

"Instead of the theaters in New York spending so much money on their orchestras and entertainers, I think it might be a good idea to spend a little money on showing their pictures properly. You hear a lot of talk about 'Greater Movie Week' and 'Better Films,' but the only way to have better pictures is to give them a chance. There is no need for a vaudeville act, a jazz band, and a ballet to get people in a theater, if the picture itself is good enough.

"My idea is to have one place where the feature picture is shown, at certain hours, and no admittance after that time. Underneath could be a smaller theater for the people who come late or for those who only come for half an hour or so. The news reel and the comedy could be shown here. It sounds rather complicated, I admit, but another theater could easily be built with the money that is spent on orchestras and entertainers.

"Until something like this is done, there need be no talk of uplifting the movies. Comedies will win easily."

"Now that we have settled what's wrong with this picture, will you answer a perfectly personal question?" I asked.

"What is it?" Mr. Griffith cautiously replied.

No Vamps in Real Life

"Why don't you have any vamps in your pictures?"

"Well, I try to have real people in them that I have seen and know to exist."

"Haven't you ever seen a vamp, or don't you think there are any?"

"I don't think there are any loose. I think they are all working for the movies."

For those who think all directors are bald and rotund, I will send this message to humanity. Mr. Griffith is not bald; and in spite of his "I remember whens," he is not old. He only harks back to such Neolithic dates as 1909. He doesn't wear puttees, and he doesn't say "what we are striving for." And oh, well, if you must have some details, he wears suspenders.

After I talked to him, I sat around for a while and watched them take some scenes in *"That Royle Girl."* Harrison Ford, who is in it, sat next to me.

"What do you think of him?" he asked me.

"I think he is wonderful. What do you think?"

"I don't think there's anybody like him. I've never seen anybody who was half as nice."

"It's too bad that he's never gotten anything out of it," I said.

"Not gotten anything?" repeated Mr. Ford in surprise. "Why he's got everything. I guess the people who work for him would do anything for him."

Just the same; I hope that some day he gets the gold doorknobs and a big diamond ring, too.

Note

1. Actually *Leather Stocking*, released September 27, 1909; Mary Pickford is not in the film.

How Do You Like the Show?

Myron M. Stearns/1926

From *Collier's*, April 24, 1926, 8–9.

[In that this piece is published in the form of an "as told to" article, it seems appropriate to treat it as an interview from which the questions have been removed.]

In one of his earlier successful motion pictures Charles Ray, as a young baseball player whose head had been turned by promotion to the majors, snubs the home-town folks who have come to honor him in the big city.[1] Beside me in the theater where I watched that film there was a pleasant old lady. At the snubbing scene, she turned to me—a stranger—and, with a voice full of apology as though the youth on the screen were her own son, she excused him: "But he's such a *boy*!"

That spontaneous remark, born of sympathy for the boy hero and apology for his shortcomings, was a tribute to the power of the picture. It left no doubt that the film had stirred the woman.

It is not often that you who flock to the movies give us such concrete and striking evidence of your reaction to a screen production. But we who make the movies, who must constantly feel the pulse of the film fans, recognize countless other signs by which you tell us whether the fruits of our efforts bore or please, thrill or amuse.

You are an unusual theatergoer, indeed, if you watch either a motion picture or a play without giving abundant indication of your unconscious reaction to what you are seeing. Upon the ability of motion-picture producers to learn and correctly interpret the signs you give [of] approval or disapproval rest your chance of having, each year, better pictures than you have ever had before.

One of the most dependable signs is coughing. If you cough frequently during the unreeling of a film, I know that you are not keenly interested. Throughout the northern part of this country, and to a slighter extent in the southern states, coughs and colds are, of course, often prevalent. At most New York and Chicago theaters, in winter, there is an almost continuous firecracker chorus of coughing—here, there, all over the house. But as interest increases the coughing stops.

Let the interest die down, let the director or playwright lose his hold on the audience by ever so little, and the coughs begin again. Listen for yourself the next time you are in a theatre.

By the way you play with your program I know whether a picture is registering with you. If a house is warm, you will undoubtedly use the pamphlet as a fan, joining in a waving sea that fills the auditorium. As interest rises the movement lessens, becomes imperceptible and, at an effective dramatic climax, ceases altogether. The picture is "getting" you then. As the interest decreases the waving recommences, becoming subconsciously less restrained.

Silence is always a sure sign of attention. Before the curtain rises at a play, before a picture is thrown on the screen, people are getting busy with this or that—getting into more comfortable positions, stowing away wraps, looking over programs, talking with the friends who have come to the theater with them. As the performance starts, this noise suddenly lowers, dying gradually away. Conversations drop at once to lowered tones or whispers, barely audible—or cease abruptly. But you will be surprised to note, if you listen for it, how the undercurrent of sound continues. No particular conversation, no outstanding rustle of paper or shifting of position, but a movement here, an added whisper there, one more look at a program beyond, combining to form a fraction of the same stir and hum that were so much more noticeable before the curtain went up.

In one of the plays that ran for only a short time recently in New York, but that has done much better in London, *The Man with a Load of Mischief* [1925, written by Ashley Dukes], the first character to appear, an innkeeper, sang to himself as he went about lighting candles. The result was almost instantaneous. There was a quick gain in audience attention. The house became quiet much more quickly than is ordinarily the case, in order to catch the words of the song, half sung, as if subconsciously, so quietly that ears were strained to follow.

Conversation stops before movement does. It takes more than passing interest in what is happening on the stage or screen to stop all movement.

The alertness with which an audience follows the details of a story, pouncing upon the explanation or comedy, is another sure gauge of interest and enjoyment. Let a really funny situation or joke come to the surface in a dull picture, and, while it will get a laugh, the response is neither as hearty nor as immediate as would be the case if the performance were going over well.

There are signs of still higher degrees of interest. Here and there people in an audience will begin to hold their breath. They will unconsciously lean forward in their seats. Unconscious of their automatic actions, they are carried along entirely by the sweep of the story they are watching. Let the situation begin to clear itself, allow the tensions to relax, and you can observe an instantaneous reaction as they sit back again, relax, begin again the ceaseless shifting into slightly different positions. The undercurrent of movement and sound, like a barometer, begins rising again to show that interest has waned.

A great tribute is paid when the unconscious response of an individual in an audience to what he sees reaches a point of actual expression. Sometimes, as when in *The Birth of a Nation*, a black fiend is creeping closer to the tragic little girl of the story, played by the Mae Marsh, the call takes the form of a definite warning to an actor on the screen: "Look out!"

At my own studios every single subtitle, every situation, every shift in scene or change in a sequence that is made in editing a film, has to go before an audience for its test before being accepted as part of the completed product. So I have learned to watch audiences closely.

But it is far more difficult for exhibitors, unversed in reading the signs so closely, to judge audience approval. Children, for instance, applaud or laugh more readily than grown-ups. The most childlike part of an audience accordingly, is most apt to express its hilarity or lose interest in the picture. The most intelligent part of the audience, the most critical, is the least demonstrative.

This is almost tragically important. It is owing to this fact that many exhibitors, relying only on the superficial evidences of audience approval, the laughter or noise that can be heard from the little box-office window outside the theater, neglect the most valuable portion of their patronage, the 10 to 15 percent that constitutes the leadership element in the community and that in the long run frequently determines whether or not the theater will be a real "first-run" house or merely one of the minor places able to draw only cheaper audiences, catering to the noisy element that will lose them in the end more money than it can ever bring in.

One of the directors whom I employed made a practice, when a picture that he had produced was to be tried out before an audience, of standing half a block or so away from the theater just before the performance began and personally asking every child that came along if he wanted to see a movie. Then he would hand out fifteen or twenty-five cents necessary to pay the youngster's admission and tell him to go ahead and enjoy himself.

That little system usually insured a couple of rows, at least, of very enthusiastic young auditors, who would collectively raise the roof at every bit of comedy that appeared on the screen, no matter how fragile. The innocent exhibitor, not knowing that I was aware of his trick, happily believed that his confidence was passed on to me.

Ordinarily film makers get the idea of what audiences like best in a picture from the eighteen thousand or more exhibitors who rent films from the big distributing corporations. They have to take their audience opinions second-hand. They trust the other fellow's judgment of what people really want. And that is dangerous.

Few producers take their pictures, as I have come to believe it is important to do, while they are still in the making, to audiences themselves. Those of us who do, have, I believe a big advantage. We take no exhibitor's word for what audiences are supposed to want. We take no distributor's word for what exhibitors think their audiences want. Even the box-office returns, the gross rentals of a picture, that would seem to be the absolute guide of popular opinion, can be in some measure thrown aside. That must come afterward. A picture has to stand or fall in the ultimate analysis on whether or not people like it.

You and I both want "better pictures." So, for the matter of that, does everybody. Only they MUST also please. They must be entertaining.

Personally, I believe it is far easier to make an artistic picture, such as would please those whom the majority consider "highbrows," than to make one that will be popular. I would enjoy making beautiful films—but how many of you would pay to see them? I consider *Sentimental Tommy* [1921, with Gareth Hughes in the title role], for instance, as a fine example of a truly artistic picture. But it was not a box-office success. The beautiful and sincere picture version that Paramount has recently made of Conrad's famous novel *Lord Jim* [1925, with Percy Marmont in the title role] is another illustration.

Now, how to combine those two things, excellence and genuine entertainment. That is where the technique of "making the audience enjoy it" comes in. And it's an exceedingly delicate and complicated technique, so difficult that the road to motion-picture successes that are at once worthwhile and deservedly popular is long and hard.

"Tell them that you're going to do it; then tell then you've done it," David Belasco is reported to have said in giving the rules for successful play production.

In one of the most successful pictures that was released in 1920–21, *Humoresque* [actually released in September 1920, directed by Frank Borzage, and starring Vera Gordon], there is an early scene sequence in which a little Jewish boy attempts to show off before the small maiden of his choice. Finally, as a climax, he wiggles his ears. It is shown on the screen in a big close-up that audiences find irresistibly funny.

For quite a while there is only a series of grimaces as the stubborn ears refuse to wiggle. Then, suddenly, the right muscles are found, and the ears work up and down splendidly. It is all done so earnestly, so confidently, with the unconscious absorption of a child, that the humor is absolutely genuine. But to the average movie fan who laughed at that little bit it will be a surprise to learn that until the film was edited the humor of the wiggling ears did not get over at all. It was this way: one of my former scenario editors was working at the Cosmopolitan studio at the time. In the projection-room, he tells me the boy's close-up was funny, but not nearly funny enough to laugh at. It was too hard to tell what he was doing. Just as a game of making "funny faces" it was too close to a failure. The audience had to be told what he was trying to do, so they could laugh with him at his efforts. One title did it.

"For nothing I wiggle my ears," they made him say—and the trick was turned. The longer they had to wait before the ears began to wiggle, the funnier, instead of more tiresome, the bit became. And when at last those ears actually *did* wiggle, there was a big laugh!

Take the trumpet calls in *The Birth of a Nation* at the gathering of the Klans. It added immeasurably to the gripping power of the picture. Take the plaintive little theme melody for Miss Lillian Gish in *Broken Blossoms*. On the other hand, one of the great box-office handicaps of *Intolerance* was that the music did not in itself have enough emotional appeal. It was too coldly classical.

Most motion-picture producers hesitate about going too near the limit of popular approval. Naturally. With so much invested in a single film, it is obvious that only disaster could attend the making of many photoplays that failed to please. And since no one knows exactly what the limit of approval in any particular instance is, the tendency of producers is, of course, to broaden the appeal, even if it means cheapening the character parts and story value of the production.

That is where those of us who make a practice of trying pictures out and studying audiences with almost scientific care have a great advantage. For since the really great returns are those which come to the photoplays that combine the greatest amount of worthwhile material and leadership with genuine popularity, that knowledge pays big dividends.

We learn, for example, that it is not necessary for a picture to have "everything."

You will respond to a combination of dramatic situation, suspense, excitement, humor, and pathos. Or to any *one* of those things. Laughter and tears are, of course, the two great tributes that are most readily detected. But interest, in the long run, will accomplish wonders at the box-office, and the key to interest is suspense. Suspense alone will often carry an entire picture.

I took *Broken Blossoms* for a tryout to Santa Ana, Cal. The story is a tragic one, in which a fragile girl of the slums dies from the effects of a beating she receives at the hands of her brutal father, a prize fighter. I have never seen an audience more nearly stunned by the picture than were those people in Santa Ana. It had beauty, but it had also grief, agony, horror

The exhibitor at whose theater the picture was shown told me he had never had such an impossible reaction.

"I've had pictures that most people liked and a few people criticized," he said, "and I've had pictures that a few people liked and most people criticized. But this is the first time I've ever run a picture that nobody liked!"

Yet, unconsciously, the Santa Ana audiences gave the evidence on which I was able, later, to build a tremendously wide distribution for the picture; from start to finish of the film each audience sat motionless. I remember seeing one man leaning forward throughout a performance. So far as I was able to observe, he never once touched the back of the seat during the hour or more that it took to run the six short reels. The picture had *suspense*.

On another tryout of that same film an amusing instance of its gripping power was afforded by the musicians in the orchestra pit. They followed the story on the screen so intently that it interfered with their best efforts in the orchestra. Finally the orchestra leader lost nearly all semblance of self-control. Over the heads of the audience his voice cracked like a whip: "Never mind the damn picture—come on with that drum."

When we develop to a still higher point the technique of putting basically fine material across, our progress toward pictures that will please more frequently the intelligence as well as the purely popular element of our ten million patrons a day will be rapid.

And the more you and your friends, who go to the motion pictures because you like them, express your opinions, the better we shall serve you.

Note

1. Griffith is thinking of *The Busher* (1919), produced by Thomas H. Ince and directed by Jerome Storm. Charles Ray (1891–1943) was a popular leading man of the 1910s and early 1920s, specializing in boyish roles, whose career as a star ended after he began to take himself too seriously.

Don't Blame the Movies! Blame Life!

Selma Robinson/1926

From *Motion Picture Magazine*, July 1926, 33, 82.

Directors come and directors go. Stars shoot into the films like comets and disappear as rapidly. Innovations in photography are treated to a brief, brilliant career and are forgotten. And throughout the bright parade, David Wark Griffith goes about his own business, seemingly unaware of anything else, yet actually following every shifting movement.

Griffith has often been called the dean of movies, and I can't think of a more fitting title. He has an air of silent wisdom, of having long ago decided to forget what other men are now discovering. It is precisely the air of a learned professor listening to the pretty theories of his young pupils. Still, his attitude isn't a conceited one. In it are combined humor, experience, tolerance, and a great urge for more knowledge—hardly the distinguishing characteristics of conceit. Nor does he look like a conceited man, with his tie knotted somewhere under his ear and his collar turning up its points.

For the fact that Griffith continues to work much as he has always worked, blame his devotion to realism. To him, nothing can be art unless it is almost indistinguishable from life. If his pictures seem romantic or sentimental or anything else, blame life.

"Voltaire said that there was nothing in fiction so dramatic, so impossible, so horrible, so banal—or so unbelievable, that it couldn't be surpassed by life itself," said Mr. Griffith. "Pick up the newspaper almost any morning and you will read of actual happenings more picturesque than anything which has been presented in the pictures. And yet on all sides there are criticisms that such and such a picture was not 'true to life.' The more I live, the more I learn that there is very little which is not true to life. Almost anything might happen in life, and almost anything does.

"And when it comes to acting, the field is even more unlimited. Given a city of six million people, and you have six million different characters, similar in many respects, it is true, but unquestionably different as individuals. Take, for example, an imaginary hold-up. If you were held up at the point of a gun, you would probably faint. That man there might punch the thief on the jaw. I might very quietly hand over everything I owned. Miss [Carol] Dempster, here, might tell the man that he ought to be ashamed of himself, holding up harmless citizens, and still another person might tell him to put his gun away and stop joking.

"There is no prescribed behavior for human beings. You remember that story by O. Henry about the two men who were discussing how they would react to a certain calamity? One fellow ridiculed the 'my God, why hast thou forsaken me' sort of thing; the other thought that profanity and slang would be inadequate to express a deep emotion. Yet when the first man came home to find his wife gone with the boarder, he gave vent to his feelings in flowery rhetoric, while the second man, confronted with a similar tragedy, burst into a string of damns."

How then, I wanted to know, could one distinguish bad acting from good, when one might be just as true to life as the other. Yes, that was true, he said; one character might weep and tear her hair where another would stand mute and dry-eyed. But, I persisted, why were critics so hard on the old school of acting when perhaps it was just as logical as the new?

"There is no old school of acting, and no new," said Griffith suddenly. "There are and have always been two schools of acting—good and bad. Bad acting was just as bad fifteen years ago as bad acting is today, and good acting was always good. Look back at some of the acting several years ago and some of the stars—Mae Marsh, Mary Pickford, Bobby Harron, Henry [B.] Walthall and many others. Miss Marsh's performance in *Intolerance* can stand up with any acting of the present, and if you could find a juvenile now whose acting would equal Henry Walthall's, he would be worth fifteen or twenty thousand dollars a week to any producer.

"On the other hand, I can mention actors tho I won't, whose art consisted of a couple of heaves, a few twitches of the eyebrows, a trembling of the chin and a clasping and unclasping of the hands. They were undeniably bad. They brought to the pictures an assortment of tricks which they used over and over again. However, you haven't very far to look to find others just as bad and even worse on the screen today. You say, perhaps, such tricks are in keeping with the character since many freaks may be true to life. Well, that would be true if the actress were playing the part of a woman who pretended to be emotional, to take that as an example. Then her obvious assuming of little tricks would be appropriate. Unfortunately, tho, the actress takes her bundle of mannerisms with her from picture to picture, whether she is intended to be waif or debutante, dancer or queen, and that is undeniably bad acting."

Good acting, in Mr. Griffith's opinion, is that which duplicates life most accurately. Of course, there are other people who believe that good acting should suggest realism, not duplicate it. There are arguments on both sides. Griffith thinks that an actor should think not in terms of himself but in terms of his character.

"We may all advance our theories, we may develop them in our own way, but the result is invariably the same," he laughed. "Good acting is good and bad acting is bad, as I said before. Coquelin, the celebrated French actor, said that it was folly for an actor to feel his part so intensely that it would dominate all his emotions; the artist should be himself at all times in order to give an intelligent impersonation. Sarah Bernhardt, on the other hand, believed that there was nothing for the actor to do but throw himself, heart and soul, into his role. And here you have two superlative artists whose opinions are diametrically opposite, yet their talents achieved the same results. I myself agree with both of them. By all means do I feel that an actor should enter into his role, but I also believe that all the emotion in the world will be powerless unless he can thru a calm, intelligent portrayal make the audience feel with him."

More attention is being paid to the repressed type of acting than formerly, Griffith said, but that is due to the change in stories. Pictures today are more subtle, less melodramatic than they used to be, and they call for more subdued acting. Mr. Griffith described the quiet methods of the late Frank Bacon which went unnoticed until he played *Lightnin'*, although he had been acting that way for twenty years![1]

"And they hailed it as acting of the newer school," Griffith said with a smile.

The dean of directors has that same smile for many present-day "discoveries," among them titleless photoplays.

"Did you know that the first pictures we ever made were without titles?" he asked.

I shook my head in surprise. *The Last Laugh* was the first picture I had ever heard of without titles and everybody declared it an innovation. Mr. Griffith kept smiling.

"Yes, we decided that titles—provided they are the right sort, held

a picture. Many important feet of film are saved by the simple expedient of using a few printed words," he explained. "Instead of showing a
man walking all the way home we found that the action was speeded up
and the story made more compact by saying that the man went home. I
think in spite of all the fuss that was made about the absence of titles in
the German film, if would have been much improved if they had been
included. Every foot of film is precious in telling a story, just as every
word in a well-knit drama should have some definite place in the scheme
of the play. Ibsen's dramas are constructed like sturdy houses and each
of his words is a brick that supports another word or another thought.
A play, whether it is on the legitimate stage or on the screen, must have
pace. It should not be allowed to lag.

"There is a distinct demand from a part of the public for better pictures and better acting, and discriminating people are quick to approve
real artistry. I have seen audiences break into applause at a beautiful bit
of photography or a fine piece of acting, whereas ten or fifteen years ago
they would applaud only when the cavalry arrived in time to save the
heroine from the Indians. Unquestionably, standards in acting have improved. More good actors are attracted to the screen today than formerly,
when motion pictures were considered beneath the notice of real artists.
But we still have our bad actors. Perhaps we shall always have them as
long as there are audiences who will accept that kind of performance.
What pictures need above everything else is a good story, for without it,
even the best acting is unavailable."

Everybody in the theater and the motion pictures also works for the
same end, but each man chooses his own method of arriving there.
Some directors rely on momentary inspiration to see their pictures
thru. Others stand and let the actors go thru their performances without interference. And Griffith rehearses his company for weeks before
he photographs a single scene. In this way alone, he feels can the actor
really understand his role. This same attention is lavished upon every
detail in the production of his pictures. On the day I interviewed him,
Mr. Griffith was testing lights and costumes for *The Sorrows of Satan*. Half
a dozen times the director ordered Carol Dempster to "sink" into her
dress, to walk about, to straighten up, so that he could study the folds of
the chiffon and avoid awkward effects. Just as I was leaving the set, Mr.
Griffith called me.

"You newspaper people are always telling us how to make pictures,"
he said; "Suppose I ask your advice. Miss Dempster is a struggling writer

in this film. At one time she had money. What sort of coat should she wear?"

He showed me the coat he had selected—a once-fashionable jacket of gray velvet trimmed with moth-eaten fur. The elbows were rubbed and the shoulders showed signs of wear. Even the lining was worn. Yet the coat was immaculately clean and neatly pressed—precisely the sort of coat that a poor but tidy girl would wear. There wasn't a suggestion I could offer. Mr. Griffith smiled once more.

"Do come and see us again, won't you?" he urged.

Note

1. Frank Bacon (1864–1922) enjoyed his greatest success at the end of his life, playing the title character in the comedy *Lightnin'*, which he co-authored with Winchell Smith, and which opened at the Gaiety Theatre, New York, on August 25, 1918.

He Might Be the Richest Man in the World

Frederick James Smith/1926

From *Photoplay*, December 1926, 30–31, 106.

[Smith notes that Griffith is living "quietly" in a hotel on New York's Broadway, and that he has not earned a cent for two years because he is paying off old debts.]

Suppose the pioneer motion picture devices had been patented as everything has been patented in the modern field of radio. David Wark Griffith would be one of the richest men in the world, and the empire of films would be turned topsy-turvy.

"Suppose I had patented the fade-out," Griffith told me sadly the other day. "I would be drawing at least a million a year in royalties. The dissolve-out is absolutely necessary to the smooth telling of a story. Try counting the number of times it is used in a single picture.

"To eliminate it would make necessary the abrupt beginning and ending of scenes. It would jar and distort the whole observation of a film drama.

"Yes, I might have patented it. You can patent anything derived from a mechanical device. I just didn't realize its significance then. We were all pioneers—and I wanted to help the business.

"I might have patented the shooting of scenes through gauze. Sometimes it is called soft focus. They used to call it 'mist photography' in the old times. That is another mechanical device.

"The revenue from the gauze appliance would have been good for another million easily each year. Only the other day I patented a new application of this device, so I know that I could have protected the original.

"It wouldn't have been possible to patent the flash-back or the close-up," Griffith went on. "Those are ideas of technique. But, with the other two devices under patent, I wouldn't have needed them. I would have my millions, anyway."

The man who laid the foundation of motion pictures looked about his hotel room. He has a little suite of living room and bedroom in a Times Square hotel. Its windows look across the west side tenements to the Hudson and to Fort Lee, the pioneer Jersey Hollywood of the films. The living room is piled high with books and manuscripts. The remainder of the Griffith records repose in the hotel basement.

"I'm not a bad business man," Griffith continued, "Honestly, I'm not. I was never in difficulties until I turned my business over to others. In California in the old days, when I both directed and managed, I got along all right. It was only when I came to Mamaroneck and turned over my business handling to others that I became involved.

"Of course, the collapse of everything at Mamaroneck nearly broke my heart. We missed success so narrowly. Bad management and bad releasing contracts caused the destruction. But when we failed, I made up my mind that the stockholders would be paid back. That's why I took the contract at Famous Players—to earn enough to pay back every cent.

"Right at this moment I have earned enough to pay back four and a half of every twelve cents I owe each stockholder. I will have the whole thing paid in another year.

"I'm not earning a cent for myself. Actually, I'm working for nothing. Last year, in fact, I went behind fifteen thousand dollars. But I will be out of servitude in another twelve months."

Another source of a possible fortune came up. Suppose Griffith had signed his various film discoveries to long-term contracts, following the custom of today. Griffith found Mary Pickford, the Gishes, Constance Talmadge, Blanche Sweet, Richard Barthelmess, and others. Suppose he had tied them up to lengthy contracts.

"It couldn't be done," Griffith told me. "Did you ever try to work with an actor who is unhappy? Did you ever try to direct an actor who thought himself underpaid, who felt that he ought to be a star? I *have*. It's a horrible experience. I wouldn't have a restless player under contract for the world. I value my peace of mind too much."

Sometime Griffith is going to write the story of his life. It will be after he finished directing, if he ever does. Griffith wants to write.

"Writers are the only ones who can express their ego," he says. "Directors can't, because pictures must be made to please the majority. We can't deal with opinions. All we can do is to weave a little romance as pleasantly as we know how."

Griffith naturally doesn't like to express comparisons. I did ask him to name the greatest actor he had ever directed.

He thought a while. "Arthur Johnson, I guess," he said. "Yes, Arthur Johnson."[1] Henry [B.] Walthall was excellent in romantic roles. Perhaps a little florid. Lionel Barrymore was vivid in those old Biograph days. But Johnson was matchless in everything—modern, romantic, comedy. He would have been a great film leader had he lived."

Griffith did not commit himself so exactly about the greatest actress he had ever directed. He obviously seems to consider Lillian Gish and Carol Dempster the greatest. I asked him about Miss Gish, in view of her more recent film roles. He countered, "Who is greater?"

Griffith doesn't believe that the public is fickle about its stars. "Stars do not slip quickly," he says, "despite the theory to the contrary. You hear that so-and-so will die if he doesn't get a good picture immediately. Consider how many weak pictures have been made by the big favorites— who are still favorites. No, the public does not like to revise its estimates. It doesn't want to go to the trouble of seeking new idols any more than the average man likes to seek a new object for his affections."

Griffith does not hold the German technique [as represented by the films of F. W. Murnau] in awe.

"Motion pictures haven't changed," he declares. "The technique of telling your story varies with passing vogues, but the photoplay remains essentially the same. It has remained unchanged since the Biograph days.

"Yes, I know it has become the custom to say that the Germans are pioneers in a new technique. Why, they are doing the things that we discarded long ago. A certain primitive virility comes of that, but it is absurd to talk of a new technique. They do things long prohibited over here. Mugging, for instance. Long scenes played right at the camera. We did all that in the beginning.

"The fact that this primitive stuff has been dressed up with superb camera work has confused observers. The Germans have a fine mechanical mind. They have perfected the camera. In fact, after the war, we found that they had gone beyond us in cameras and camera equipment. In lighting, too.

"But this new German technique is all bosh. We make better pictures in America. Sacha Guitry, the French playwright-producer, once said that the Biograph film drama revolutionized the stage. The effect of films upon the spoken drama must be obvious to everyone. The Germans haven't revolutionized our screenplay—not yet, anyway."

Griffith has been called a recluse. He was for a time, when collapse confronted him at Mamaroneck. He goes to many films but seldom to screen premieres. His amusement tastes are various. I have seen him dancing happily after the theater. I have seen him enjoying himself as a ringsider at big prize fights. But I have never seen him enjoy himself so completely as he does when he is directing. Griffith says he would like to spend his days in a sailboat on the Chesapeake. But I know he is kidding himself. He likes pictures too much.

Note

1. Arthur Johnson (1876–1916) is a strange, unfathomable choice. Griffith ignores his best known leading men, including Richard Barthelmess, Robert Harron, and Henry B. Walthall, and selects an actor whom he directed at the Biograph Company between 1908 and 1910.

His Best Pictures Were the Least Expensive, Says "D. W."

Tom Waller/1927

From the *Moving Picture World*, September 24, 1927, 232.

"My best pictures were my least expensive pictures."

That's what D. W. Griffith told the writer the other day on the set of *Drums of Love* [1928], this pioneer director's first effort under his renewed affiliation with United Artists.

Broken Blossoms [1919], which he regards as one of the greatest achievements, was lowest of all his pictures in production costs, he said.

Sounding Griffith on Hollywood's economy wave secured this information about his own productions.

That artistry cannot be confined within rigid limitations is one of the reactions this writer got from Griffith's observations between a ham sandwich and a cup of coffee which he was enjoying at a studio luncheon given in his honor, at which members of the press were guests.

Relaxed on a wooden bench, Griffith was allowed to concentrate for a few minutes longer, during which he also told the writer:

"Give the greatest director a bad story and he'll get a lousy picture. The first important thing in making a picture is the author. Upon the author rests 80 per cent of the outcome of the picture at the box-office."

Griffith mentioned one of the last pictures he had made before rejoining United Artists, as a picture that he had made against his will.

"I couldn't even read the script," he said. "I had to lock myself in a room in my attempt to decipher it. A director cannot be expected to make a good picture under such circumstances as this."

Knowing your theme, doing your perspiring before you start shooting, and not attempting to experiment in long European shadows when they are not needed, is Griffith's interpretation of logical production economy.

D. W. Griffith Addresses the Academy of Motion Picture Arts and Sciences

AMPAS Bulletin/1928

From Academy of Motion Picture Arts and Sciences October Bulletin, October 19, 1928, 2–3.

[Many will question the inclusion of this little-known piece in that it is not perhaps an interview. I will argue that it is close to an interview, and too good not to be reprinted here.]

The Directors Branch of the Academy conducted a discussion on talking pictures, at the Hollywood Roosevelt Hotel on Monday night, October 15. Chairman J. Stuart Blackton introduced D. W. Griffith. . . .

Mr. Griffith responded in a somewhat facetious vein, apparently intended as a protest against a predominance of commercialism in motion picture production. He wondered what the Academy was all about, why the high sounding name, and why he should discuss talking pictures, concerning which he knew nothing. He questioned the right of motion pictures to any claim of art and declared the science of the pictures was mostly the science of making money. Therefore, he thought that it should be called a business and not a science or an art. Perhaps, he added, the talking pictures may in time bring true art into this business of quickies and squawks and moans, when the poetry of Keats and Shakespeare and the beauty of the great master painters may be paralleled through something like the theatre medium, with talking pictures produced not for money but solely for beauty and truth. What was needed, he claimed, was a new deal of the cards before the real art can be expected and he ventured to hope that this dream may be brought about by talking pictures.

[After Griffith comments, director William C. de Mille expressed his admiration and respect, but chose to differ. "Mr. Griffith questions the art of the motion picture," said de Mille, "when he, himself, is the one man who has done more to make it an art, than almost anyone else. I don't think he can have looked at his own pictures." Griffith left the meeting after de Mille's remarks, returning to the United Artists studio where he was in the middle of shooting.]

"I hope you did not take my remarks too seriously. I did not take them seriously myself. I wanted to give you something to talk about."

Walter Huston Interviews D. W. Griffith

Walter Huston/1930

From the prologue for the sound reissue of *The Birth of a Nation*, filmed spring 1930.[1]

Walter Huston: Is it generally known that you're a Southerner?

D. W. Griffith (laughs): I should think it should be. It's been advertised enough. Yes, my father was a colonel in the Confederacy.

Walter Huston: Now I want to ask you a question.

D. W. Griffith: Go ahead.

Walter Huston: When you made *The Birth of a Nation*, did you tell your father's story?

D. W. Griffith: No, no, I don't think so. Well, after you mention it, perhaps I did.

Walter Huston: How long did it take you?

D. W. Griffith: How long does it take to make anything. I suppose, oh I suppose, it began when I was a child. I used to get under the table and listen to my father and his friends talk about the battles they'd been through and their struggles. Those things impress you deeply. And I suppose that got into *The Birth*.

Walter Huston: Do you feel as though it were true?

D. W. Griffith: Yes I feel so. True as that blade [of a Confederate sword that Huston presents to Griffith]. That's natural enough, you know. When you've heard your father tell about fighting, day after day, night after night. And having nothing to eat but parched corn. And about your

187

mother staying up night after night, sewing robes for the Klan. The Klan at that time was needed. It served a purpose. Yes, I think it's true. (sighs) But as Pontius Pilate said, "Truth? What is the truth?"

Walter Huston: Well, it has stood the test of time, still considered to be the best picture that was ever made. Does it make you feel proud?
D. W. Griffith: Thank you very much for that. If I thought you really thought it was the best picture ever made, I would be tempted to be a little proud. But I don't know. You never get into those things, you know. You never get into those things, the things that you expect to get, the things you ought to get.

Walter Huston: It has a fury of life in it. I mean, it made your blood tingle.
D. W. Griffith: Well, maybe there was something in it. But I don't think I deserve the credit. It was about something. You can tell easily a story about something. It was about a tremendous struggle. A story of people that were fighting desperately against great odds, great sacrifices. Suffering. Death. It was a great struggle, a great story. A story where young girls used to wear cotton for ermine, and where the boys imagined. Did you read about Pickett's charge at Gettysburg? Pitiful thing. There were boys, like in many a battle. When the fathers dropped the guns, these nothing but children picked them up and went on fighting, and they fought to the bitter end. It's easy enough to tell that kind of a story. All you have to do is . . . Anybody can do that. It's a story in itself . . . that tells itself.

Note

1. It is still in doubt as to whether this prologue was ever actually screened with *The Birth of a Nation*. The sequence begins with three children, Byron Sage, Betty Heisler, and Dawn O'Day (later known as Anne Shirley) creeping up on Griffith and Huston as they talk. Huston presents Griffith with a confederate cavalry sword, and, because it is a "sharp" gift, the director gives him a quarter as payment. As far as can be ascertained, the prologue was actually directed by D. W. Griffith. In a piece titled "The Re-Birth of a Nation" by Campbell MacCulloch, published in *Motion Picture Magazine*, October 1930, Griffith is quoted (page 98) after seeing the new version, "Those were great days . . . That was a great cast. Four of them are passed on to larger things—Bobby Harron, Jennie Lee, George Siegmann, and Wally Reid have gone. And it was a great story. If I could only find such another story and such another cast! But I must not see this picture often— perhaps never but once more. It awakens too many memories."

David Wark Griffith Tells 'Em

Motion Picture Herald/1933

From *Motion Picture Herald*, April 22, 1933, 17.

The business of motion pictures is being run by individuals displaying the mentality of children, according to D. W. Griffith, "old maestro" of production. While scores of executives from both coasts have been fighting the Battle of Hollywood, trying to figure ways and means of putting the industry on a sound operating basis, attempting to solve problems through numerous "conferences," talking about dictators to oversee all production, and physical distribution mergers, the maker of *The Birth of a Nation*, *Way Down East*, and *Intolerance* from his apartment high up in the Park Central Hotel, New York, snaps his fingers and says: "There is only one problem to be considered, drooping box-offices."

Surveying on his right hand the Broadway scene and on his left, a broad expanse of the Jersey shore and the North River, D. W. spoke still with the authority of a master of matters pertaining to the industry, its foibles, and its good and not-so-good points.

Blames Poorly Constructed Stories

"I say that the industry is in the hands of children because they have made no particular steps forward technically since the inception of sound," he declared. "They do not consider their public, and their stories in nine cases out of ten are so badly constructed that if a person happens into the middle of a show he is completely lost. There is no possible way in which he can make head or tail out of the plot, and if he sits through the rest of the bill until the picture starts again, there have been so many disturbing influences in the meantime that it is out of the question for him to pick up the threads of the story from the end, where he started, back to the beginning. It's ridiculous on the face of it. How long would a magazine, which started its stories at the end and worked back to the beginning, survive? What would happen if a theatrical producer decided to start the evening performance with the last act first? The theatre-going public simply wouldn't stand it."

And this, Mr. Griffith believes, is only one of the many problems which have a direct bearing on falling grosses. He feels that the star system should be partly done away with and that ultimately good stories, competently produced and acted, with less emphasis on the players will prove more consistent box-office winners.

"Of course, I realize that stars draw many persons," the producer said, "but the fact remains than in view of the current desire on the part of producers and distributors to readjust the earning power of stars in proportion to lower average grosses, they might well give a little more thought to creating stories in which the players are secondary. By so doing they would partly solve the star problem. How many people today can remember what players appeared in *The Birth of a Nation*, *Hearts of the World*, *Way Down East*, *The Covered Wagon* [1923], *The Big Parade* [1925], *The Four Horsemen of the Apocalypse* [1921], that have taken their place in screen history as among the greatest successes of all time?

All motion picture theatres should present their shows on a time schedule, Mr. Griffith said, as patrons then would be able to see a complete performance without the disturbing influence of interrupted thought. He added that these schedules should be widely publicized in theatre advertising, that it is not the business of the picture patron to find out for himself what time the picture goes on.

Wants Time Schedules Advertised

"This interrupted thought does not apply to musical pictures or comedies where the plot is of minor importance," D. W. said. "But as long as drama is the backbone of the entertainment business, a considerably amount of time and thought should be given to this phase of it. I have stood in front of many theatres and heard people coming out say, 'How miserable motion pictures are getting.' And why do they say it? Simply because they have been unable to assimilate all of the value the picture has to offer."

Mr. Griffith belittled the oft-expressed opinion that, because of the depression, it is impossible for pictures to make big grosses.

"Good pictures will always make money," he said, "and roadshows could be just as successful today as they ever were. Of course, you must have the picture for this, and quite frankly, there hasn't been a single 'legitimate' roadshow attraction in the past two years."

Little Technical Progress, He Says

Asserting that there is an insufficient amount of experimentation in film laboratories today, Mr. Griffith pointed out that it took years to build up the technique of the silent film and that with the inception of sound a completely new technique had to be devised. He feels that the industry has not made much progress in the development of the new art, with due allowance for generally unsettled conditions.

"There should have been a glimmering of a new process of some nature by this time," he declared. "So far there has been none, and with radio an ever-increasing source of competition and worry, it's high time Hollywood began to do something about it. Radio has made gigantic steps forward in every respect, far greater in proportion to the length of its existence than has the motion picture."

Talking of the days when roadshows were reaching the height of popularity, and business all over the country was booming, Mr. Griffith pointed out that *Way Down East* grossed $1,380,000 in the first five and one-half months of its roadshowing. And he is convinced that the same thing can be done today.

"But where, oh where are the stories, the showmen, and the ability to put them across," he asks.

The Star-Maker Whose Dreams Turned to Dust

Mildred Mastin/1934

From *Photoplay*, May 1934, 50–51, 95–97.

[The interviewer here obviously borrows heavily from Frederick James Smith's December 1926 interview in *Photoplay*, "He Might Be the Richest Man in the World."]

At the window of a tall Manhattan hotel, a man stood looking down at Broadway. From the window, twenty-two stories above the street, he watched hundreds of dancing, burning electric signs, screaming the names of movies and their stars.

For twenty years the man had been the outstanding creative genius in motion pictures. He was idle now. Out of the game.

"Movies," he commented slowly, "are written in sand. Applauded today, forgotten tomorrow. Last week the names on the signs were different. Next week they will be changed again."

It was a theatrical statement, made by a man who has a talent for expressing simple truths in a melodramatic way.

The man was David Wark Griffith.

Recently, a columnist wrote that the director is broke, in need. If that is true, Griffith does not admit it. He points with pride to several rare pieces of antique furniture in his apartment; to his library, its walls lined with finely bound books. He speaks casually of a winter vacation in Florida, of the pleasant, leisurely hours he is spending now, rewriting some plays.

Thus, subtly, he denies rumors that he needs financial help. For he is intensely proud.

Griffith should be wealthy today. He is not, because, like most artists, he lacks good business sense.

Many major improvements in picture making were invented or initiated by David Wark Griffith. A clever business man would be collecting royalties. Griffith collects nothing—except occasional praise, when someone is feeling sentimental.

There was a time when motion pictures were jerky, jumping awkwardly from one scene to another. Griffith strove to find a way to smooth them out. He made a little gadget with the top of a cigar-box. And the "fade-out" was born.

Griffith was delighted. Sequences could be ended artistically now, fading out, merging smoothly into the next scene.

"It improved pictures tremendously," he says enthusiastically. Then adds, "I never thought of patenting it."

If he had, the royalties would be running into millions. For the fade-out is used in every picture that is filmed today.

It was Griffith who first conceived the idea of taking a close-up. His rivals and associates thought them very funny—filling the screen with a single face or detail. But they couldn't laugh Griffith down. Perfecting the idea took time and money. Only Griffith believed that the close-up would permit dramatic expression, a still kind of beauty, that movies must have, if they were to exist as an important medium of entertainment. And Griffith was right.

It was Griffith who first gambled on lengthening pictures. In the early days, all pictures were one-reelers. Quick, flashy, too short to tell a story. Griffith decided to make a two-reeler. People thought he was mad! The two-reeler was made.

Exhibitors refused to show it. Finally they put it on—one reel one night, the second reel the next night. That, incidentally, was also the beginning of the serial.

The first picture that might properly be called of epic dimensions was a Griffith gamble—*The Birth of a Nation*. Griffith did not produce this picture because he thought it would make money. (And, of course, he got little money out of it. He doesn't even own the film today.) He planned it because, he says, he wanted to tell the North the truth about the South. As a child he had sat in a Kentucky schoolhouse and read, with bitter resentment, the story of the Civil War, always written by a Northerner. Some day, he promised himself, *he*, a Southerner, would tell the story.

Every important picture that Griffith made was born of a great human impulse. If it was expensive to express the thing he had to say, Griffith did not economize. But he was never extravagant in the spectacular, superficial way that some others have been.

He produced over four hundred films. And the total cost of making them was approximately $12 million. The gross profits from the pictures were five times that—slightly over $60 million. Only a small part of these profits ever found their way back to Griffith. When they did, he usually tossed the money, with reckless courage, into another picture.

The only picture he ever "cleaned up on" was *Way Down East*. It made money, not because it had been cheap to produce, but because it was phenomenally popular. He put tremendous sums of money into the making of it, went heavily into debt. He paid $175,000 for the story, in the first place. Then, with customary care, he insisted on filming it in New England, and waiting for each of the four seasons to roll around so that none of the scenery would need to be faked. The company started to work in the fall. Production continued during the bitter cold New England winter, through spring, and into the summer.

Griffith was rewarded by seeing his picture run for over a year in a Broadway theater at a five dollar top!

In part, his screen glory was due to his canny ability to spot talent.

Two girls came knocking at the door of the old Biograph studio one day to see Gladys Smith—Mary Pickford, of course. Griffith answered the door. The girls were Lillian and Dorothy Gish.

Griffith approached a young man in a theater lobby one night and urged him to go into pictures. The man was Doug[las] Fairbanks.

Once a freckle-faced youngster sneaked into the studio to watch her sister play an extra bit. Griffith saw the girl—plain, unattractively dressed. Her name was Mae Marsh.

Griffith gave Wallace Reid his first chance in *The Birth of a Nation*. He launched Constance Talmadge on her movie career in *Intolerance*.

He noticed an electrician on the set one day, took him off the job and gave him a featured role in a movie. The man was Charles Emmett Mack.

Henry B. Walthall, Miriam Cooper, Carol Dempster, Ralph Graves, Blanche Sweet, Seena Owen, Erich von Stroheim, Richard Barthelmess, Robert Harron, Mildred Harris, Gladys Brockwell—all were Griffith-made stars.

But Griffith never grew rich on these "finds." And the stars, incidentally, rarely found happiness in the success that Griffith gave them. Tragic deaths cut short the careers of four of them—Wallace Reid, Mack,

Gladys Brockwell, and Robert Harron. And sorrows and misfortunes accompanied the others.

Today, a number of the famous people once associated with Griffith have slipped into oblivion or, like the director himself, are living in comparative obscurity, hoping they may still be given a chance to "come back." The exceptional Richard Barthelmess alone among the erstwhile protégés of Griffith has enjoyed uninterrupted movie stardom. The Gish sisters are much better known to the New York stage than to pictures now. Fairbanks and Pickford still are prominent names, of course, but they have been in retirement for lengthy periods in recent years.

For himself, Griffith says he doesn't want to "come back."

"I am tired of movies! To suggest my making another film is like asking a pensioned bricklayer to build another wall."

But his dreams belie words.

And, finally, he admits that he does think of yet another picture of the South. It would be a story of the great Southwest, with romantic, adventurous Sam Houston as the central character.

A pioneer in introducing startling ideas, new developments in pictures making, Griffith now has only one plan for improving pictures. And that, strangely enough, has nothing to do with the producing of movies, but rather with exhibiting them. He wants, by some means, to make sure that everyone who sees a picture, observes it from the beginning. He feels that good feature pictures are carefully built, and that the artistic and dramatic effect is lost when the latter part of the picture is seen first.

In large theaters, Griffith would have a second auditorium where shorts and news reels would be shown to late-comers, while they waited for the next feature showing to begin. The plan is expensive, but Griffith, as usual, is thinking of the artistic effect—not of the money bags!

Griffith is not bitter because others reaped the fortunes that his pictures made. He laughs when he tells you that he worked at Biograph for only fifty dollars a week, because he thought his pictures weren't making money, and afterward discovered that a few men there were cleaning up on his productions. For him the weeks of toil without salary on *The Birth of a Nation* were filled with adventure. And the debt he plunged into to make *Intolerance* was well worth while, because the picture was an outstanding example of cinematic technique.

So now a columnist has written that David Wark Griffith is broke, in need. Certainly, many of the brilliant names, once associated with his, are forgotten. And his old movie masterpieces, when run off on the new and faster modern projectors, jump and flicker foolishly [being shown at the incorrect speed].

His glory is in the past.

Griffith knows that. He wishes they wouldn't revive his pictures. He wishes editors wouldn't speak grandly of his past productions as "works of art."

"They aren't!" he says. And adds dramatically, "When motion pictures have created something to compare with the plays of Euripides, or the work of Homer or Shakespeare or Ibsen, or the music of Handel or Bach, then let us call motion picture entertainment an art—but not before then."

Film Master Is Not Proud of Films: "They Do Not Endure"

Daily Express/1935

From [London] *Daily Express*, May 24, 1935.

"I am prouder that a magazine printed a two-verse poem of mine, for which they paid me fifteen dollars, many years ago, than I am of any film I have made."

So says great director, conversationalist, and arch-sentimentalist Griffith, who reached the Savoy [Hotel, London] from far places last night.

"The movie is not an art," says Griffith. "It is a beautiful business. So transient it cannot endure for a year. Why, the greatest films of the greatest masters of movie, made five years ago, shown today look ridiculous. I haven't made a film myself that can endure. Words, painting, sculpture last."

It is three years since the greatest made a picture. When he goes to the cinema now, which is rarely, he finds that the masters of the talkie art are just creeping up to the standard of photographic ingenuity again that he had perfected a decade ago. Talk has made the whole thing so simplified.

He has come to London to see about the making of his famous silent film *Broken Blossoms* into a modern talkie. He doesn't know as yet whether he will direct it himself.

"After all," says [Griffith], "a shadow's a shadow . . ."

D. W. Griffith Tells Plans Which Include Picture Making

Grace Kingsley/1936

From the *Los Angeles Times*, March 14, 1936, A7. Copyright © 1936, *Los Angeles Times*. Reprinted with Permission.

To interview D. W. Griffith, giant of the films of other days, is also to interview his lovely young bride [Evelyn Baldwin]! And she is a charming chatelaine to any interview.

And so it was while smiling down on her, in their suite at the Ambassador [Hotel], and telling her to "run away and put on the red shoes, because they match your red neck bow," that we got under way as to his future plans.

Looking in the very pink of condition, it is easy to believe that the famous pioneer is quite ready to undertake new enterprises, but he declares that "never again will I film any story in which I do not believe, though I had to do it a few years ago in order to complete a contract."

"But I shall," he went on, "make pictures again, either here or in England. The reason I didn't make *Broken Blossoms* in England was because I could not find a proper cast without waiting perhaps for months. It would not have been easy to replace Dick Barthelmess, Lillian Gish, and Donald Crisp. Besides, I'll confess, critics, including Hannen Swaffer [at that time with the *Daily Herald*], dissuaded me, saying that people carried the old picture in their memories, and that even if I made a better picture in the talking version, they would always say it was not as good.

"I have been asked to remake *The Birth of a Nation* as a talker, but frankly I'm scared, and for the same reasons. How could I replace Mae Marsh and Henry Walthall? Besides the old silent film is still running."

Radio, too, is calling Griffith, but he seems not to have warmed much to it. His heart, it is plain to be seen, is still with pictures, although he did several weeks of radio in New York last year.

Asked what was needed to bring pictures back nearer to the hearts of the public—that nearness to which Griffith himself was the first to bring them—he answered diplomatically and obliquely.

Repeating Not Good

"One reason I got out of the business was because I found myself repeating formulas, instead of getting life and real human beings into my pictures. I got out of it all to study life. That is the great thing—humanity— that is the thing that can never be exhausted, and you must take time to drink at that fountain to really create anything worthwhile. There are only five or six plots, to be sure, but life itself—men and women—they are inexhaustible sources of live, breathing story material. A director must stop awhile to get back to life. While I was in the South, I went into courtrooms and took notes, just in order to get the kind of talk that people really talk when it comes out of their vital experiences. I lived with the country folks.

"And when I married," he went on, with another smile at Mrs. Griffith, "I married a regular little home girl instead of an actress! And we were wed by the presiding elder in the Methodist Church!"

Mrs. Griffith is a dainty demi-blonde, with a quiet little sense of humor. She very much resembles Claire Windsor.

Asked concerning their romance, Griffith declared he met the present Mrs. Griffith ten years ago, when she was not much more than a child, at a charity bazaar in New York, with her mother, "making a pretty picture as they sat on the side-lines, holding hands. A friend introduced us then and there, and I was invited down to their Long Island home. The friendship with the whole family has persisted ever since. But I came near losing my chance of getting into the family once. That was when I cooked a Southern dish for dinner when I was at their home! I got excited and put too much pepper in it. But Mrs. Griffith proved equal to the strain, and I managed to ingratiate myself again!"

Speaking of Charlie Chaplin's reported marriage and also of his latest picture, Griffith declared that he admired Paulette Goddard very much, and liked her performance [in *Modern Times*] because it reminded him of those of his heroines!

"How marvelously efficient your studios out here are!" he exclaimed.

"And how grand! You know the first studio I handled here, the old Biograph, consisted of a few yards of reflector cloth. Big financial problems bothered me in those days—I had to pay Mary Pickford $25 a week and Lionel Barrymore $7.50 a day!"

Return of a Master

Herb Sterne/1939

From the *New York Times*, September 3, 1939, X4. Copyright © 1939 Herb Sterne. Reprinted with permission of Anthony Slide, executor of estate of Herb Sterne.

Frantically manufacturing new gods for public worship, Hollywood soon forgets the names of the haloed ones of yesterday. Several weeks ago a terse item, relegated to the subsequent pages of the daily press, announced that "D. W. Griffith, director of silent films, has been signed as supervisor by Hal Roach." No adjectives. No fanfare. Ignored was the fact that the motion picture, as we know it today, was founded and developed by Griffith. Overlooked were the technical devices—the close-up, the flash-back, the moving camera shot, narrative story-telling on the screen—which he introduced. Of no seeming interest to any one was his gift for star-making or the fact that among the players he developed were Mary Pickford, the Gish girls, Robert Harron, Blanche Sweet, Henry [B.] Walthall, Douglas Fairbanks, Mae Marsh, Rudolph Valentino.

Almost completely slighted by columnists employed in recording film news were Griffith's great classics, *The Birth of a Nation*, *Intolerance*, *Way Down East*, and *Broken Blossoms*, pictures that pleased millions and made millions. Drama lurks behind the return of Griffith to Allied Artists, an organization which he helped found in the days when his name was a synonym for directorial greatness.

Back in 1920 he started the company with Pickford, Chaplin, and Fairbanks. They were known as "The Big Four." Success at first with such hits as *Orphans of the Storm*, *Way Down East*, and *Hearts of the World*; then financial reverses, and Griffith was forced to sell out his interest. Quick and complete oblivion followed. Now after eight years of retirement, the master is attempting a comeback with the same organization, but this time as a humble employee.

There was no difficulty getting past the gate of the Roach studios, but once inside, there was difficulty in locating Mr. Griffith. His name was unlisted on the board dedicated to studio employees of importance. "Griffith?" People on the lot couldn't place the name. However, the publicity office found him readily enough, on the top floor of the same building.

In a single, one-room office, the old master sat hunched in a swivel chair. His official age is 59, which he looks. He twiddled the same type of Panama hat made familiar by photographs taken during the years of his great success, but his hair has grayed, grown sparse. On seeing me enter he tilted back in his chair, placed his feet, encased in high brown shoes with brass eyelets, on the desk. The sole of the right shoe frankly gaped.

Griffith talks in a tired voice that still retains a trace of the blue grass of Kentucky, his native state. There is more than a hint of weary philosophy in his words. He is still consumingly interested in motion pictures: the man who started working in them at the old Biograph studios in 1908 still considers the filming of a super-colossal [production] the most important thing in the world.

Since his retirement, Griffith has been writing. An autobiography is just about complete. He has also written a number of stage plays, as yet unproduced. "Maybe," he comments, "not the best plays in the world, but there have been bad ones before." He smiled and shrugged his shoulders.

"A number of people think it strange that I should write plays. I started as a stage actor. I also was the first to use dialogue in a feature film. That was in *Dream Street*, released in 1921. The recording was on discs, like the early Vitaphone. *Dream Street* opened at the Town Hall in New York replete with passages of talk and even a theme song recorded by the Kellum process.[1] We had to 'dub in' the vocalizing, for [leading man] Ralph Graves couldn't sing. I tried to sell the idea of talking pictures to Adolph Zukor as I didn't have enough money to finance the project myself. Zukor told me I was crazy."

Of the two all-talking films Griffith made he only cares to mention *Abraham Lincoln*, starring Walter Huston. In that he feels he did a good job of balancing speech and action. As a matter of fact, it was the first audible film that managed to capture the fluid quality of the silent medium. *The Struggle* Griffith would as soon forget. Never generally released, it was taken off after a two-day run on Broadway and shelved. "No use," he commented, "in going in for alibis. If a picture hasn't the stuff no amount of explanation will help."

Griffith's biggest hit was the unforgettable *The Birth of a Nation*, which was shot in a little over two months and cost $110,000. To date it has grossed $16 million, and although made in 1914 is still being shown. His pet picture of them all, however, is *Intolerance,* an expensive venture, an artistic success, but a staggering financial flop. It was the first sociological picture to be produced in America. Griffith, despite its lack of public approval, followed it with other humanitarian sagas, including the story of postwar Germany, *Isn't Life Wonderful.* Today he is no disciple of the "message" on the screen. Only casually interested in the worth of such subject-matter as *Of Mice and Men* and *The Grapes of Wrath* as fodder for celluloid, he contends that though most of his pictures were harangues, he believes, primarily, in entertainment. "A good story is a good story, no matter what it's about."

"Producers complain of low picture grosses today. Films have had such cycles before. I honestly don't believe that the radio and the motor car have robbed us of the public's attention. In the old days the bicycle, vaudeville, and the stage were still competition. When a picture comes along that is good enough to arouse comment people will rush to see it, depression or no depression. Pictures need more actual backgrounds, less process work which lends an air of unreality. The audience must believe what it is seeing. And the picture business needs more young blood, youngsters with a sense of adventure and the spirit of experiment."

The telephone rang. Griffith answered. "It's the projection room. They're going to run *Topper Takes a Trip* for me. Guess they'd like me to take a look at what present-day screen magic is like." We walked down the stairs together; shook hands.

Griffith continued to the projection room. His head was bent forward, his shoulders were bowed, the spring gone from his step. The studios of today are vastly different from those of the 'teens and twenties. The come-back trail is a difficult road to ascend. Particularly when one has been a god.

Note

1. Developed by Orlando E. Kellum in 1913; Griffith's introduction to *Dream Street* is preserved at the UCLA Film and Television Archive.

Griffith Back to Live Here "for Half Century"

James Warnak/1944

From the *Los Angeles Times*, April 17, 1944, 9. Copyright © 1944, *Los Angeles Times*. Reprinted with Permission.

"Winston Churchill and the late Gabriel D'Annunzio are the smartest scenario writers I ever met," said David Wark Griffith, producer of [*The*] *Birth of a Nation* and other cinema classics in an interview yesterday at the Roosevelt Hollywood [Hotel], at which he and Mrs. Griffith are guests.

"Unfortunately, I could not produce either the story outlined to me by Mr. Churchill in 1917, nor the one offered by the Italian poet," said Mr. Griffith. "Their production would have cost more money than I had at the time. Besides, Churchill's story contained too much thought, while D'Annunzio, then in his sixties, wanted to act the hero in his play."

Here for Fifty Years More

Looking almost as young as he did when he was producing his spectacular silent dramas here thirty years ago, Mr. Griffith, who, incidentally, produced the first sound film ever made in New York, has come to Los Angeles to live "the next half century of my life."

Mr. Griffith has not lived in Los Angeles for the past "ten or twelve years, although I visited here four years ago," he said. "I haven't had any permanent home during that time but have been traveling around the country. You see," he added, "I like to travel."

Douglas MacArthur's Age

"How old are you now, Mr. Griffith?"

"Same age as Douglas MacArthur," he replied. "One of my aunts lived to be 112, and an uncle topped a hundred years, so I see no reason why I shouldn't stick around another fifty years. Poor old uncle! An irreconcilable Southern gentleman! He has never written to me since I produced *Abraham Lincoln* . . ."

"To what do you attribute your health, Mr. Griffith?"

"'The good die young, while those whose hearts are dry as summer's dust burn in the socket,'" quoted the dean of producers. "Seriously, one secret is maintaining an interest in life, developing the capacity to live in the past, the present, and the future. My main object just now is to finish a novel I began when I was eighteen. On the side I hope to write a few plays."

Tomorrow's Pictures

"What about motion pictures of tomorrow?"

"They'll continue to be bad," he answered laughing. "Oh, perhaps, they'll make a few good ones,"

"What is a good picture?"

"One that makes the public forget its troubles," he replied. "Also, a good picture tends to make folks think a little, without letting them suspect that they are being inspired to think. In one respect, nearly all pictures are good in that they show the triumph of good over evil."

Human Mind Must Change

"How about war—when will it end?" asked the interviewer.

"If I were the Almighty I might be able to tell you—but probably wouldn't," said Mr. Griffith. "Of course this war will end, but wars never will cease until human beings change their dispositions."

"And when will that be?"

"Perhaps within the next twenty thousand years," he said. "Don't be impatient. Humanity has only been civilized or half civilized for about five thousand years. We're still infants, morally and spiritually. Give the poor human race a little time."

"Cinema's Fullest Scope Still Ahead"—D. W. Griffith

Fred W. Fox/1947

From *Hollywood Citizen News*, May 7, 1947, 11, 12.

David Wark Griffith, who made what is probably the most ambitious mistake in motion picture history, also gave to the world the most memorable of all films, *The Birth of a Nation*, which many authorities claim is the greatest money-making photoplay ever produced. Gross of *The Birth*, estimated as high as $48 million since it was first screened more than thirty years ago, no doubt is the largest return per dollar invested in cinema annals, since its production cost was only $90,000.

The "mistake," however, was not *The Birth of a Nation*, but the fourteen-reel spectacle *Intolerance* that followed. The "mistake" was that Griffith made *Intolerance* in 1915 instead of three decades later. He was ahead of his time.

Griffith told me about *Intolerance* the other afternoon in his Beverly Hills home. Among the 320 pictures he has made since 1909, it is the one that seems to have the strongest hold upon his memories, perhaps because it was an ugly duckling, financially, for him. He almost lost his shirt over it, but more astute businessmen who inherited it coined handsome profits. When it was reissued ten years after it was produced, it won acclaim from the public that had at first been denied, except by a few discerning critics.

Implications Unrealized

Those among us of an older generation who felt the impact of the early Griffith movies when they were first shown and who have nurtured a sentimental remembrance of them, may not have realized then the implications of *Intolerance*. We were overwhelmed by its dramatic sweep and the vastness of its staging.

Yet there was something beyond pictorial grandeur that made *Intolerance* significant and too advanced for its day. The movies' novelty still held a public not ready for the story of *Intolerance*. Ten years later was a more propitious time, and today's audiences might have made it a success from the outset.

Documentary films, so much in vogue today, were paced by *Hearts of the World*, a Griffith film of the World War I period that had many authentic scenes made on French battlefields. The picture dramatically pointed up the battle against Kaiserism, as modern films have depicted the war against totalitarianism. Griffith's films did much to spearhead global supremacy for American movies. They were seen by millions who had never heard a word of English spoken.

D. W., an inveterate screen fan, sees an average of four pictures a week. He doesn't dwell in the past and his thinking isn't dated. He does believe, however, that talkies are in their infancy; that they have not yet bridged the gap between silent film skills and talkie technology.

"Moral Obligation"

"Talkies have not yet achieved the rhythm, the movement and flow of the silent drama," he observed. "The perfect blending of the silents' effortless storytelling and the effectiveness of sound and dialogue is yet to be attained.

"The industry has a moral obligation to turn out a few films that are wholly artistic, without thought of the box-office. This is not too heavy a burden for some of our prospering film companies to assume, and I feel that in the long run it will prove profitable for them.

"Talkie dialogue has encroached too much upon acting and cinematography. Beautiful lines are well spoken by players, but expressions of faces and bodies too often are not reflective of the words uttered. In the silents, thoughts were photographed. Now, there is a tendency to photograph dialogue and movement too much," Griffith stated.

"The cinema is the ideal medium, compared to the stage. Movies have a world-wide scope for settings, but they need poetry and beauty after the idea of Keats. Beautiful scenery, slow tempo, careful creation of musical settings are some requisites."

Large Casts No Boon

"Except by dialogue, you cannot put a battle between two nations on the stage. You can portray the world on film, so why waste so much of pictures' potentialities by confining them to studios? Even in the battle between human ethics, the stage is limited, but the cinema can run the whole gamut without hindrance.

"Yet breadth to use large casts of actors is no special boon for films. You can have millions of people, but they are of no avail without a story and the people who can tell the story," D. W. asserted.

He feels that the present apathy of audiences needs to be "cured" by a return of pictures that stir people.

Forty-Seven Questions from Seymour Stern to D. W. Griffith

Seymour Stern/1947

November 25, 1947. Copyright and reprinted with permission of Ira Gallen.

[On November 25, 1947, Seymour Stern prepared a list of forty-seven typewritten questions for D. W. Griffith, and recorded his replies in longhand. Many times, the director has no answer, other times, the response is well-known and not worthy of record. I have listed the questions with the most interesting or unusual responses.]

What was your boyhood like? Was it a happy one?
Very happy.

Was it entirely spent in La Grange and Louisville?
House was on stock farm—was in country, not in La Grange itself. About eighteen miles from Louisville, seven or eight from La Grange village on a rural turnpike. Best farm in Oldham County. Worth $30,000 today. At thirteen, went Louisville for first time.

Did you go to public (grammar) school?
Passed exam for second year high school, but didn't go. . . . Chief intellectual influences: father and moreso the sisters.

Apart from school, what was the chief cultural and intellectual diet of (a) your boyhood, (b) your youth?
Literary evenings and literary societies. Shakespeare, Dickens, Thackeray, Keats, Tennyson, and the other English poets. Especially *Pickwick Papers*.

When did you go with the stock company? Names some places?
Jeffersonville, Indiana, and small towns.

When and with what company did you try again in the theatre?
In about '97 or '98, returned to Louisville and soon after joined Meffert
Stock Company. Oscar Wilde and popular plays from New York. Oscar
Eagle and Esther Lyon, Robert and Ralph Cummings [were principals in-
volved]. Robert fired D. W., but next day Lyon took over the company
and when Eagle returned, D. W. was restored. In '99, D. W. went to Chi-
cago for a few weeks with Eagle's own company and played lead role in
Abraham Lincoln.

When and why did you leave Biograph?
1912 [incorrect]. He wanted ten percent of profits. J. J. Kennedy of Empire Trust Co. told Griffith he, D. W., was only a "cog in the machine."

Year, date and place of your meeting with Linda Arvidson?
Met Linda in 1905 or '06 in San Francisco, where he was playing in Market Street Stock Company, probably run by [David] Belasco. Linda was an
actress, but not in D. W.'s troupe.

Marriage did not last?
Date of separation is 1911. Professional incompatibility.

When did you meet H. E. Aitken?
Right after he left Biograph. Aitken got in touch. He was a promoter
then, not yet a producer.

When did you first meet Thomas Dixon?
He had played about 1907 in one of Dixon's plays. Dixon went along
with traveling company. D. W. knew him well.

Where did you live in Los Angeles while you were directing (a) *The Birth
of a Nation*; (b) *Intolerance*; and (c) *Hearts of the World*?
Alexandria Hotel. Had a corner suite. Kid McCoy came down to help
D. W. in trim boxing.

How much part, if any, did Thomas Dixon have in filming *The Birth of a
Nation*?
None. Never saw production. Was in East during shooting.

What were the terms of your financial arrangement with Epoch regarding your share of the profits from *The Birth of a Nation*?
D. W. was to get forty percent of the profits, but was talked into accepting twenty-two percent.

Who helped finance *The Birth of a Nation*?
[W. H.] Clune put in $15,000; stock was sold in Pasadena and L.A.

Who financed *Broken Blossoms*?
Famous Players put up $80,000; U.A. bought if from Famous Players for $250,000. Production itself entirely independent.

Flash-Back to Griffith

Ezra Goodman/1948

From *PM*, May 19, 1948, M12-M13.

[This interview was reprinted in a different format as part of Ezra Goodman's *The Fifty-Year Decline and Fall of Hollywood*, New York: Simon and
Schuster, 1961. On page 12 of the book, Goodman notes that the interview was rejected by one editor after another, from *Harper's* to the *New
York Times* as too "rough." It was eventually accepted by Ed McCarthy,
Sunday editor of *PM* and published as a lead article. On April 1, 1948, Seymour Stern wrote to Goodman that Griffith was "much pleased with it. I
rushed over with it to the hotel at noon, and at his request read it aloud.
The old man chuckled and laughed; then when he found his eyeglasses,
which had fallen under the couch, he read the whole thing through
himself. He told me to express his great appreciation to you."]

David Wark Griffith, the father of films, the maker of *The Birth of a Nation, Intolerance, Broken Blossoms*, and *Way Down East*, sat in a hotel room
overlooking the heart of Hollywood. He sat in an easy chair, attired in
pajamas and a patterned maroon dressing gown, his lordly aquiline features surmounted by sparse white hair. Standing about the room were
several trunks. On one of them reposed Griffith's floppy felt hat, against
it leaned his cane. In the kitchen stood two large cans of film containing
a rare, good print [presumably 16mm] of the twelve reels of *Orphans of the
Storm*, his successful silent epic of the French Revolution, made in 1922
with Lillian and Dorothy Gish and Joseph Schildkraut.

D. W., as he is called, picked up a double gin at his side and said in his
rhythmical, resounding speech:

"I am seventy-three years of age. I can say anything I want about Hollywood. You can print anything you please. What's the difference? I
don't give a hoot what anyone says about me.

"I was a reporter once myself. You know, they will not print any of this. But I don't care. I am seventy-three years old and I can say anything I like about the movie business.

"It's all nostalgia. I would love to be again at 44th and Broadway and love again to see George M. Cohan walking down the street. I would love again to see that. But most of all I would love to see John and Lionel Barrymore crossing the street as they used to be, when they were young and full of youth and vitality, going to a Broadway theater. They'd stop traffic, arm in arm, when they were young, in the blessed days when they were young."

D. W. sat down his glass on an endtable. The room faced out on a shadowy alleyway in the early evening. The [Knickerbocker] Hotel was one block from the crossroads of the cinema city at Hollywood and Vine. An internationally known giant of the screen, Griffith has not made a movie since 1931. Though library shelves are weighed down with books, monographs, and magazine and newspaper articles about him, he lives a secluded and practically unnoticed existence in the Hollywood he largely helped to create.

"There is a dreadful sameness in the sunshine out here" said D. W. "I love the rain and the sun. I love the change of seasons. I would love to be in New York again. The most brainless people in all the world live in Southern California. No one here has any brains except he comes from the East. But, for certain financial reasons, I am exiled from New York.

"When I first went to New York—I was spoiled in my youth: I had my first poem, better say 'verse,' and my first play and story published at the same time. . . . I thought I was a great genius. That was a lot of baloney. Today nobody is interested in D. W. Griffith. I don't kid myself. They don't know who I am."

The Wolf of Poverty

"*D. W. Griffith and the Wolf*—that's my autobiography—it's lousy. I stopped writing it after eighty or ninety pages and I don't know where it is now.[1] *The Wolf* is poverty. Nothing is so sad as poverty. My story would be the story of a fellow who is very poor, whose family lost all its money. In Louisville, Ky. Now, that's a story—not the young fellow becomes a cheap ham actor and makes a fortune which he loses. That's what they might be interested in, but not in D. W. Griffith who once made movies."

Obviously, he has never seen the jam in the Museum of Modern Art's theater whenever his pictures, enshrined in the museum's film library, are shown.

Further evidence that interest in him continues is that his life is being written by Seymour Stern, film critic and Griffith's disciple, who is three-quarters through a 1800-page biography entitled *Griffith*, which he has been assembling for eight years.[2] Stern's authoritative *An Index to the Creative Work of David Wark Griffith*, will soon be published by Harcourt, Brace.[3] Sidney Skolsky,[4] who produced *The Jolson Story*, has an option to do the Griffith film biography. Skolsky believes that Griffith has been largely neglected by Hollywood and that his story would be the story of the movies, of Hollywood itself.

Stern, who is Preston Sturges's story editor, accompanied this interviewer to see Griffith. D. W. is rarely accessible to either reporters or anyone else. Occasionally, he can be seen promenading down Hollywood Boulevard, his tall, lean figure crowned with the battered hat and sporting the perennial cane, moving unrecognized through the pedestrian traffic as he gazes into shop windows.

At the other end of Hollywood Boulevard, at another hotel,[5] lives Mack Sennett, the famed king of custard pies in the silent slapstick days of the screen. Sennett is also "retired" from moviemaking and lives modestly and quietly. Sometimes the two men encounter each other on the boulevard. Griffith gave Sennett his first job as an actor at the old Biograph Studio on 14th Street in New York about forty years ago.

This interview was obtained after a good deal of effort by the expedient of slipping a note under the door of Griffith's hotel room. He was not acknowledging telephone calls and his mail box was crammed with three weeks' letters. He finally got on the phone and agreed to be interviewed after some persuasion on the part of Stern and the writer, who had spoken to him some years previous. After a while he warmed up to the idea of an interview.

"I never read a letter or answer a telephone," he said. "If it's important, they get to you. I go out sometimes to see movies. I haven't seen a picture in some time now. The best pictures I did were not popular. The lousy one, like *The Birth of a Nation*, only a cheap melodrama, were popular, and *Way Down East*—they got three dollars for that one in New York, about a girl floating over Niagara Falls and being rescued.

"I think *The Miracle of Morgan's Creek* [1944] is the greatest comedy I have ever seen in a long time. I saw *Gone with the Wind* twice and thought it better than *The Birth of a Nation*—not really, of course. I saw *The Seventh Veil* four times.[6] That [James] Mason is a great actor. *It's a Wonderful Life*

[1946] was a piece of cheese, *Duel in the Sun* [1946] a good melodrama. *The Best Years of Our Lives* [1946] just okay. *My Darling Clementine* [1946] lovely. The best directors today are Leo McCarey, Frank Capra, and Preston Sturges, the best actors Spencer Tracy and Lionel Barrymore, and the daintiest, sultry-eyed beauty that Russell girl—not Jane, but Gail.

"I loved *Citizen Kane* [1941] and particularly loved the ideas he (Orson Welles) took from me. The various cycles, the goddam German pictures. I loved them all. I could see all the stuff they stole from me, because being very modest—George Bernard Shaw said any man who pretends to be modest is a darn fool. No one is modest. I am the only producer on stage and screen who knew Plato and the Vedic hymn[s], the first religioso published,[7] the Talmud, too."

Branded Racial and Dangerous

"You can print anything you please. What's the difference? I'm seventy-three years old. This Washington business, the investigation [the House Committee on Un-American Activities], that's a lot of baloney. I was called a Communist myself in my youth, when *Intolerance* was branded radical and dangerous. It's an old idea. All this stuff gives me a pain in the neck. I wrote *The Rise and Fall of Free Speech in America* to answer my critics. The movies should have the same freedom of speech as the press. There should be no censorship. According to the Constitution, you are allowed to say anything you please, but you are responsible for your speech and conversation by law and may be punished. No one is really allowed to say what he pleases."

Griffith, a titan of the screen in his time, earned big money as well as world-wide artistic prestige. His best pictures, like *Intolerance*, embodied a boldness of technique and a moral fervor almost entirely absent from the screen today.

Scholars and critics alike call Griffith's work "the greatest single contribution toward the development of the motion picture." He took the storytelling line Edwin S. Porter employed in *The Great Train Robbery* [1903] and gave it humanity, realism, and unusual technique. Griffith was the first to exploit the close-up, the flash-back, and cross-cutting extensively. He did not hesitate to cut from a contemporary scene to ancient times and back again to tell his story. This plus his sense of pageantry, his use of a thousand or more extras to recreate history in dramatic grandeur, broadened the movie medium and influenced other moviemakers.

Used Documentary Technique

Griffith is credited also with having been one of the first to recognize the possibilities of the semi-documentary technique used in current films like *The Search* [1948], *Naked City* [1948], *The Kiss of Death* [1947], *Call Northside 777* [1948] and *Boomerang!* [1947]. For his *Isn't Life Wonderful*, a story of post–World War I Germany, he took a troupe of Hollywood actors to actual German locations. His *Dream Street*, made in 1924, three years before *The Jazz Singer*,[8] was one of the first talking pictures. *Dream Street* used the [Orlando] Kellum process in which a phonograph behind the screen synchronized dialogue with the action to give the illusion of [stars] Ralph Graves and Carol Dempster singing. His last film, *The Struggle*, produced in 1931, was a violently realistic film about the evils of liquor in a slum setting that makes *The Lost Weekend* [1945] look like cinematic near beer. The picture received poor critical notices and Griffith has not worked in the movies since then. His wife [Evelyn Baldwin] divorced him last year and he lives alone today.

Money has always been a bother to Griffith. He lost the fortune he had made from *The Birth of a Nation* on *Intolerance*, because he believed in the latter's message of good will toward men. *Intolerance* was a box office failure, but is today recognized as a milestone in the history of motion pictures. When the Alexandria Hotel in Los Angeles, where Griffith had lived when he first came to Hollywood, went bankrupt and was gone over by auditors, a packet marked *D. W. Griffith—Personal* was found in one of the vaults with $26,000 in cash that he had completely forgotten. Recently, Griffith's lawyer brought him a check for $3,000, representing certain income. The check was never deposited and was apparently thrown out with the wastepaper.

Atom on Tail of a Louse

Griffith leaned back. "It is my ambition to see *The Treadmill* produced," he said. "It's a play that I have been writing over the years. It is so beautiful, it is too good for anyone to see. It is a story of the beginning of life to the end of life. It is a play about the earth and solar system, with the idea of eternal recurrence. I began it when I was eighteen or nineteen. It says the universe is nothing but foredoomed to annihilation, of the essence of dust. It is the greatest dream any man has had, ah, the superb egotism of this old man in a cheap hotel.

"It says that no man is God, but woman, the poor mother of the skies, and she has an ugly duckling running around her backyard and she is worried because the great son, Orsus, is streaming through the skies, streaming fecundity, for twice 3,000 trillion miles. And then all the little planets are drinking up the fecundity and each little planet is revolving and re-revolving through the great Heavens. And then the poor mother wonders and says, 'Where is my great son lost in the depth of eternity?' And then she finds one of the little planets, a trio of little ducklings, lost, a little duckling—his name was Earth—the ugliest duckling of them all—Earth, an atom on the tail part of a louse.

"There has been no improvement in the movies since the old days," D. W. Griffith from his easy chair. "We did Browning and Keats then, *Pippa Passes*. Today you don't dare do those things. Imagine anyone doing Browning today. They have not improved in stories. I don't know that they've improved in anything.

"What the modern movie lacks is beauty—the beauty of moving wind in the trees, the little movement in a beautiful blowing on the blossoms in the trees. That they have forgotten entirely. They have forgotten that no still painting—not the greatest ever—was anything but a pallid still picture. But the moving picture! Today they have forgotten movement in the moving picture. It is still and stale. The moving picture is beautiful, the moving of wind on beautiful trees is more beautiful than a painting. Too much today depends on the voice. I loved talking pictures properly done. Sometimes the talk is good, often very bad. We have taken beauty and exchanged it for stilted voices.

"In my arrogant belief," said D. W., "we have lost beauty."

Notes

1. Edited and annotated by James Hart, who had worked with Griffith as a ghostwriter on the autobiography, published as *The Man Who Invented Hollywood: The Autobiography of D. W. Griffith* (Louisville, Ky.: Touchstone Publishing Company, 1972).

2. Seymour Stern (1917–2009) was, arguably, the most fanatical of Griffith's followers.

3. *An Index to the Creative Work* of David Wark Griffith was published in four sections as a special supplement to *Sight and Sound* by the British Film Institute between April 1944 and May 1947. The series is incomplete in that it ends with *Hearts of the World*.

4. Sidney Skolsky (1905–1983) is best remembered as a Hollywood columnist who claimed to have invented the term "Oscar" for the Academy Award. He produced two biographical film, *The Jolson Story* (1946) and *The Eddie Cantor Story* (1953).

5. The Garden Court Apartments.

6. The Seventh Veil, a 1945 British film, directed by Compton Bennett, and starring James Mason, Ann Todd, and Herbert Lom. It is surprising that Griffith should have seen it, let alone singled it out for commentary.

7. Hindu texts.

8. Actually, *Dream Street* was released in 1921, and *The Jazz Singer* in 1927.

The Writings of D. W. Griffith

[The 1929 *Motion Picture News Blue Book*, p. 85, contains a full-page advertisement, listing four "signed stories" by D. W. Griffith, available for sale, "The Motion Picture—Today and Tomorrow," 2200 words; "How the Movies Are Made," 1500 words; "From Nickelodeon to Picture Palace," 1500 words; and "The Future of Motion Pictures," 1500 words.]

"The Motion Picture and Witch Burners" and "The Future of the Two-Dollar Movie," promotional, syndicated pieces publicizing *The Birth of a Nation*, reprinted in Fred Silva, ed., *Focus on The Birth of a Nation*, Englewood Cliffs, N.J.: Prentice-Hall, 1971, pp. 96–101.

"*The Birth of a Nation* Controversy," a letter dated April 6 to the editor, *New York Globe*, April 9, 1915. [reprinted in Fred Silva, ed., *Focus on The Birth of a Nation*, Englewood Cliffs, N.J.: Prentice-Hall, 1971, pp. 77–78]

"Defense of *The Birth of a Nation* and Attack on the Sullivan Bill," *Boston Journal*, April 26, 1915. [reprinted in Fred Silva, ed., *Focus on The Birth of a Nation*, Englewood Cliffs, N.J.: Prentice-Hall, 1971, pp. 88–90]

The Rise and Fall of Free Speech in America. Los Angeles: The Author, 1916. [reprinted Hollywood, Calif.: Larry Edmunds Book Shop, 1967]

"Pictures vs. One-Night Stands," *Independent*, December 11, 1916, pp. 447–48. [reprinted in Harry M. Geduld, ed., *Focus on D. W. Griffith*, Englewood Cliffs, N.J.: Prentice-Hall, 1971]

"Where Griffith Got His Clouds for *Intolerance*," Philadelphia *Evening Public Ledger*, December 30, 1916, p. 5.

"What I Demand of Movie Stars," *Motion Picture Classic*, February 1917, pp. 40–41, 68. [reprinted in Harry M. Geduld, *Focus on D. W. Griffith*, Englewood Cliffs, N.J.: Prentice-Hall, 1971]

"Griffith in London," *Moving Picture World*, May 26, 1917, p. 1270. [transcript of Griffith's speech at London opening of *Intolerance*]

"Mr. Griffith's Great Speech against Censorship," *Exhibitors Trade Review*, April 16, 1921, p. 1781. [a complete transcript of speech in oppo-

sition to censorship delivered at a legislative hearing in Albany, N.Y.,
on April 5, 1921]

"Motion Pictures: The Miracle of Modern Photography," *The Mentor*,
July 1, 1921, pp. 2–12.

"Youth, the Spirit of the Movies," *Illustrated World*, October 1921, pp.
194–96. [reprinted in Harry M. Geduld, ed., *Focus on D. W. Griffith*,
Englewood Cliffs, N.J.: Prentice-Hall, 1971]

"Are Motion Pictures Destructive of Good Taste?," *Arts and Decoration*,
September 1923, pp. 12–13, 79. [reprinted in Harry M. Geduld, ed., *Focus on D. W. Griffith*, Englewood Cliffs, N.J.: Prentice-Hall, 1971]

"The Real Truth about Breaking into the Movies," *Woman's Home Companion*, February 1924, pp. 16, 138.

"The Movies 100 Years from Now," *Collier's*, May 3, 1924, pp. 7, 28. [reprinted in Harry M. Geduld, ed., *Film Makers on Film Making*, Bloomington: Indiana University Press, 1967, and *Boxoffice*, May 1994, pp.
14–16]

"Pace in the Movies," *Liberty*, November 13, 1926, pp. 19, 21. [reprinted in
Liberty, Spring 1975, pp. 28–30]

"The Greatest Theatrical Force," *Moving Picture World*, March 26, 1927, p.
408.

"The Motion Picture Today and Tomorrow," *Theatre*, October 1927, pp.
21, 58.

[letter], *Register of the Kentucky State Historical Society*, vol. XXVI, no. 76,
1928, pp. 92–93.

"Tomorrow's Motion Picture," *The Picturegoer*, June 1928, p. 11. [reprinted in Harry M. Geduld, ed., *Focus on D. W. Griffith*, Englewood Cliffs,
N.J.: Prentice-Hall, 1971]

"What Is Beauty in Motion Pictures," *Liberty*, October 19, 1929, pp. 28–29.

"Griffith Picks Fifty Finest All-Time Films for *N. Y. Evening Post*," New York
Evening Post, August 12, 1930, p. 12.

[foreword], *How I Broke into the Movies by Sixty Famous Screen Stars*. Hollywood, Calif.: Hal C. Herman, 1930.

"An Old-Timer Advises Hollywood," *Liberty*, June 17, 1939, p. 18.

The Man Who Invented Hollywood: The Autobiography of D. W. Griffith, ed.
James Hart. Louisville, Ky.: Touchstone Publishing, 1972.

Index

Printed in the United States
by Baker & Taylor Publisher Services